PHYSICOCHEMICAL DYNAMICS OF RESONANCE CAVITATION AND TORSION-ORIENTED TURBULIZATION PHENOMENA

Dr. Lev Amusin, Ph.D.

iUniverse®

PHYSICOCHEMICAL DYNAMICS OF RESONANCE CAVITATION AND TORSION-ORIENTED TURBULIZATION PHENOMENA

iUniverse books may be ordered through booksellers or by contacting:

iUniverse
1663 Liberty Drive
Bloomington, IN 47403
www.iuniverse.com
844-349-9409

ISBN: 978-1-6632-4408-6 (sc)
ISBN: 978-1-6632-4413-0 (hc)
ISBN: 978-1-6632-4409-3 (e)

Print information available on the last page.

iUniverse rev. date: 08/31/2022

CONTENTS

ABSTRACT 8

CHAPTER 1
GENERAL OUTLOOK 12

1.1 INTRODUCTION 12

1.2 TORSION-ORIENTED PHENOMENA 22

1.3 THERMODYNAMICS OF DISPERSION SYSTEMS 24

1.4 TORSION-ORIENTED TECHNOLOGICAL PROCESSES 28

1.5 LAW OF ENERGY CONSERVATION FOR DISPERSION SYSTEMS 29

1.6 NATURE OF ORIENTENTION'S MOMENTS 36

CHAPTER 2
VIBRATION PROCESSES 42

2.1 PHYSICOCHMICAL VIBRATION TECHNOLOGY 42

2.2 PHYSICOCHEMICAL DYNAMICS 45

2.3 PRELIMINARY EXPERIMENTAL STUDIES 47

2.4 ANALYSIS OF PRELIMINARY STUDIES 54

2.5 REACTORS FOR IMPMENTATION OF THE SUBJECT PHENOMENON 62

2.6 CYLINDRICAL REACTORS 64

2.7 SINGLE CAVITY HYPERBOLICAL REACTOR 64

2.8 SECTIONAL REACTORS 66

2.9 PRACTICAL USAGE OF THE TORSION-ORIENTED TURBULIZATION 67

2.10 PROCESSING OF ALLOYS IN TURBULIZATION MODE 69

CHAPTER 3
DYNAMICS OF THE RESONANCE CAVITATION AND TORSION-ORIENED TURBULISATION PHRNOMENA 71

3.1 DYNAMICS OF THE FIRST HALF-A-CYCLE OF THE VIBRATION PRIOR TO ARISING OF RESONANCE 71

3.2 BEGINNING OF THE FIRST HALF-A-CYCLE 72

3.3 1-st PERIOD: THE BEGINNING OF THE FIRST HALF-A-CYCLE 73

3.4 CAVITATION 74

3.5 2-nd PERIOD: DEVELOPMENT ZONES WITH DIFFERENT INTERNAL PRESSURE 75

3.6 3-rd PERIOD: ZONES WITH MAXIMUM AND MINIMUM INTERNAL PRESSURE 76

3.7 4-th PERIOD: BEGINNING OF BACKWARDS MOTION 76

3.8 5-th PERIOD: FORMATION ZONES WITH ELEVATED INTERNAL PRESSURE 77

3.9 JUSTIFICATION THE POSSIBILITY TO CONSIDER A DISPERSION SYSTEM AS A SPECIAL CASE OF A THEMODINAMIC SYSTEM 80

3.10 THE FLUID DINAMICS OF A MIXURE INSIDE THE REACTOR 83

3.11 6-th PERIOD: THE COLLAPSE OF THE CONTINUUM OF A LIQUID MEDIUM 85

3.12 A PHENOMENON OF THE RESONANCE CAVITATION 87

3.13 EQUATION FOR THE MOTION OF THE LIQUID MEDIUM DURING 6-the PERIOD 88

3.14 THE FLUID HAMMER IMPECT 89

3.15 FORMATION OF DISPERSION SYSTEMS 96

3.16 ANALYSIS OF FORCES THAT ARE ACTING DURING FORMATION OF DISPERSION SYSTEMS 99

3.17 A PHENOMENON OF THE TORSION-ORIENTED TURBULIZATION 104

3.18 FORMATION OF DISPERSION SYSTEMS (continuation) 107

3.19 TURBULIZATION MOTION OF THE DISPERSION PHASE 108

3.20 THE EQUATION OF HEAT BALANCE FOR THE TORSION-ORIENTED TURBULIZATION 121

3.21 VECTOR ANALYSIS OF THE MOTION OF THE MEDIUM OF DISPERSION SYSTEMS 124

3.22 SURFACE TENSION AND INTERFACE BETWEEN PHASES OF DISPERSION SYSTEMS 127

3.23 DISSIPATION OF ENERGY DURING TORSION-ORIENTED TURBULIZATION 131

3.24 THE SUMMARY OF THE CHAPTER 3 134

CHAPTER 4

THE RESEARCH OF INFLUENCE OF THE EXTERNAL FIELD OF VIBRATION ON THE RESONANCE CAVITATION AND THE TORSION-ORIENTED TURBULIZATION PHENOMENA 136

4.1 THE WORKING MODEL OF THE VIBRATION MACHINE WITH REACTOR 136

4.2 FLUCTUATION OF THE MATERIAL POINT 141

4.3 TASK No.1: FLUCTUATION OF A SINLE MATERIAL POINT 144

4.4 TASK No.2: FLUCTUATION OF A MATERIAL POINT WITH CONSIDERATION OF THE RESISTANCE A DISPERSION MEDIUM 150

4.5 TASK No.3: FLUCTUATION OF A MATERIAL POINT THAT IS UNDER THE INFLUENCE OF AN EXTERNAL REVOLTING FORCE, BUT WITHOUT CONSIDERATION OF THE RESISTANCE OF THE DISPERSION MEDIUM 155

4.6 TASK No.4: FLUCTUATION OF A MATERIAL POINT THAT IS UNDER THE INFLUENCE OF AN EXTERNAL SINUSOIDAL FORCE, BUT WITHOUT CONSIDERATION OF THE RESISTANCE OF THE DISPERSION

MEDIUM 156

4.7 TASK No 5: Solution 1 157

4.7a TASK No 5: Solution 2 158

4.8 TASK No.6: FLUCTUATION OF A MATERIAL POINT THAT IS UNDER THE INFLUENCE OF AN EXTERNAL SINUSOIDAL FORCE, AND A FORCE OF THE RESISTANCE OF THE DISPERSION MEDIUM, THAT IS PROPORTIONAL TO THE SPEED OF THE MOTION 159

4.9 TASK No.7: FLUCTUATION OF A MATERIAL POINT THAT IS UNDER THEINFLUENCE OF AN EXTERNAL SINUSOIDAL FORCE, AND A FORCE OF THE RESISTANCE OF THE DISPERSION MEDIUM 161

4.10 TASK No 8: ANALYSIS OF THE MOVEMENT OF ELEMENTS OF THE DISPERSED PHASE IN THE VIBRATIONAL FIELD 164

4.11 TASK No.9: FLUCTUATION OF A MATERIAL POINT THAT IS UNDER THE INFLUENCE OF AN EXTERNAL SINUSOIDAL FORCE, INCLUDING THE ELASTIC COMPONENT OF THE DISPERSION PHASE 167

4.12 SUMMARY OF THE CHAPTER 4 171

CHAPTER 5
PHYSICOCHEMICAL DYNAMICS OF THE DISPERSION SYSTEM 172

5.1 DEVELOPMENT OF MOLECULAR-SURFACE FORCES DURING FORMATION OF A DISPERSION SYSTEM UNDER MODES OF RESONANCE CAVITATION AND TORSION-ORIENTED TURBULIZATION 172

5.2 FORMATION AND STABILITY OF DISPERSION SYSTEMS 175

5.3 ELECTRIC DOUBLE LAYER 176

5.4 ELECTROSTATIC REPULSIVE FORCES OF DISPERSED PARTICLES 180

5.5 ENERGY OF THE INTERACTION OF DISPERSED PARTICLES 182

5.6 MOLECULAR INTERACTION OF DISPERSED PARTICLES 186

5.7 SPHERICAL PARTICLES 188

5.8 PLANE-PARALLEL PLATES 189

5.9 PHYSICOCHEMICAL DYNAMICS OF BUBBLE FORMATION 190

5.10 RESEARCH ON THE FORMATION OF DISPERSION SYSTEMS IN THE MODEL OF A VAPOR-GAS BUBBLE 194

5.11 RESEARCH ON THE CAPILLARY-SURFACE PHENOMENA 201

5.12 ANALYSIS OF FORCES ACTING ON THE SURFACE OF GAS BUBBLES DURING FORMATION OF DISPERSION SYSTEMS 207

5.13 SUMMARY OF THE CHAPTER 5 222

CHAPTER 6
EFFICIENCY OF THE REALIZATION OF RESONANCE CAVITATION AND TORSION-ORIENTED TURBULIZATION PHENOMENA 223

6.1 SPEED OF FORMATION OF DISPERSION SYSTEM 225

6.2 GENERAL EQUATION OF THE FORMATION OF DISPERSION SYSTEMS IN A HOMOGENEOUS ENVIRONMENT 230

6.3 ASSESSMENT OF THE AVERAGE SPEED OF THE FORMATION OF DISPERSION SYSTEMS 233

6.4 PROCESS OF FORMATION OF DISPERSION SYSTEMS AND COLLATERAL CHEMICAL REACTIONS AT THE PERMANENT INTERNAL VOLUME OF THE REACTOR 236

6.5 CONSIDERATION OF THE CONTINUOUS FORMATION OF DISPERSION SYSTEMS 239

6.6 GAS ABSORBTION BY THE LIQUID MEDIUM IN TORSION-ORIENTED

TURBULIZATION MODE 242

CHAPTER 7

DIRECT METHOD OF MEASUREMENT OF THE INTERNAL PRESSURE DURING THE FORMATION OF DISPERSION SYSTEMS 249

7.1 ANALYSIS OF FORCES ACTING ON THE SURFACE OF A SENSITIVE ELEMENT OF THE DEVICE FOR THE MEASUREMENT OF THE INTERNAL PRESSURE 249

7.2 DIRECT METHOD OF MEASUREMENT OF INTERNAL PRESSURE 264

7.3 CALCULATION OF A RELATIVE ERROR OF SPHERICAL CAPSULES AND FLAT MEMBRANES 268

7.4 CALCULATION OF A RELATIVE ERROR OF CYLINDRICAL CAPSULES AND FLAT MEMBRANE 271

7.5 CALCULATION OF A RELATIVE ERROR OF CYLINDRICAL CAPSULES AND CORRUGATED MEMBRANE 273

7.6 ANALYSIS OF THE SYSTEMATIC ERROR OF MEASUREMENTS OF THE INTERNAL PRESSURE 275

CONCLUSION 285

REFERENCES 286

LIST OF AUTHOR'S PUBLICATIONS RELATED TO THIS SUBJECT 304

ABSTRACT

The purpose of this monograph is to conduct a physical and mathematical analysis of resonance cavitation and torsion-oriented turbulization phenomena from the position of physicochemical dynamics. The practical use of the considered phenomena in discrete and continuous modes offers breakthrough technological solutions for the formation of dispersion systems of the following types: liquid–liquid, liquid–gas, liquid–liquid–gas, liquid–solid particles–gas, and so on. This is an extremely promising direction in the development of chemical technology processes using the powerful energy of vibration to form dispersion systems and to create composite materials and alloys with unique properties [1–7].

Resonance cavitation and torsion-oriented turbulization phenomena occur in a single cavity hyperbolic chamber of the chemical reactor that is installed on a vibration machine, which forms a rigid mechanical vibrator–reactor system [1–7]. The reactor, with components of the resulting dispersion system loaded into it, is exposed to the indignant influence of a force field at accelerations of 20 to 50 times greater that of usual terrestrial gravity acceleration. When the frequency of the indignant oscillations from vibration machine approaches the frequency of the natural oscillations of the loaded mixture, a mechanical resonance develops in the system that is followed by the fluid hammer impacts. Shock waves extend throughout the internal volume of the reactor and lead to the violation of the dispersion phase's continuity and to the explosion-like occurrence of gas bubbles. This phenomenon is called resonance cavitation.

When the quantity of bubbles reaches a critical amount, units of bubbles forms within the system. When each individual bubble collapses, additional shock waves are formed, which propagate inside the reactor also. Shock waves occur as the result of individual fluid hummer impacts. In front of the rapidly moving shock wave are forming areas of increased pressure, while areas of reduced pressure are formed behind the wave. These shock waves, superimposed on each other, in turn cause secondary discontinuities in the liquid dispersion medium, forming a heterogeneous dispersion system. Moreover, this process develops explosively.

Macroscopic volumes arise inside the reactor. The subject volumes characterized by the development of internal pressures in them. The values of internal pressures in each separately allocated volume, due to the difference in the density due to presents of bubbles, do not coincide with the value of the internal pressure of the adjacent allocated volume. Because of this, internal tension arises between them. The process of changing the specific density of each allocated volume changes continuously, the internal stresses between each adjacent macroscopic volumes change continuously also.

Thus, during a short period of time, measured in fraction of second, centrifugal forces develop in each selected macroscopic volume of the processing dispersion system, with continuously changing values of the modules of these forces. As a result of a complex configuration of the difference in the internal pressure between adjacent volumes, that resulting of the difference in the moments of inertia between adjacent allocated volumes. Considering the complexity of the curvature of the inner surface of a single cavity hyperbolic, it leads to a myriad of continuously changing short-lived bubbles begin to rotate in a horizontal plane around the vertical axis of the reactor's chamber, gradually enticing internal volumes in horizontal sections of the reactor.

As the indignant forces from the vibration machine continue to act upon reactor, the influence of gravitational forces in comparison with the indignant forces decreases. Finally, at some point in time, in the central part of the reactor, all bubbles begin to rotate in a vertical plane relative to the horizontal axis. A funnel is formed in the reactor, resembling a tornado. Thus, the emerging phenomenon can be represented as a torsion-oriented turbulization.

This phenomenon became possible to observe only because the vertical shell of the reactor was transparent. Moreover, the design of the vertical shell of the reactor was as rigid and strong that, it allowed the material of the vertical shell to remain in the zone of elastic deformations, under the action of indignant forces. It allows to keep the process at a constant volume. Also, the energy of dissipation was observed as the temperature of reactor's shell increases.

The following results are given in this monograph:

- The study offers mathematical models of resonance cavitation and torsion-oriented turbulization phenomena.
- The study considers the mathematical model of gas bubble development dynamics and the processes occurring at an interface of phases.
- The study considers the design and results of research into the processes of heat exchange and mass transfer in a physical model of a single gas bubble.
- The author carries out a mathematical justification and develops a technique for measuring internal pressure fields during the formation of dispersion systems.
- The author carries out a mathematical analysis of measurement errors.
- The study offers different designs for chemical reactors to realize the phenomena in question. Reactors could be designed as modular systems in the form of a single-cavity hyperboloid, a straight cylinder, or a multi modules stepped cylinder of a diameter different from that of the reactor's other modules. This constructional flexibility allows reactors to be designed for work in batch and continuous modes.

The phenomena considered differ from orthodox processes in their development of uniquely large surface of separation between phases. This interface creates new technological capabilities to produce dispersion systems, composite materials and unique metal alloys. Those breakthrough technological methods can be applied in producing artificial blood, creating artificial fuel based on of carbon dioxide retrieved from the atmosphere, and producing ferromagnetic and electronic liquids, as well as being used in the processes of, for example, dissolution, emulsification, extraction, and homogenization in either batch or continuous mode. Some of these applications are as follows:

- In processing of electronics, biochemicals, the paints and varnishes, and other branches of chemical technology
- In macro-, micro-, and nanotechnological processes
- In environmental protection processes, such as the dissolution and saturation of various liquids with hazardous waste, including the trapping

and dissolution of carbon dioxide (including but not limited to sewage flotation, sorption release of substances from solutions, recovery of a collateral chemicals, and iodine recovery from water solutions, etc.)

- In extraction processes in the production of herbal medicines
- In producing and manufacturing of various types of food products including dairy products, sauces, mayonnaise, and flavors and flavorings
- In fermentation processes for producing alcohol and alcoholic drinks
- In removing riveting metals in diamond cutting
- In producing protective coatings against environmental influences

The offered breakthrough technology can be used in fabricating composites from materials that are normally incompatible. Such new products would differ from existing materials in terms of their mechanical and physical properties. For example, a porous ceramic or a spongy titanium could be filled with substances that create a new product with significantly improved or new properties. Another direction for the presented phenomena is their use in creation of multicomponent, high-performance alloys that otherwise cannot be processed in terrestrial environments. Such alloys could be produced under acceleration greater than 20 to 50 times that of terrestrial gravity.

The fact that indignant vibrational forces acting upon melting pot practically eliminating influence of terrestrial gravity. That makes possible to melt together metals like aluminum and lead, that is impossible to do it because of difference of their specific gravity.

Alloys that possessing such essentially new properties could then be used in special conditions, such as hostile environments (e.g. high or low temperatures, chemically aggressive conditions), fossil energy production, chemical processing, and underwater shipbuilding, as well as in air and space applications.

This phenomenon became possible to observe only because the vertical shell of the reactor was transparent.

CHAPTER 1

GENERAL OUTLOOK

1.1. INTRODUCTION

Existing orthodox methods of physicochemical technology applicable to the formation of homogeneous and heterogeneous materials have already been developed to a high degree of perfection. The further improvement of any technologies, based on the use of additional energy, is limited and any attempts to improve the existing technologies are impossible in principle. At the same time, for a variety of reasons, thorough research is lacking regarding the influence of the fields of the physical, physicochemical and mechanochemical nature on the formation the subject materials, including composites and exotic alloys. The use of resonance cavitation and torsion-oriented turbulization phenomena can compensated for this lack.

The existing technological methods, including mixers and blenders use blades of different shapes and forms that placed inside processing products and rotated. This is a problem for contamination and causes processing equipment cleaning and disinfection difficulties. The equipment for realizing the offered technology has no moving parts. It makes this process an ideal for processing of nanoemulsions and nanosuspensions applicable for the pharmaceutical, cosmetic and coating industries as well as many other applications. An additional positive side of the offered vibrational technology is its low energy consumption through the combine action of mechanical resonance and hydraulic hammer impacts, which activate highly energetical molecular-surface forces.

Another extremely important characteristic of the torsion-oriented turbulization is the development of exceptionally large surface of separation between phases. Considering a fact that all chemical reactions and physicochemical processes, including mass transfer and heat exchange, occur mainly at the surface of phase separation, this technique opens new technological opportunities for producing macro-, micro-, and nano-dispersion systems.

In the material world there are existing fields of power of various natures. These forces are determined by their corresponding characteristics: mechanical (e.g., gravitational), physical and mechanical (e.g., friction), physical (e.g., thermal and electromagnetic); physicochemical (e.g., molecular-surface forces) and, finally, chemical (e.g., interatomic interaction) [1]. The first three of these can be perceived by the human senses or devices (gravitational, friction, thermal and electromagnetic). These forces can interact with one another, producing work. Forces of a physicochemical and chemical nature, however, are determined by using special methods and instruments. In addition, these forces can act on the crushed particles of matter and interactions between molecules and atoms to create new substances and compounds that did not exist in nature.

Torsion-orientated turbulization, considered a fundamentally new process of physicochemical technology, is based on the powerful energy of vibration [2–7]. It is different from other physicochemical processes in its unique ability to develop a substance with the exceptionally large surface of separation between phases. This is important because in the processed dispersion system, particles of solid matter (in suspensions) or droplets of liquid that are immiscible and insoluble in other liquid that form a dispersion phase (in emulsions) are very small, which triggers an increase in the influence of molecular-surface forces that in turn, leads to a significant minimization of the dispersed phase. Thus, the offered technology enables to process dispersion systems with improved quality and extend shelf life of the final products.

In general, all dispersion systems consisting of two or more components. If there are no collateral reversible chemical reactions occur during the formation of such systems, then the number of components is equal to the number of substances that make up the system. If these systems form with irreversible chemical side reactions, the number of system components is equal to the difference between the number of parts that make up the system and the number of independent reactions.

Dispersion systems form as the result of action of molecular-surface phenomena caused by the influence of the fields of external forces. During formation of the dispersion systems the particles of the dispersed phase distributed in the dispersion medium in which they are embedded.

Dispersion systems, depending on the number of components (phases), are considered to be two- or three-phase systems. They can be classified as follows:

Dispersion Environment	**Dispersed Phase**	**Common Description**
Gas	Liquid Droplets	Aerosol, Mist, Fog
Gas	Solid Particles	Smoke, Aerosol
Liquid	Gas	Foam
Liquid	Liquid Droplets	Emulsion*)
Liquid	Solid Particles	Suspension, Colloidal Solution
Solid Particles	Gas	Solid Foam
Solid Particles	Liquid	Solid Emulsion, Gel, Paste
Solid Particles	Solid Particles	Alloy, Powder

Note: *) Emulsions are dispersions systems formed by minimized drops of immiscible and insoluble liquids and the dispersion medium in which they are embedded.

The interaction of the components of a dispersed phase and the dispersion medium defines the formation process, stability and rheological characteristics of dispersion systems.

Nanoemulsions and nanosuspensions are dispersion systems that occur during the interaction of molecular-surface force fields, which interact with particles of solid matter and liquid droplets sizes from 10^{-6} to 10^{-8} meters. Those compounds have special properties, that are important for effectiveness of consumption by patients of medications and organoleptic characteristics that are imported for an example, cosmetic cremes and pastes and special coatings, etc.

The criterion for the similarity of the motion of heterogeneous dispersion systems is the Froude criterion $(\boldsymbol{Fr})$, which can be used in cases where the influence of external disturbing forces is significant. The Froude number characterizes the ratio between the inertia force and the external force in the field in which a movement occurs, acting on the elementary volume of components of dispersion systems:

$$\boldsymbol{Fr} = \frac{\omega_{flow}^2}{gL},$$

where ω_{flow} is the speed of the flow, [m/s]; g is the acceleration characterizing the action of external (gravity) force: the gravity acceleration, [9.8 m/s^2]; and L is the size of the area in which the flow is considered.

The offered physicochemical processing method is based upon resonance cavitation and torsion-oriented turbulization phenomena, which occurs upon the action of vibrational forces. Implementing the subject phenomena allows use of processing reactors without and internal parts. This technological process is realized in a single-cavity hyperbolic chamber of the chemical reactor that is installed on a moving table of a vibration machine. The reactor's housing is sealed with bottom and upper covers. The reactor and mobile table, forming the uniform vibrator-reactor system. The design of the reactor's housing provides a rigidity capable of resisting considerable external mechanical forces. This rigidity influences the deformation of the shell elements that continue to remain in the elastic tension zone.

Before we discuss of the subject phenomena, we should consider concept of oscillation itself. In physics, it is customary to call oscillations processes that repeat exactly or approximately at regular intervals. Oscillations can occur when there are changes in fields of mechanical or electromagnetic forces. A different type of oscillation occurs when the stability of the internal state of equilibrium of systems changes because of the influence of external disturbing forces, changes in the heat balance or volume of systems, and the tension in the internal pressure fields. Fields of internal pressure arise because of the pressure difference between adjacent volumes of the system. Such conditions are usually called natural or own oscillation. This kind of oscillation, as a rule, cease to operate when the balance is restored.

Natural or own oscillations are the most common form of the existence of substance and the basis of the theory of oscillations. They are the most important type of oscillations, given the conditions for the occurrence and the nature of all other types of oscillations that may arise in the system and depend on the nature of the own oscillations of dispersion systems. When the frequency of the disturbing external vibrational forces approaches the frequency of the natural oscillation, the amplitude of the components of the dispersion system to be formed can sharply increase, causing the occurrence of the phenomenon called resonance.

To form a dispersion system, the components of the planned system are loaded in the reactor. The reactor and mixture of components are exposed to low-frequency vertically directed reciprocating sinusoidal disturbing forces with frequencies in the 30- to 150-Hz range, amplitudes in the 1- to 4-mm range and acceleration in the 20- to 50- G (gravity acceleration) range. When the frequency of the vibration approaches the frequency of the mixture's self-oscillation, mechanical resonance occurs that causes an essential increase in the amplitude of components processing dispersion system. Thus, the mass of this system comes up at high speed and strike the bottom surface of the top cover of the reactor, causing a rapid change of speed for the subject dispersion mass. In this case, the conditions for the occurrence of resonance require special consideration of the rheological and physicochemical characteristics of the processing dispersion system. In this case, it is fair to use the theory of the impact of a liquid on a rigid surface, when the impulses acting on a liquid and a rigid surface are determined. Knowledge of those impulses is necessary for calculating the rigidity and strength of the reactor's housing and reactor's covers.

Mathematically, the problem of the impact of an incompressible dispersed mass with density ρ_0 on a rigid surface is reduced to finding the velocity potential

$$\upsilon = \frac{\wp_i}{\wp_0},$$

where $\wp_0$ and $\wp_i$ are an impulsive pressure and υ is the harmonic function subject to the boundary conditions

On the liquid's free surface $\wp = 0$, and on the contact surface of the dispersed system with the inner surface of the upper cover of the reactor $\frac{\partial \wp}{\partial n} = a_n$, where a_n is the projection of the velocity of a given point on the surface of the dispersion system onto the normal. In the considered particular case of the vertical impact of the dispersion system on the bottom surface of the reactor's upper cover, the system receives a vertical velocity a_y, in a direction opposite to the movement of the dispersion mass. The amount of motion of the dispersed mass I_y and its kinetic energy K are determined by the expressions:

$$I_y = m_y a_y;$$

$$K = \frac{m_y a_y^2}{2} = \frac{I_y a_y}{2},$$

where m is the generalized mass of the components of the emerging dispersion system.

As a result of the impact of the dispersion mass on the rigid surface of the upper cover, a shock wave is formed. It propagates through the dispersion mass in the opposite direction of the movement of the subject mass with supersonic speed. This shock wave represents a thin transition layer inside a dispersion system in which there is a sharp increase in the density, pressure and velocity of the substance.

The thickness of the transition layer is equal to the length of a free path of molecules. In the subject under question, shock waves are of interest only in which the direction of the velocity of the substance are perpendicular to the surface of the wave's front. When shock waves are passing through gas-air bubbles and liquid media, the parameters of these substances change in a discontinuous manner.

The values of physical and physicochemical characteristics of dispersion systems on both sides of the shock wave are in ratio to one another arising from the laws of mass conservation, momentum and energy. It should also be noted the transition of shock waves changes the entropy of the substance. In this case, the jump in entropy is determined only by the law of conservation, which admits the existence of two modes: a jump in compression and a jump in relief of tension. However, in accordance with the second law of thermodynamics, the modes exist only when entropy increase.

As the shock wave propagates through the unperturbed mass, with the supersonic speed D is equal to:

$$D = |\alpha_0| > \alpha_0.$$

The supersonic speed increases when the value of the intensity of the shock wave is greater and when the difference of pressure is greater on both sides of the shock wave. Also, an area of increased pressure is formed in front of the rapidly moving shock wave, while an area of reduced pressure is formed behind the wave. Thus, the shock wave is mechanically stable because any disturbances cannot penetrate the unperturbed medium, get ahead of the shock wave, or blur its front. With respect to the compressed matter located behind the front, the shock wave propagates at a subsonic speed that causes the thermodynamic regime behind the front of the shock wave to affects its amplitude. With an unlimited increase in the amplitude, the compression behind the front remains limited.

All the above applies to the very first shock wave that reaches the reactor's bottom cover, is reflected by it, and begins to move in the opposite direction. Because the external disturbing forces act on the reactor with a certain frequency, the first shock wave is followed by the second, which is superimposed on the reflected first shock wave. The second wave is followed by third wave, and so on.

These waves arise, move from the reactor's upper cover, and reach the reactor's bottom cover, which reflects them. These waves move through an already disturbed medium, that is, through zones of compression and depression. Shock waves meet and are superimposed upon one another, which causes the resonance cavitation phenomenon.

Considering the dimension of the bubbles and the thickness of the films of the dispersion medium surrounding the elementary volumes of solid particles, it is easy to assume that the forces acting on the surface of the bubbles are capillary–surface forces.

In this state the dispersion system is unstable. The number of forming bubbles grows rapidly. They group together, forming a zone in the central part of the reactor in which bubbles are most active. They vertically and horizontally oscillate, rotate, and collapse. The shock waves generated during their ruptures create a reduction in pressure inside the reactor, which contributes to the emergence of countless new bubbles.

In general, regardless of any origin, the cavitation phenomenon represents a disparaging process caused by continuity violation of the liquid environment and its transformation into a two–phase system liquid–gas, whereas pressure in the liquid becomes equivalent to the pressure of saturated vapor of this liquid. At the same time, from a hydrodynamics perspective, any cavitation represents the process vapor-gas bubble formation in a volume of liquid resulting from the powerful influence of the external field of mechanical forces. In a broad sense of physicochemical dynamics, cavitation is the process of bubbles emerging in the exasperated liquid. Otherwise, it is a process of violations in a continuity of liquid that occurs without change in the ambient temperature.

Cavitation is indicated by a noise caused by the collapse of bubbles and is defined by the so-called cavitation number [8]:

$$\kappa = \frac{2(\mathcal{P} - \mathcal{P}_V)}{\rho V^2} \quad \text{or} \quad \mathcal{P} = \frac{\kappa \rho V^2}{2} - \mathcal{P}_V,$$

where κ is the cavitation number; $\mathcal{P}$ is the pressure inside the liquid, [H/m^2]; $\mathcal{P}_V$ is the pressure of the steam, which is saturated by the liquid, [H/m^2]; ρ is the liquid's density, [kg/m^3]; and V is the speed of liquid flow, [m/s^2].

The meaning of formula (A) is that cavitation bubbles begin to form when pressure in the liquid, $\mathcal{P}$, falls below a critical value: $\mathcal{P}_{Cr}$ $(\mathcal{P} << \mathcal{P}_{Cr})$. In a liquid, the critical pressure, $\mathcal{P}_{Cr}$, is determined by the saturated vapor pressure inside the liquid at a certain ambient temperature and atmospheric pressure above the free surface of the liquid.

Because a certain amount of dissolved gas is constantly present in the liquid, under the condition $(\mathcal{P} < \mathcal{P}_{Cr})$, microscopic caverns are formed in the liquid volume. Those caverns are filled with the vapor of the dissolved gas and by the evaporation of the liquid itself, which penetrates because of diffusion. If the pressure inside the liquid falls below a certain value corresponding to the liquid's boiling point, intense evaporation of the liquid into the bubbles occurs through the interface. If the pressure inside the liquid remains below what the pressure is during boiling, gas prevails inside the bubbles.

As a result of the movement of the bubbles in the fluid flow, the growth of the bubbles that have fallen into the high–pressure zone is limited and, under certain conditions, the bubbles are compressed to the dimensions corresponding to the surface pressure in the films surrounding them. Moving from one zone to another, these bubbles can change its size several times. However, in the areas of reduced pressure, the vapor-gas bubbles change their size with great speed and, as a result, collapse. This causes the fluid hammer impact also. This phenomenon is accompanied by a relatively loud sound impulse. The resulting shock wave propagates through the surrounding liquid. Moreover, the stronger the fluid hammer impact, the less vapor there is in the volume of the bubble.

Several known mechanisms that lead to the emergence of cavitation bubbles. The first type of cavitation consists of development in the flow of the liquid that is moving in the pipeline under the influence of an external source of a force field. Any flow restrictions cause the differences in internal pressure in the adjacent zones, between which tensions are formed. This is likely explained by the deficiency of the liquid that results from the movement through the pipes of various sections. The quantity of liquid is simply not enough to maintain a continuous stream of liquid through the entire internal volume of a pipeline.

The second type of cavitation consists of the formation of bubbles in the flow of the liquid moving under the influence of an external force field (for example, a ship screw or a pump impeller). As a result, differences in internal pressure form between adjacent zones of liquid, thus creating tension between these zones. However, these phenomena differ in that variations in pressure arise at the expense of the varying speeds of a stream's elementary volumes.

The third type of cavitation occurs under the influence of heat. When heating the tank containing the liquid, conditions are created on the hot surfaces of the device in the areas adjacent to the heat sources. Under these conditions, some volumes of liquid transition to a vaporous state. Other reasons for this type of cavitation are the effects of ultrasound, high-frequency electric discharge and flow around a surface with a high-speed gas stream (e.g., the surface of the fuselage or the wing of an airplane).

One shared fact among the above types of cavitation is that this phenomenon arises only in local volumes of liquid, adjacent to external borders of liquid or gas. In this work, there is no need to examine in detail all the emergence mechanisms of the abovementioned types of cavitation nor to conduct detailed research on their nature.

1.2. TORSION-ORIENTED PHENOMENON

Until recently, physics considered four levels of reality of matter: solid, liquid, gaseous and plasma, including fields of various natures and elementary particles. Recently, theoretical physics has been mastering the fifth level of reality: the physical vacuum. A. Akimov [9] and G. Shipov [10] proposed the opinion that the main state of any kind of matter, as well as the source of all particles and fields without exception, is a physical vacuum: that is, what remains in space when all gas and all elementary particles are removed from it.

The concept of torsion fields was first used by the French mathematician Elie Cartan in 1913. He was the first person to say quite definitely, "There must be fields based on rotation in nature."

The first scientist to develop a method for studying torsion fields was N.K. Karpov; the literature includes references to the works of the experimenters V. Kasyanov and F. Okhatrin who obtained photographs of the fields under consideration. A great contribution to the study of torsion fields was made by E. Fradkin [9], D. Gitman [12,13], V.Bagrov [13-15]; D. Ivanenko, who participated in the creation of a hydrogen bomb [16]; I. Buchbinder [17-19] and other scientists.

Since the mid-20th century, the Department of Theoretical Physics of the Physics Faculty of Moscow State University has been studying torsion fields. Data also exist from research in this area carried out by scientific groups led by physicists D. Radin [20], A. Jafari [21], N. Nausaka [22], S. Imoushi [23], D. Sabbata [24, 25] and other researchers. The discovery of new possibilities in physics and the development of vacuum physics bring changes to a wide variety of areas of knowledge: mechanics, quantum mechanics, astrophysics, physics of elementary particles and fields, and cosmology.

Recently, a whole range of torsion technologies have been developed in several laboratories. These technologies cover all sectors of the economy. The area of torsion technologies comprises torsion energy, torsion transport, torsion communications and communications, torsion production of structural materials, torsion geology and geophysics, chemical production, ecology, disposal of nuclear waste and cleaning of territories from radioactive contamination, agriculture and medicine. In Russia, dozens of organizations are engaged in scientific and experimental research on the use of torsion fields. Some of these technologies have already been commercialized and put into production.

Also, changes in the structure of metals under the action of the torsion effect have been investigated. The first technology brought to the production stage was the production of aluminum — silicon alloy called silumin (AI+Si). When torsion fields are applied to the silumin melt at the outlet without any alloyed additives, an alloy is obtained 1.5 times stronger and three times more plastic, with greater corrosion resistance and higher fluidity of conventional silumin, which is especially important when casting parts of complex shapes.

After the researchers discovered that torsion fields could change the structure of crystals, experiments were carried out to change the crystal structure of metals. These results were obtained when the dynamic radiation of a torsion generator was applied to melts of some metals in a Tamman furnace. This furnace is a vertical cylindrical crucible made of refractory steel. Above and below the cylinder is closed with covers. The metal under study was placed in the crucible inside the furnace. After the metal had melted, a torsion generator located outside the crucible was turned on. For 30 minutes, the torsion generator irradiated the metal melt. During this time, it was cooled from 1400 ° C to 800 ° C. Then it was cooled and cut, and a physicochemical analysis was performed, the results of which showed that the crystal lattice pitch of the metal irradiated by the torsion field changed throughout the ingot volume, and

Changes in torsion fields are accompanied by a change in the characteristics of dispersion systems and is accompanied by the release of energy. A torsion field is formed around a rotating object and is a set of micro-vortices of space. Because matter consists of atoms and molecules, and atoms and molecules have their own moment of rotation, the matter always has a torsion field. A rotating dispersed system also has a torsion field. Torsion fields can arise due to the special geometry of space. Torsion charges of the same sign (direction of rotation) are attracted (i.e., like attracts like). The main properties of torsion fields are as follows:

- Torsion fields can interact, exchange information, combine.
- Large torsion vortices can absorb small ones, and small ones can merge into one large one.
- Streams swirling in one direction attract; differently swirling streams are repelled.
- One large vortex creates around itself many small vortexes, which are acting in opposite direction.

1.3. THERMODYNAMICS OF DISPERSION SYSTEMS

The condition of the dispersion systems is characterized by an excess of free energy. Moreover, the integration of particles of the dispersed phase happens spontaneously, causing the reduction of free energy U. Thus, dispersion systems are unstable in a thermodynamic sense. Their temporary stability depends on the existence of the power barrier to prevent rapprochement and the fixing of elementary volumes and particles at rather small distances from each other (aggregation), the full association of droplets in emulsions and fogs, or the association of bubbles of gas in foams (coalescence). In a dispersed state, although steady for coalescence, separate solid particles are united in somewhat large units and form a so-called coagulative structure. They keep their identity from the dispersion liquid. Destruction of the films of surface separation causes the full associations of elementary volumes of the liquid phase in foams and emulsions or the emergence of direct contacts between microscopically small solid objects in suspensions or colloidal solutions.

The influence of modes on the formation of different kinds of dispersion systems and on their stability is especially important. The primary feature of the systems in question is the existence of a highly determined surface of separation among elements of the dispersed phase and the dispersion phase with the coefficient of surface tension $\boldsymbol{\sigma}$. The main contribution to the change of free energy caused by minimization of substances of system components comes from atoms located on the surface among phases. The number of atoms is comparable to their number in the volume of the substance that forms the dispersion environment.

As we considered earlier [5], the physical characteristic of a turbulent state is the potential difference of the internal pressure developing between the elementary volumes of the dispersion medium. At the same time, the considered turbulent state of a moving dispersed system is characterized by an indefinite compressibility of the liquid phase, the presence of numerous, constantly changing and indefinite discontinuities in the continuity of the dispersion medium, as well as an indefinite motion of particles of a solid and a gas-liquid mixture, which have six degrees of freedom. Obviously, such a movement cannot be described by analytical methods. The only way to describe the nature of the motion of such a system in the first approximation is vector analysis.

Before continuing the mathematical and physicochemical analysis of the initial stage of vibration impact on the reactor, it is necessary to consider the question: *IS IT* possible to consider a dispersion system as a thermodynamic system?

A thermodynamic system is any macroscopic system (in any state: solid, liquid or gaseous, and as well as a multicomponent mix) that is in equilibrium from a thermodynamics position, or close to it [24,25]. However, such a definition does not exclude the possibility of a system condition in which one or several of its parameters within elementary volumes or points of this system differ from one another.

The condition of strength of the dispersion systems is characterized by an excess of free energy *U*. Moreover, the integration of particles of the dispersed phase occurs spontaneously and causes the reduction of free energy U. Thus, in the thermodynamic sense, dispersion systems by their nature, are unstable. Their temporary stability is based on the existence of a power barrier, capable to prevent rapprochement and fixing of elementary volumes and particles of solid matters at rather small distances from each other (aggregation), the full association of droplets in emulsions and fogs, and the association of bubbles of gas in foams (coalescence).

In a dispersed state—but steady in coalescence— separate solid particles are united in rather large units to form a coagulative structure. They maintain an identity and are divided by layers of the dispersion medium. The destruction of the surface films of separation between phases causes the full associations of elementary volumes of the liquid phase in foams and emulsions, or the emergence of direct contacts between microscopically small solid objects in suspensions or colloidal solutions.

For instance, we could assume the existence of systems in which temperature changes from one point of measurement to another; as well as systems (gas, liquid, or system gas–liquid) in which the internal pressure in various elementary volumes differs from one another. It is obvious that, in these systems, the phenomena of heat exchange and a mass transfer would be observed. Such conditions do not remain invariable over time if they are not supported by an additional inflow of energy. Otherwise, after some time, a state is established in which the parameter values at all points or elementary volumes of the system remain unchanged for an arbitrarily long time if external conditions do not change and there is no influx of additional energy. Such states considered to be in equilibrium.

The process of a thermodynamic system transition from a state of nonequilibrium to equilibrium is called a relaxation. For averaging or otherwise, aligning values of each parameter in all volumes of a system, there is a characteristic time that is called a relaxation time for this parameter. The total relaxation time falls on the longest of all relaxation times. Estimations of the relaxation time for various processes cannot be made within the framework of thermodynamics. Physical kinetics deals with this issue.

Now, let us consider that a process in a thermodynamic system proceeds with a speed significantly lower than the speed of relaxation. This means that, at any point in such a process, all parameters would begin to level. Such a process represents a chain of equilibrium states indefinitely close to one another. These rather slow processes can be called equilibrium or quasi-static processes. It should be noted that, during equilibrium processes, the gradients of all parameters are equal to zero at any moment. It follows from this that, because of symmetry, the process in the system can go in both directions—any system parameters can increase or decrease. Therefore, in the direct process, alignment can be reversed in time. In this regard, equilibrium processes can be considered reversible.

Thus, at the initial stage of the formation of dispersion systems in the mode of resonance cavitation, the system quickly goes into equilibrium upon the termination of the disturbing force. It is possible to apply standard thermodynamic methods to analyze these systems.

At the next stage of the formation of dispersion systems upon transition from resonance cavitation into the torsion turbulization mode, opposing hydraulic hummer shocks and, consequently, multidirectional shock waves arise. This situation is complicated by the fact that hydraulic hummer shock impacts and shock waves are physically different in nature. Hydraulic shock impacts arise upon impact of the mixture components on the top cover of the reactor, whereas shock waves result from the collapse of the vapor–gas bubbles. This mass formation, development and rupture of vapor-gas bubbles could become relatively irreversible.

Under such conditions, in the presence of chaotic shock waves, it is not possible to talk of the temperature of the mixture at a certain point (to consider this process as isothermal), nor it is possible to talk about a low rate of temperature change, constant pressure, or the reversibility of an isothermal process. Under these conditions, the concepts of entropy or enthalpy, as well as thermodynamic potentials, need additional definitions—if this is even possible in principle.

Consequently, upon transition to the resonance turbulization regime, characterized by the simultaneous and combined mechanical resonance action and fluid hammer phenomena, the process of forming dispersion systems becomes irreversible. In this case, they cannot be analyzed using regular thermodynamic methods. At the same time, all dispersion systems, regardless of how they are framed, are separated over time into constituent initial components after the termination of the action of an external perturbing force—relaxation. Therefore, for a final solution to this issue, additional research is required.

1.4. TORSION–ORIENTED TECHNOLOGICAL PROCESSES

At present, in astronomy, mechanics, and physics, a lot of observations have been accumulated related to the spontaneous ordering of the mutual arrangement of rotating subjects. These and many other experiments indicate the dependence of the energy of the system on its total rotation. Because in these experiments only the direction of the rotations changed, but not their magnitude, then in this case it is necessary to consider not only torsion interactions, which consist in the transfer of angular momentum of rotation, but also processes that can be called torsion-oriented processes.

According to Dr. V. Etkin, who contribution greatly to theoretical studies of torsion-oriented processes [28, 29], interest in them has increased in connection with the search for the so-called fifth force, that is, the total interaction of force fields that differ from gravitational and electromagnetic ones. Meanwhile, a huge number of facts underlying the thermodynamics of irreversible processes [30] indicate that any real process arises under the action of all forces acting in the system (Onsager's theorem) so that its character and direction is determined by the ratio of these forces and their degree of involvement in a particular process.

Onsager's theorem [31], is one of the main theorems of thermodynamic irreversible processes, establishes the symmetry property of the kinetic coefficients for cross phenomena. In thermodynamic systems (in which there are gradients of temperature), concentrations of components and chemical potentials, irreversible processes of mass transfer, heat exchange, and chemical reactions arise. These processes are characterized by mass and heat potential, rates of chemical reactions, etc. They are called by the general term flows, and the causes that cause them (deviations of thermodynamic parameters from equilibrium values) are called thermodynamic forces.

This is especially true for the processes occurring at the junction of the phenomena when the indicated forces have a different physical nature. Therefore, it would be correctly to speak about a specific process that arise under the action of already known forces, that lead to the order of the orientation of rotating systems or their parts, instead of an unknown force generated by an unknown interaction of various kinds of forces.

If a specific process of forming a dispersion system is associated with the transfer of the rotational acceleration of this system to elements of the dispersed phase, Dr. V. Etkin proposed to call them torsion-oriented processes [32]. Consideration of these processes, in his opinion, is advisable to consider from the standpoint of thermo-kinetics, as a unified theory of the mass transfer and internal energy [33], as well as from the energy dynamics and its further influence on the processes of conversion of various forms of energy [34].

1.5. LAW OF ENERGY CONSERVATION FOR DISPERSION SYSTEMS

It is known that classical thermodynamics expresses changes in the internal energy of the system U as a reversible (quasi-static) process. In general, the product of the total (generalized) potential Ψ_i (temperature T, pressure P, chemical potential of the k-th substance M_k, so on) by the change in the generalized coordinate of the physical parameters

θ_i (entropy $\mathbb{S}$, volume $-V$ (with the minus sign), the mass of the k-th substance M_k, and so on) [30, 31]:

$$dU = Td\mathbb{S} - PdV + \sum_k \mu_k dM_k = \sum_i \Psi_i d\theta_i \ , \quad (1.1)$$

where $i=1,2, \ldots ,n$ and n is the number of degrees of freedom of the equilibrium system; TdS is the elementary heat exchange of the system dQ; PdV is the elementary work of expansion dW; and $\mu_k dM_k$ is the energy transfer the k-th substance across the boundaries of the equilibrium system (energy exchange) dU_k.

For equilibrium systems expressed in general form by equation (1.1), the change in the generalized coordinate is due to the transfer of a certain amount of it across the boundaries of the system. This allows expressing the change in the parameters θ_i over time t to be expressed as:

$$\frac{d\theta_i}{dt} = -\int j_i n df, \qquad (1.2)$$

where $j = \rho_i w_i$ is the flux density of the physical parameter θ_i through the closed surface of the system f in the direction of the outer normal n; $\rho_i = \frac{d\theta_i}{dV}$ is the density of the parameters θ_i; $w_i = v_i - v_m$ is the speed of movement of its element $d\theta_i = \rho_i dV$ with respect to the center of mass of the elementary volume dV; and $v_i = \frac{d\overrightarrow{\mathfrak{r}_i}}{dt}$ and $v_m = \frac{d\overrightarrow{\mathfrak{r}_m}}{dt}$, $\overrightarrow{\mathfrak{r}_i}$ and $\overrightarrow{\mathfrak{r}_m}$ are the radius vectors (respectively) of the element of the i-th physical parameter $d\theta_i$ and an element of mass dM in a fixed system of coordinate.

Substituting (1.2) into (1.1), there is:

$$\frac{dU}{dt} = -\sum_i \Psi_i \int j_i ndf \quad (1.3)$$

The equation (1.3) is a consequence of a general expression:

$$\frac{dU}{dt} = -\sum_i \int \psi_i j_i ndf. \quad (1.4)$$

For a particular case of a homogeneous system, when the local value of the function ψ_i of the generalized potential, then Ψ_i is equal at all points of the system and therefore can be taken outside the integral sign, where $\psi_i j_i$ is the i-th component of the internal energy density $j_u = \sum_i \psi_i j_i$ through the element df of the surface of the system located relative to the fixed system of coordinate.

Based on the Ostrogradsky-Gauss theorem [35], expression (1.3) could be reduced to an integral over the volume of the system, the expression for the energy conservation law for an arbitrary region of the continuum can be written in the following form:

$$\frac{dU}{dt} = -\int divj_u dV. \quad (1.5)$$

If:

$$divj_u = \sum_i div(\psi_i j_i),$$

that the expanded form of equation (1.5) could be presented as the sum of two terms:

$$\sum_i \psi_i divj_i + \sum_i j_i grad\psi_i.$$

Or:

$$\frac{dU}{dt} = -\sum_i \psi_i div j_i + \sum_i \text{i} X_i j_i, \quad (1.6)$$

where $X_i = -\,grad\psi_i$ is the driving force of the i-th process, called in the theory of irreversible processes thermodynamic force in its energy representation.

In comparison with (1.1) equation (1.6) contains a doubled number of terms. Those additional members are related to processes that are not characteristic of homogeneous systems. First of all, these are processes of energy dissipation, leading to a spontaneous change in a number of thermodynamic parameters (entropy $\mathbb{S}$, volume V, mass of the k-th substance M_k, etc.) due to friction (viscosity), expansion into cavities, chemical reactions, etc.

The balance equations of these quantities:

$$\frac{d\rho_i}{dt} = -\,\mathrm{div}\,\mathrm{j}_i + \sigma_i, \qquad (1.7)$$

are considered by introducing the density of internal sources of this quantity σ_i [30]. The div j_i reflects the change in the quantity ρ_i because of the transfer of the physical parameters θ_i across the boundaries of the system, which takes place during mass transfer, heat exchange, volumetric deformation, etc. Also, by taken (1.7) into account equation (1.6) takes the following form:

$$\frac{dU}{dt} = \sum_i \int \psi_i(d\rho_i/dt)dV + \sum_i \int \psi_i\,\sigma_i\,dV + \\ + \sum_i \int X_i j_i\,dV \qquad (1.8)$$

It is easy to see that in equilibrium (externally and internally) systems in which the thermodynamic force $X_i = 0$ and the function of the generalized potential $\psi_i = \Psi_i$, and there are no internal sources σ_i, this equation transforms into (1.1). Consequently, the terms of the third sum (1.8) can refer only to the work W_i by the system being performed in addition to the work of the extension.

For the sake of simplification, let us consider the thermodynamic force X_i and the speed of displacement v_i constant over the volume of the system and, therefore, taking them outside the integral sign, we have:

$$\int X_i j_i \, dV = \int X_i v_i \, d\theta_i = F_i v_i, \quad (1.9)$$

where $F_i = \theta_i X_i$.

This expression (1.9) corresponds to the definition of the work (power) of the i-th process $N_i = \frac{dW_i}{dt}$ as the product of the resulting force F_i by the speed vi of the object of application of this value v_i. As a result, the thermodynamic force X_i becomes simple and understandable in the Newtonian understanding of the force referred to the i -th physical quantity ($X_i = \frac{F_i}{\theta_i}$).

According to equation (1.8), in the process of doing work, energy can pass from one (for example, i-th) form to any other form (for example, j-th), including thermal (so, the energy can dissipate). This circumstance makes the equation (1.6) valid for processes with any degree of dissipativity, and allows one to obtain from equation (1.8) the expression that is fundamental in the theory of irreversible processes for the rate of entropy occurrence in stationary processes ($\frac{dU}{dt} = 0$) [33].

Thus, the proposed form of the law of conservation of energy differs from the form of the law used in mechanics of continuous medium and thermodynamics of irreversible processes [30], taking into account additional processes of energy conversion, accompanied by the performance of useful work W_i including energy dissipation.

In case, when the system performs rotational motion, then an additional term is added to the right side of equation (1.1):

$$\sum \mathfrak{G}_{\alpha}\, d\theta_{\omega\alpha}\ ,$$

where $\mathfrak{G}_{\alpha}$ and $\theta_{\omega\alpha}$ are the components of the angular velocity vector $\overrightarrow{\mathfrak{S}_{\alpha}}$ (at $\alpha = 1,2,3$) and the angular momentum $\theta_{\omega} = I\mathfrak{S}$, where I is the moment of inertia of the body.

Thus, the term appears in the second sum of equation (1.6) $X_{\omega\alpha}Jj_{\omega\alpha}$, where $X_{\omega\alpha} = -\overrightarrow{\mathbb{N}}\omega_{\alpha}$, $j_{\omega\alpha} = \rho_{\omega}w_{\omega}$ are the components of the vector-gradient of the angular velocity $\overrightarrow{\mathbb{N}}\mathfrak{G}$ and the tensor of the flux density of the angular momentum, where $\rho_{\omega} = \vec{I}\,\theta_{\omega}/\vec{I}\,V$, and w_{ω} is the relative velocity of moment transfer amount of motion.

These terms characterize the processes of transfer of the rotational momentum in systems with an inhomogeneous field of angular velocity of rotation.

It was suggested to call this kind of interaction torsional [9, 10]. It should be noted that, according to equation (6), the transfer of vorticity [32] — in particular, turbulent transfer of momentum—possible in media with a moment of inertia, when $I \neq 0$.

When considering processes occurring in inhomogeneous systems, it can be carried out, that the radius vector $\overrightarrow{\mathfrak{r}_{\iota}}$ of the element $d\theta_i$ is expressed by the product of the basis (unit) vector $\overrightarrow{e_{\iota}}$, which is characterizes by the modulus $|r_i|$ of this vector. Therefore, in the general case, its change is expressed by two terms:

$$d\overrightarrow{\mathfrak{r}_{\iota}} = d_{\varphi}\overrightarrow{\mathfrak{r}_{\iota}} + d_{r}\overrightarrow{\mathfrak{r}_{\iota}} = e_i d\overrightarrow{\mathfrak{r}_{\iota}} + \overrightarrow{\mathfrak{r}_{\iota}} de_i . \quad (1.9)$$

In equation (1.9), the first term on the left-hand side $d_{\varphi}\overrightarrow{\mathfrak{r}_{\iota}}$ characterizes the transfer of the element $d\theta_i$ without changing the transfer direction e_i, and the second term $d_r\overrightarrow{\mathfrak{r}_{\iota}}$ characterizes the change in the direction of this vector.

It is more convenient to express the value of $d\mathbf{e}_i$ through the vector of the rotation angle φ, normal to the plane of rotation formed by the vectors $\overrightarrow{e_i}$ and the increment of this vector $d\overrightarrow{e_i}$ [33]. In this case, the increment $d\mathbf{e}_i$ is determined by the product of vectors $d\overrightarrow{\varphi_i}$ and $\overrightarrow{e_i}$, that:

$$r_i d\mathbf{e}_i = [d\boldsymbol{\varphi}_i, \mathbf{r}_i] \quad \text{and} \quad \mathbf{X}_i \times [d\boldsymbol{\varphi}_i, \mathbf{r}_i] = d\boldsymbol{\varphi}_i \times [\mathbf{r}_i, \mathbf{X}_i].$$

Taking into account (1.7) and (1.8), the equation (1.6) could be presented as:

$$\frac{dU}{dt} = \sum_i \int \psi_i (d\rho_i / dt)\, dV + \sum_i \int \psi_i\, \sigma_i\, dV +$$
$$+ \sum_i {}_i \int \mathbf{X}_i \cdot \mathbf{j}_i^c\, dV + \sum_i \int \mathbf{M}_i\, (d\varphi_i / dt)\, \rho_i dV \qquad (1.10)$$

where $\mathbf{j}_i^c = r_i \mathbf{e}_i \dfrac{dr_i}{dt}$ is the displacement of the flux density of the element $d\theta_i$ relative to the center of mass of the system; $M_i = r_i X_i$ is the moment of force X_i; and $\dfrac{d\varphi_i}{dt}$ is the angular velocity of rotation of the element $d\theta_i$ relative to the center of mass of the system.

Equation (1.10), according to Dr. V. Etkin [32], is the most general and at the same time the most detailed of the known mathematical formulations of the energy conservation law. In addition to the processes of energy dissipation, mass transfer and heat exchange in the considered theory of irreversible processes and physical kinetics, the equation (1.10) describes the processes of *reorientation* of displacement vectors $d\overrightarrow{r_i}$, arising in the presence of moments M_i of thermodynamic forces X_i. Moreover, it contains two types of members responsible for rotation.

First, these are the terms of the third sum (1.10) containing the "rotation" forces $X_{\omega\alpha}$, which are rotational components of the vector-gradient of the angular velocity $\overrightarrow{\mathbb{N}}\mathfrak{G}$. These terms characterize the processes of transfer of the angular moments of motion, caused by the inhomogeneous distribution of the density of the angular moment of rotation of subject (as well as their angular velocity ω).

The terms of the fourth sum of equation (1.10), containing the moments of forces M_i, determine the work done by the moment of force M_i per unit of time when the element $d\theta$ is reoriented at a speed $X_e j_e$. However, in accordance with (1.9) and (1.10), these moments disappear when the direction of the vectors $\overrightarrow{X_i}$ and $d\overrightarrow{r_i}$ coincides. Therefore, according to Etkin [30], these moments of force should be called not rotation moments of forces but orientated moments of forces.

Unlike torsional, the orientation processes do not change the angular momentum of the system and its kinetic energy of rotation, affecting only the orientation of dispersed particles relative to external elements or fields (angle φ_i) (i.e. to a part of their potential energy $U(\varphi_i)$), which depends on their mutual orientation. In accordance with the thermodynamic principles of the classification of processes (distinguishing processes not for reasons causing them, and not for the physical nature of the interaction, but for their consequences), such processes should be called oriented.

1.6. NATURE OF ORIENTATION'S MOMENTS

A feature of the formation of dispersed systems (as a special case, inhomogeneous systems) under conditions of joint and simultaneous action of mechanical resonance and the impact of numerous shock waves arising from exploding vapor-gas bubbles is the shift of the center of the extensive parameters θ_i. Those parameters are relative to the center of mass of the total dispersion system. This, to a certain extent, coincides with what was shown in Etkin's work [34].

It is known that the position of this center, the radius vector of which is designated $\overrightarrow{\mathbf{R}_1}$ and is equal to:

$$\overrightarrow{R_i} = \frac{1}{\theta_i}\int \overrightarrow{r_i}\, d\theta_i \qquad (1.11)$$

Let suppose that position of the center of the parameters θ_i in the homogeneous (equilibrium) system R_{io} is taken as the origin of the current coordinate r_i. In this case $\Delta R_i = R_i - R_{io}$. So, for any equilibrium state the external R_m and the internal position R_{io} are coincide, ΔR_i will determine the displacement of the center of parameters θ_i from the center of mass of the system R_m. Thus, under the action of the forces X_i in a dispersion system, a certain "moment of distribution" $\mathbf{Z}_i = \theta_i \Delta R_i$ of the parameter θ_i looks like:

$$Z_i = \theta_i \Delta R_i = \int \overrightarrow{r_i}\, d\theta_i\,. \qquad (1.12)$$

The redistribution of the parameters $\int \overrightarrow{r_i}\, d\theta_i$ can cause that some of the forces acting in the system with respect to the mass of the system to act *off-center*. Those forces, after being brought to the center of mass of the system, form oriented moments that tend to reorient the increment of the center of mass position ΔR_i in such a way that the forces $\mathbf{X}_i$ tend to act *in-center*.

A less obvious reason may be the presence of several oppositely directed forces X_i in the emerging dispersion system. According to the basic proposition of the theory of irreversible processes, each of the flows j_i arises under the total action of all forces of the same tensor rank X_j in the system (for $j = 1, 2, \ldots n$). This assumption is in full compliance with the Onsager's principle [31]:

$$j_i = \sum_i L_{ij} X_j\,, \qquad (1.13)$$

where L_{ij} are so-called phenomenological coefficients characterizing the conductivity of the system. The particular cases of equation (1.13) are the well-known laws of heat exchange (Fourier's), electrical conductivity (Ohm's), mass transfer (Fick's), filtration (Darcy's), viscosity (or friction) (Newton's), and so on.

Thus, in accordance with modern concepts, forces of different nature, generating one or another independent process, are generally equal to the number of nonequilibrium degrees of freedom of the system. Because of that, they cannot be reduced to the four known types of fundamental interactions. In this case, equations (1.13) reflect the interrelation of processes arising as a result of the imposition of dissimilar forces X_j. This superposition leads to the emergence of numerous phenomena (thermomechanical, thermochemical, mechanochemical, etc.) [30. 31].

In particular, as it follows from (1.13), the process of displacement of any parameter θ_i (for example, electric current) can arise not only from the forces of electrical nature, but also under the action of the thermo-motion force $X_j = -\vec{\nabla}T$. The last force, as is known, along with the magnetic component of the Lorentz force, bends the trajectory of the electric charge and leads to the appearance of an electric field E in the direction of the force X_j. This phenomenon is called the thermo-magnetic phenomenon [10].

Similarly, the process of redistribution of electric charges can also cause mechanical stresses X_{Mech} (piezoelectric phenomenon). Thus, equations (1.6) and (1.10), instead of searching for a unified field theory, propose a unified method for finding clearly distinguishable driving forces of various physicochemical processes, including the processes of heat transfer, mass transfer, transformation of rotational motion, and reorientation of inhomogeneities that are present in the system. These last processes arise under the action of the moments M_i tending to reorient the increments of the vectors $\overrightarrow{\Delta \mathbf{R}_1}$ in the direction of their decrease. Since the vectors $\overrightarrow{\mathbf{M}_1}$ and $\mathrm{d}\overrightarrow{\boldsymbol{\varphi}_1}$ were the result of the expansion of the second sum in equation (6) and reflect two sides of the same process of redistribution of the parameter θ_i, any equation similar to

(1.12) could be written for the generalized rates of the reorientation process as:

$$\frac{\overrightarrow{d\boldsymbol{\varphi}_1}}{dt} = \sum K_{ij} M_j, \quad (1.14)$$

where K_{ij} are phenomenological coefficients characterizing the compliance of dispersion systems to rotation.

As in equation (1.13), the equation (1.14) reflects the fact that the process of reorientation of the dispersion system can be caused by any of the moments M_j. In particular, this means that the process of orientation is influenced by various fields of forces: temperatures, differences in internal pressures between adjacent elementary volumes (the internal tension), and so on. Reorientation processes can also produce torsion fields characterized by the antisymmetric part of the tensor $\boldsymbol{\nabla}\mathfrak{G}$.

During conducted experiments, inside of the central part of the reactor, the tornado-like formation of floating and simultaneously rotating vapor-gas bubbles was observed. It is quite probable that this behavior of dispersed particles was caused by the action of some of the moments $\mathbf{M}_i$ on the rotating particles of the dispersed phase. This explains the occurrence of motion, in which the system forms a figure that look like hyperbola. Thus, there is every reason to assume that such a distribution of dispersed particles coincides with the torsion-oriented field contours.

It is also known that the moment of force M_i, which must be applied to the axis of rotation to rotate it through an angle $d\varphi_i$ in time dt, is equal to the rate of change of the angular momentum θ_ω [36]:

$$M_i = \left|\frac{d\varphi_i}{dt}\right| \times |\theta_\omega| \sin \varphi_i. \quad (1.15)$$

Thus it follows that for the same value of the disturbing moment M_i, the angle φ_i is the smaller, the higher the angular moment θ_ω. Therefore, when an additional angular moment θ_ω is imparted to the subject, the angle φ_i decreases (i.e. the orientation of the axes of rotation of subjects becomes more organized). Thus, the change of the angular moment is also accompanied by a reorientation of the angular moment of the rotating components of the dispersed phase. It is these processes that V. Etkin called torsion-oriented [32]. This allows the subject process of formation of dispersion systems to be considered as torsion-oriented turbulization as well.

From equation (1.10), any forms of ordered energy transfer and mass exchange can include components that perceive by dispersion systems as their oriented polarization. This circumstance makes it superfluous to consider additional influences to explain the phenomena associated with this. According to the above, the existence of torsion and oriented interactions directly follows from the energy conservation law applicable to dispersion systems. Regardless of their nature, these interactions give rise to processes of orderly energy exchange, such as the ability to perform work.

Consideration of torsion-oriented processes and the corresponding interactions are of a purely thermodynamic nature. That statement does not claim to be a fully described of all details of the subject process and therefore does not require the establishment of the nature of the mentioned interactions, or a structure of the system, or a mechanism of the energy transfer. This approach makes it possible to draw a clear line between torsional and oriented phenomena. From a standpoint of energy dynamics, torsion interactions are generated by an inhomogeneous field of angular velocities of rotation of media possessing mass and a certain moment of inertia. In this case, the oriented impact is transmitted by known force fields.

Consideration of oriented processes is a definite step toward the study of the process of formation of dispersion systems. It provides a key to understanding the origin of such processes, to finding their driving forces and to clarifying their influence on the functional capabilities of nonequilibrium systems. When some relaxation processes occur in some parts or degrees of freedom of a polyvariant system, their other parts or degrees of freedom can move away from equilibrium, which ensures the possibility of a long-term development of such systems, bypassing the state of equilibrium.

This is because the fact that the approach of the system to equilibrium is accompanied not only by energy dissipation, but also by a useful transformation of energy. The internal work performed at the same time ensures the maintenance of a temporary order in the system, called dissipative structures. It is characteristic that in the most inhomogeneous system such useful transformations of energy can be caused not only by external force fields (electromagnetic, gravitational), but also by the fields of temperatures, internal pressures (stresses), concentrations, etc.

This is of particular importance for understanding the causes of the emergence of the so-called processes of self-organization, which is due to the performance of useful internal work of some parts of the system on others with the inevitable irreversibility (presence of losses) in both. In particular, equation (1.10) reveals the reasons for the emergence of the so-called dissipative structures, (i.e. ordered states maintained by dissipative processes in the system). In this case, the stationary state of partially ordered systems arises through the mutual compensation of two opposite processes - orientation (when performing work) and disorientation (caused by energy dissipation). It is especially important to understand that torsion-oriented turbulization can be spontaneous.

CHAPTER 2

VIBRATION PROCESSES

As noted earlier, this monograph is devoted to the study of the occurrence of resonance cavitation and torsion-oriented turbulization.

The resonance cavitation phenomenon is similar in nature to common cavitation but differs in that it develops not only on a free surface that limits the volume of liquid (i.e., inside the pipeline) but in the total volume of the components located inside a hermetically sealed reactor. The reason for the occurrence of the resonance cavitation phenomenon under consideration is the simultaneous and combined actions of resonance impact and fluid hammer impact, arising from the effect of an external disturbing field of vibrational forces. Cavitation does not change the volume of the mixture because this mixture fills the entire internal space of the reactor. The reactor's shell and covers are the external boundaries of the formed dispersion system.

If the size of the power influence at each timepoint causes many bubbles to arise, develop, and burst in the dispersion environment, there is an intensive hashing and power impact on dispersion medium external borders. The greatest effect is reached when the force operating on the reactor result from the impact of the compelled fluctuations whose frequency approaches the frequency of the natural fluctuations of the mix, that is, in the mode of a mechanical resonance.

Thus, the development of the processes of chemical technology to use the power of vibration for the formation of dispersion systems seems extremely promising.

2.1. PHYSICOCHEMICAL VIBRATION TECHNOLOGY

In chemical technology, there are known processes for hashing bulk powders by passing air through them are reminiscent of the process of boiling. However, the processes of hashing and drying in the vibration boiling layer are more effective when intensive hashing is created by the influence of low-frequency vibrations. In this case, hashing happens at any speed of gas or liquid, even without a supply of gas under a powder layer. Hashing could also be achieved in a vacuum.

In 1963, researchers at the Institute of Physical Chemistry of the Academy of Sciences of the USSR, researched aerodynamic properties of powders and found out that bulks in the vibration boiling layer, rather than showing resistance to the filtered gas, are sucking the gas by themselves and, like a pump, are transferring this gas up to the upper surface of a layer [38].

These experiments were conducted in a device whose internal chamber was divided by a screen. The device was installed on a vibration platform that vibrated in the vertically. The layer of the powders studied was loaded on a horizontal screen. The pressure of the gas in the device was measured using differential micromanometers installed under the screen. Similar measurements were taken by the device with a flat metal bottom, where the studied powder was laid. The pressure that developed under the powder layer was measured using thin tubes connected to micromanometers.

It was found that the vibrating quasi–boiling layer created in the device showed a steady difference in the gas static pressure. At the same time, there was a discharge in the area under the powder layer. The scientists discovered that the influence of various factors on the difference in static pressure and the mechanism of its emergence process in the vibration boiling layer.

It was proven [38] that the difference in the static pressure inside the layer of material arises at the time of transition from a condition of vibration fluidization into one of vibration boiling. This transition results from the acceleration of the vibration platform when it equals the acceleration the gravity of particles in a layer. When vibration parameters, including amplitude, frequency, and acceleration, exceed a critical point, the static pressure difference of gas increases. At the same time, the decrease in gas permeability resulting from the increase in a layer's thickness or the reduction of the size of particles, also leads to an increase in the difference of the static pressure of the gas. The increase in the effective viscosity of the powder's layer, resulting from the roughness of the surface of particles or an increase in the humidity of the material, reduces the difference of the static pressure. Researchers found that periodic changes occur in the density of the powder in the horizontal plane of the vibration boiling layer [38]. Moving up from the lower layers, layers with the higher density transport the gas ahead of themselves, creating a static discharge of gas beneath themselves and increasing the static pressure above.

The application for this discovery, titled "The Phenomenon of the Emergence of Difference of the Static Pressure of Gas in the Vibro-boiling Layer" for discovery was submitted to the State Register of Discoveries in the USSR, No. 138 with priority date June 4, 1963. It was submitted with following claim: "The phenomenon of the emergence of static pressure difference of the gas, unknown earlier in the vibro-boiling layer, which is formed as a result of the cyclic change of porosity of the dispersed material subjected to vertical vibration influence with the acceleration exceeding the acceleration of gravity of the material in this environment, is experimentally established".

From 1970 to 1979, the research on vibration processes was conducted at the Institute of Physical Chemistry of the Academy of Sciences of the USSR [39–42]. However, later, for subjective reasons, these research studies in Russia were later discontinued.

These conducted research studies [39–59] showed the following:

- The preparation time for cosmetic creams, shampoos, and pastes, depended on their components that are a part of them, but did not exceed 1 to 2 minutes. The quality of the products, measured against the production requirements was excellent, according to the Quality Control Laboratory.
- The process of mayonnaise homogenization continued for no longer than 2 minutes. Its rheological and flavoring properties conformed to standard requirements, but the organoleptic properties were much

higher than those of mayonnaise with a similar structure that was produced using the standard technique.

- The preparation of dough took 3 to 5 minutes, but bread freshness lasted significantly longer.
- The process of the forming of butter from milk took no longer than 30 to 60 seconds. Moreover, it became possible to prepare butter with a fat content of less than 50% fact content as well as what was essentially a new product: hard sour cream with a fat content of 20% to 30%.
- Extraction from raw vegetable materials for pharmaceutical applications ended in only minutes. The amount of the extracted substances was close to theoretical.
- The washing of diamond powder and diamonds to remove the riveted metals in the mixture of sulfuric and hydrochloric acids was fully completed within 10 to 15 minutes.
- The process of liquid saturation by soluble gas in the cultivation of microorganisms was completed within 5 to 30 seconds. During this process, the liquid was saturated with air micro-bubbles. This all occurred in the intensive hashing of the nutrient medium, which that is extremely essential to ensuring deep processes. The consumption of gas was cut between 50 and 100 times.

These research studies [39–59] noted that power- and labor-intensive processes were accelerated 10 to 50 times. Moreover, the quality of the final products surpassed that of similar products processed using orthodox techniques. Now, subjective circumstances allow for research on these phenomena to be continued in the US.

2.2. PHYSICOCHEMICAL DYNAMICS

Classically, physicochemical dynamics is considered a branch of colloidal chemistry that studies mechanical, physical, and other properties of dispersion systems and the processes of formation, stability, destruction, deformation, and minimization [60–69].

Physicochemical dynamics covers the comprehensive study of the molecular, structural, rheological, and thermodynamic characteristics of materials and nonlinear behavior with variation in thermodynamic conditions; it also carries out physical, and physicochemical experiments and pilot studies of processes using mathematical modeling.

Research has continued in Russia and the USA on vibration processes, including the formation of dispersion systems [70–81] and the design and development of chemical reactors [82–95].

All existing publications of patents and results of research and development (R&D) on vibration methods and applicable hardware can be divided into the following groups:

- The first group: Patents related to the general methods and reactors that allow an increase in the interface between phases of the processed systems [96–98],
- The second group: Patents related to the methods and reactors that use the mixing devices and allow for an increase in the interface between phases of the processed systems [99–102],
- The third group: Patents related to the methods and reactors that use bubble columns (with both an open and closed tops) and allow for an increase in the interface between phases of the processed systems [103–109],
- The fourth group: Patents related to the methods and reactors that use vibration mechanisms and allowing for an increase the interface between phases of the processed systems [110–112],
- The fifth group: Patents related to the technological techniques and reactors that use various physical methods including cavitation, and allow for an increase in the interface between phases of the processed systems [113–133],
- The sixth group: Patents related to the methods and reactors that use mechanical and physical methods, including cavitation, for the purposes not related to increasing an interface between phases [134],
- The seventh group: Patents related to methods and reactors that use mechanical and physical methods, including cavitation allowing for

increasing the interface between phases of the processed systems [135],

- The eighth group: Patents related to the methods and reactors that use various vibration methods for processing dispersion systems [136–147].

Along with mechanochemistry (a science that studies the physicochemical and chemical phenomena that occur under the influence of fields of a mechanical and physical-mechanical nature), the resonance cavitation and the torsion-oriented turbulization are significantly affecting the intensification of heat transfer and mass exchange resulting from absorption of mechanical vibrational energy. One reason for the activation of the formation of dispersion systems is the absorption of vibrational energy that is transmitted through a hydrodynamic field. By analogy with ordinary cavitation, we also observe the development and collapse of gas bubbles, discontinuities in the liquid component, and the formation of vacuum caverns distributed in a dispersion medium. When the bubbles of the vapor–gas mixture and vacuum cavities burst inside the dispersion phase, gas and vapor molecules transfer vibrational energy and their association and dissociation.

2.3. PRELIMINARY EXPERIMENTAL STUDIES

To define the conditions of the emergence of torsion-oriented turbulization, there were carried out experiments on 3.5– and 5.5–liter reactors. The shells of the reactors were made of transparent 6.5 mm thick PYREX® glass made by Corning Inc. This material has a high rigidity and a low coefficient of temperature expansion. The reactors were made with rigid elements capable of remaining in a zone of elastic deformations under the influence of an external disturbing force. The top and bottom covers of the reactors were made of chemically resistant 12.0 mm thick 316L stainless steel (Fig. 2-1 to Fig. 2-7). The ratio of the internal diameter of the reactor to its height was 1:6 (Fig. 2-1) [2–4]. During assembly, all point of connection were filled with a liquid silicone sealant. All sealing gaskets were made of silicone.

The parameters of the reactors were as follows:

- Reactor #1: The height was 558.8 mm, the outer diameter was 101.6 mm, and the internal diameter was 88.90 mm. The weight of the empty reactor was approximately 10 kg.
- Reactor #2: The height was 685.8 mm, the outer diameter was 127.0 mm, and the internal diameter was 114.3 mm. The weight of the empty reactor was approximately 15 kg.

All tests were carried out at Independent Testing Laboratories (Costa Mesa, CA). The electrodynamic vibration machine MB Electronics C-50 was used as a source of external vibration impact for the reactor. The vibration machine was capable to generate harmonic oscillations from 3 to 2,000 Hz at an acceleration of up to 50 G.

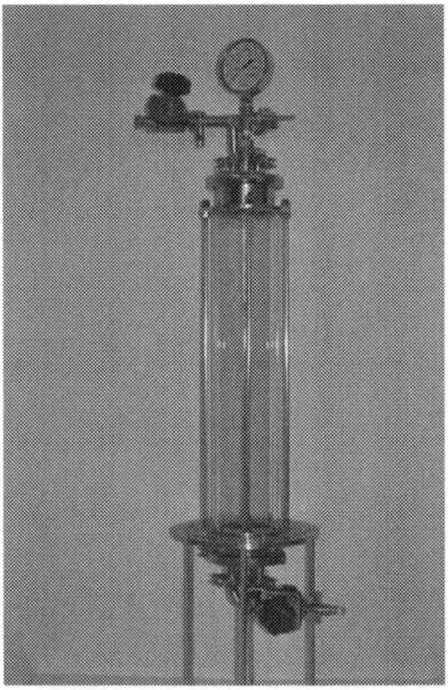

Figure 2-1. The Experimental Reactor

The vibration machine was controlled by a Dell computer equipped with the computer program "The Data Physics, DP-350, QA Manager," developed by the US company Signal Star.

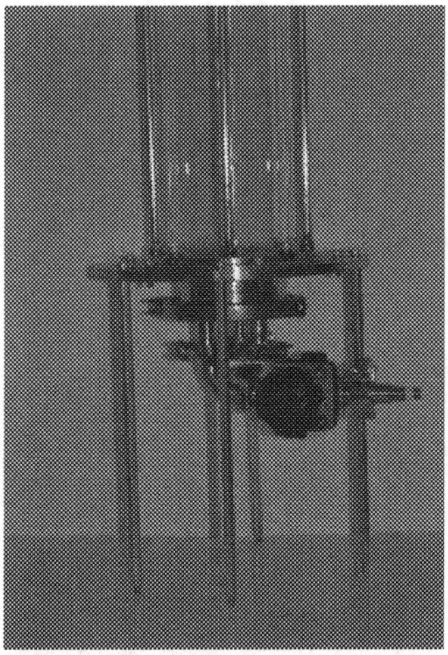

Figure 2-2. The Lower Part of the Reactor

The vibrating machine consisted of a movable platform connected to the housing by a mechanical system that allowed for perpendicular reciprocating motion, strictly ensuring a single degree of freedom for the reactor. The machine included a magnetic coil, which creates a high magnetic flux density. The coil of the solenoid was rigidly attached to the platform and was located inside the magnetic coil. When electric current passes through, the solenoid experiences a pushing force proportional to the magnitude of the flowing current. The developing force is then transmitted to the solenoid, causing it to move in the axial direction relative to the winding. In this process, because the high density of the electromagnetic field, the elements of the vibrating device are heated. The air cools the electrical windings of the vibrating machine.

The vibrating machine consisted of a movable platform connected to the housing by a mechanical system that allowed for perpendicular reciprocating motion, strictly ensuring a single degree of freedom for the reactor. The machine included a magnetic coil, which creates a high magnetic flux density. The coil of the solenoid was rigidly attached to the platform and was located inside the magnetic coil. When electric current passes through, the solenoid experiences a pushing force proportional to the magnitude of the flowing current. The developing force is then transmitted to the solenoid, causing it to move in the axial direction relative to the winding. In this process, because the high density of the electromagnetic field, the elements of the vibrating device are heated. The air cools the electrical windings of the vibrating machine.

The reactor was installed on the vibration table of the vibration machine (Fig. 2-3).

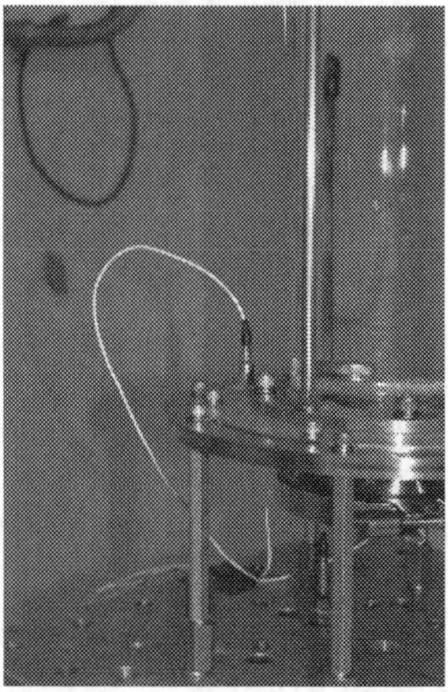

Figure 2-3. Sensors of Vibration Parameters

Tests were carried out in the mode of harmonic oscillations in the range of frequencies in the 30- to 80-Hz frequency range and the 1.25- to 3.00-mm amplitude range, developing acceleration from 20 to 50 G.

For the purpose of receiving two-phase liquid-air dispersion systems in the mode of resonance cavitation, the liquid component of the subject heterogeneous systems was loaded into reactor, filling about 92% percent of its internal chamber (to a height of approximately 550 mm). The remaining space was filled with air.

Let us consider, from the physical point of view, a system that is at the initial stage of the process. All components of the future dispersion system loaded into the reactor are under the influence of the gravitational force. The possible actions of other force fields of a physical nature could be neglected. Under such circumstances, the components have a certain quantity of energy, which could be defined by the condition of the force fields at each point in time.

Components of the heterogeneous system contain the mass of liquids and gases and, in some cases, solid particles. All of them fill the internal volume of the reactor; in essence, the space is filled with material points. Thus, there is no doubts about the balance of the equation:

$$G = mg, \tag{2.1}$$

where G is the weight of the liquid, [N]; $m = \pi \rho r^2 (h_L - h_R)$ is the mass of the liquid, [Kg]; g is the acceleration due to the gravity at point of measurement [m/s^2]; π = 3,14; ρ is the liquid density, [kg/m^3]; r is the internal radius of the reactor, [m]; h_L is the cumulative height of components of the planned disperse system filling of the reactor, [m]; and h_R is the internal height of the reactor, [m].

If the reactor is installed on the vibrator's moving platform, the force field changes when the vibrator acts on the reactor that is filled with components of the planned dispersion system. Experiments were carried out in the zone of harmonic oscillations: that is, in those zones in which the physical quantity changes over time according to sinusoidal law.

The kinematic equation of such harmonic oscillations is:

$$x\ (t) = A\ sin\ (\omega t + \varphi) \text{ or } x\ (t) = A\ cos\ (\omega t + \varphi),$$

where x is the shift of the fluctuating point from the equilibrium position at the time t, [m]; A is the amplitude of fluctuations, [m]; ω is the cyclic frequency, [Hz]; $(\omega t + \varphi)$ is the full phase of fluctuations, [Hz]; and φ is an initial phase of fluctuations, [Hz].

The differential equation describing harmonic oscillations is:

$$\frac{d^2x}{dt^2} + \omega^2 = 0.$$

Any uncommon solution of this differential equation is a harmonic oscillation with a cyclic frequency ω.

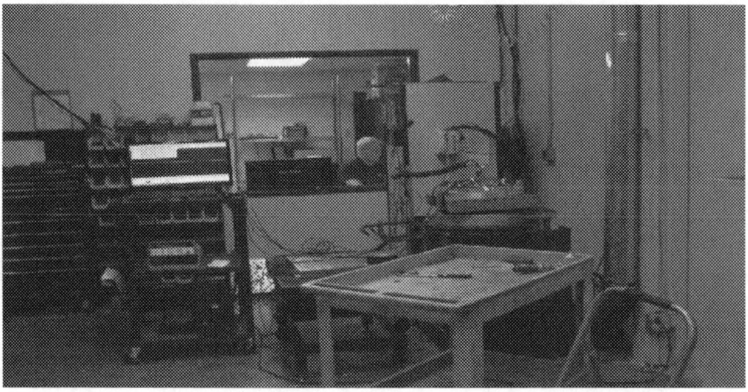

Figure 2-4. General View of the Testing Laboratory

Figure 2-5. The Lower Part of the Reactor with Sensors of Fluctuation Parameters

At the onset of the vertically directed sinusoidal oscillations of the reactor, the components located in the reactor begin to move, creating a certain material flow inside the reactor related to the internal cross section of the reactor at each moment in time. In this case, the force field inside the reactor changes, adding a disturbing force that acts on the reactor. The perturbing force changes the direction of the action according to the frequency of oscillations. Thus, it is a function that depends on time. As a result of the action of the disturbing forces of vibration transmitted from the vibrator to the reactor, the dynamic pressure forces, $\mathcal{P}_{\text{Pr}}$, are equal to:

$$\mathcal{P}_{\text{Pr}} = \frac{\mathcal{M}w}{S} \qquad (2.2)$$

where: $\mathcal{M} = \frac{\pi\rho r^2}{t}(h_L - h_R)$ is the mass of a moving stream at the time t, [kg/s]; w is the linear speed of the stream, [m/s]; and $S = \pi r^2$ is the area of the cross section of the stream equal to the area of the internal cross section of the reactor, [m^2].

In equation (2.2), the pressure $\mathcal{P}_{\text{Pr}}$ is measures by the force $\mathcal{F}(t)$ and is distributed over the internal cross section of the reactor. This pressure is equalized in section $S = \pi r^2$ of the stream, with the consumption of the mass and with the linear speed w. The force $\mathcal{F}(t)$ is equal to:

$$\mathcal{F}(t) = \mathcal{A} sin(\omega t + \varphi) \text{ or } \mathcal{F}(t) = \mathcal{A} cos(\omega t + \varphi).$$

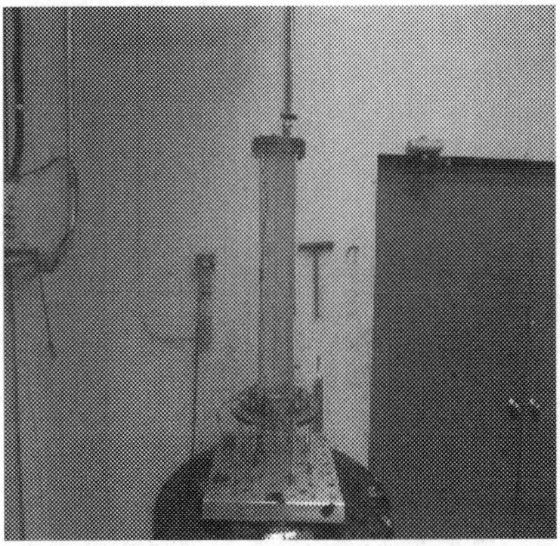

Figure 2-6. The Reactor Installed on the Testing Machine

Equation (2.2) defines the relationship between force and mass during the change of the condition of the heterogeneous system as a response to the change in the force field. When changing the condition of the system, the force is determined by the amount of energy that measures the ability to perform a certain amount of work. The direct change of a state in the equation (2.2) is expressed by the consumption of mass $\mathcal{M}$, in units of time.

2.4. ANALYSIS OF PRELIMINARY STUDIES

Conducted experiments showed that the phenomenon of resonance cavitation arises in the chemical reactor while it is under the influence of the external indignant forces. All components loaded into the reactor were under the influence of the gravitational force. Upon impact of the external indignant force, which acts upon the reactor with the liquid loaded in it at the low frequencies of oscillation and at small amplitudes, small ripples were observed on the free surface of the liquid.

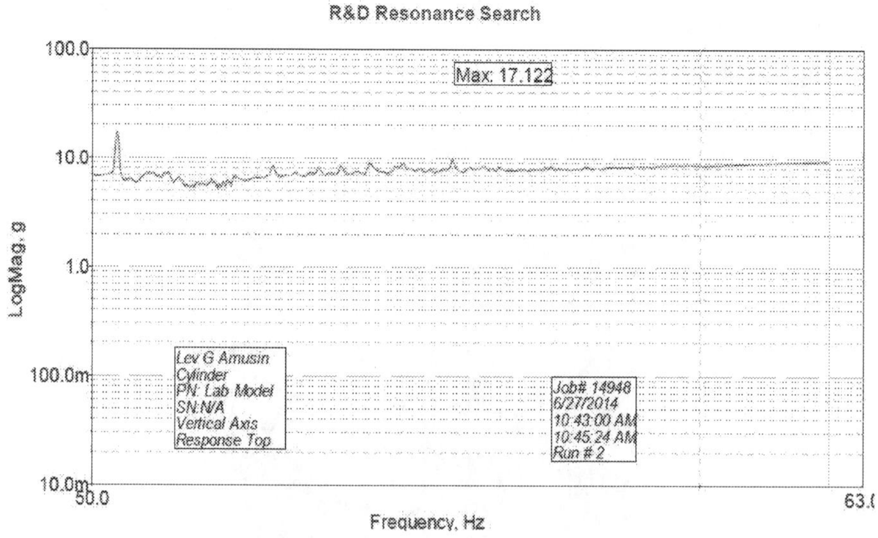

Figure 2-7. Part of the Registration Tape with the Allocated Resonance Mode

The motion of the uniform liquid in the middle part of the reactor was noticeable because the laminar component prevails near the reactor's transparent walls. It explains the observations at this stage of the displacement of small volumes from the center to the periphery on the free surface of the liquid. A further increase in the vibrational frequency brought the liquid to a more excited state, characterized by the development and chaotic movement of separate bubbles, as small as approximately 1 mm, inside the liquid located at the bottom of the reactor.

Each elementary volume of the dispersion phase makes oscillatory movements. These wave motions act upon the elements (particles of solid matter and/or elementary volumes of liquid) of the dispersed phase, distributing them in such a way that these elements' centers of mass move to one side with respect to the elementary volumes of the dispersion medium. Figuratively speaking, waves in the liquid generate one-sided directed movements of the elements of the dispersed phase. Moreover, the directions of these movements depend on the position of the particles of the dispersed phase inside the cylindrical reactor. For this, there are two possible cases:

1. If the dispersed phase elements are inside the annular layer (Fig. 2–8), crossing the lower part of the cylinder along the outer ring and the upper part of the cylinder along the inner ring, the waves that arise inside the dispersion medium contribute to the downward movement of the particles of the dispersed phase.
2. If the dispersed phase elements are outside the annular layer, the waves that occur inside the dispersion medium facilitate the upward movement of the dispersed phase elements in the opposite direction, (i.e., upward).

As the frequency approached, zones formed in the internal volumes of the liquid medium in the central part of the reactor in which there was increased activity in the bubbles' critical values. Bubbles, like a swarm of bees, stray together. Single bubbles increased in volume and were interconnected, forming aggregates. They were separated from the walls of the reactor and from one another by layers of the liquid medium. This chaotic mixture of liquid and gas, comprising large, asymmetric and small bubbles, was in the central part of the reactor. Ultimately, all bubbles either float up and burst or burst while they are developing. This process resembles the nucleation of bubbles during boiling.

It should be noted that, for some amplitude and frequency values that differ from resonance, bubbles move to the bottom of the reactor. If there are solid particles with a density greater than that of the dispersion medium, they float up to the free surface of the liquid. A similar phenomenon was described earlier by V. Chelomey [147].

With a further increase in the frequency of vibrational exposure, there comes a moment when the frequency of the external disturbance coincided with the frequency of the internal oscillation of the components of the mixture in the reactor. At this point, a state of turbulization arose in the reactor. The components of the mixture, as though exploding, filled the entire internal space of the reactor and, hitting the reactor's top cover, caused a fluid hammer impact.

Previously, we conducted those experiments in a reactor whose 6 mm thick walls were made of transparent polyacrylonitrile (also known as organic glass or plexiglass), with the top and bottom covers made of polycarbonate, also known as LEXAN®. Both materials absorb shock energy, stretching in the direction of the forces developing inside the reactor. In such a reactor, it was impossible to create a torsion-oriented turbulization mode.

This phenomenon can take place only when the reactor's shell and both the top and bottom covers are rigid enough to keep the deformation of the reactor's components within the elastic zone. Only under this condition are they capable of withstanding the development of shock influences. From this moment onward, the processes proceeded at a constant volume [2-5].

The analysis of the results received of the above experiments— and their comparison with the results of similar research conducted at the Scientific Center of Nonlinear Wave Mechanics and Technologies of The Institute of Engineering of the RF Academy of Science [titled: "Resonant Processes in Confined Spaces": www.nwmtc.ac.ru/basis/home01.htm] —showed that fluctuations with 1 degree of freedom are capable of significantly improving the quality of the homogenization of heterogeneous dispersion systems (Fig. 2-7). Harmonious influences of the external indignant force can produce complicated movements in the dispersed phase and elementary volumes of the dispersion media. Such modes can intensify the processes of the formation of dispersion systems.

Fig. 2-8 schematically shows one of the motions of the individual particles in the dispersed phase, suspended in a dispersion medium located in a cylindrical reactor [titled: "Resonant Processes in Confined Spaces"]. At both ends of the reactor, the regions of instability that repulse particles of the dispersed phase are marked in pink, and the regions of stability that attract them are shown in green–blue.

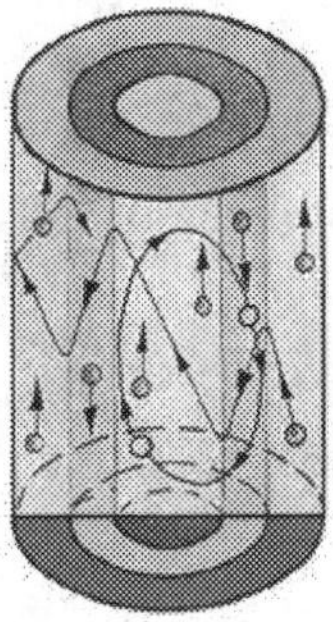

Figure 2-8. Scheme of the Movement of Elements of the Dispersed Phase

The external disturbing effect led to a multidirectional motion of the elementary volumes of the dispersed phase distributed in the dispersion medium. Moreover, particles that had transverse velocities unequal to zero at the initial moment, falling into different zones of the reactor, could acquire velocities with different directions in the vertical component—first in one direction, and then in the other. Thus, the vibrational effect of a disturbing force acting upon the dispersion medium can be the cause of various forms of motion of the dispersed phase's mixing, separation, localization, and stabilization, etc. In this case, the motion of the dispersed phase itself can change substantially. This kind of movement contributes to the intensification of the formation of dispersion systems.

Fig. 2-9a shows the process of filling the dispersion phase with air bubbles. Fig. 2-9b shows the status of the vibrational cavitation mode. These figures show the stages of the transferring the "liquid-gas" system into the turbulization mode. In the first stage, the bubbles filled with liquid— in the "violation" of the Archimedes principle—sank and gathered on the bottom of the reactor as a “swarm” (Fig. 2-9a). That is, the mode of wave stabilization of gas bubbles formation was realized. In the next step, the system switched to motion in turbulization and intensive mixing. The energy transferred to the system by external periodic influences to the system was rather small.

Figure 2-9a

Figure 2-9b

The photographs in Figs. 2–10a, 2–10b, and 2–10c shows the process of mixing two immiscible and insoluble liquids: oil and water. The first photograph (Fig. 2–10a) shows a mixture of oil and water before being processed in the torsion-oriented turbulization mode. The liquids are separated oil there is in the upper part of the reactor and water is in the lower part.

The photograph in Fig. 2–10b shows the phenomenon of vibrational cavitation. Under certain regimes of frequencies and amplitudes of vibrational influence, a uniform emulsion with a dispersion of the order of 2 mm is created almost instantly in the reactor. In this case, a heterogeneous dispersed structure fills the entire internal volume of the reactor. The amplitude of the oscillations needed to maintain the regime is within a range of a few millimeters.

Vibrational cavitation phenomenon involves several nonlinear mechanisms of wave motions of inclusions in liquids with the formation of the so-called stable and unstable surfaces located in a volume occupied by an excited multiphase dispersion medium. After the cessation of external influences, the emulsion does not exfoliate for a long time.

The third photograph (Fig. 2–10c), shows the beginning of the emulsion separation process.

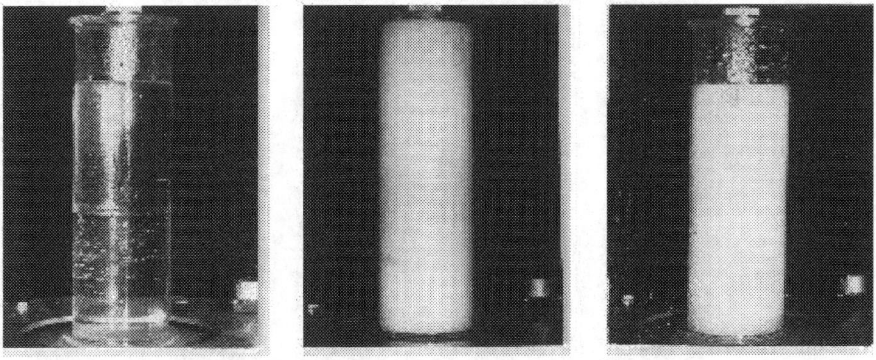

Figure 2-10a **Figure 2-10b** **Figure 2-10c**

Figure 2-11a. The Initial Stage of the Vibration Process

The photographs in (Figs. 2-11a, 2-11b, and 2-11c) show certain periods in which the phenomenon under consideration occurs. At the very beginning of the process, bubbles develop at the bottom of the reactor (Fig. 2-10a).

Then, as vibrational cavitation stabilizes, when the minimum pressure moves to the middle part of the reactor, the bubbles also move to the center (Fig. 2-10b). Finally, at a moment of resonance, the system explosively forms a dispersion system, filling the entire space of the reactor (Fig. 2-10c).

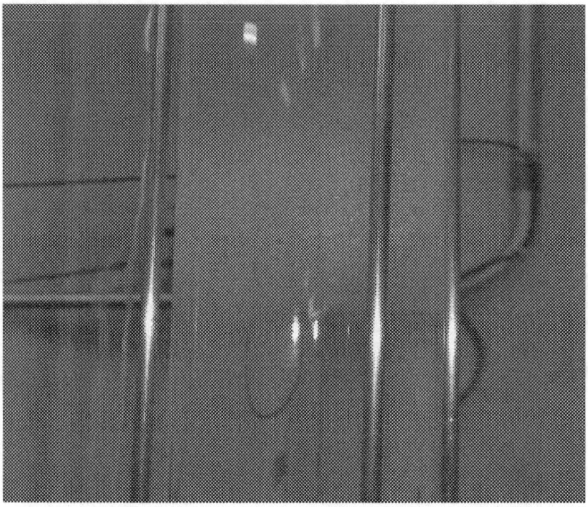

Fig. 2-11b. The Stabilization of the Process—Resonance Cavitation

The above experiments helped define the condition(s) of the existence the resonance cavitation. This effect is accompanied by several unique phenomena:

- In a dispersion medium, we observe the intense emergence, development, and collapse of vapor-gas bubbles, which leads to the emergence of very significant local pressure pulsations.

- In some regimes, the processes of dispersion of inclusions are significantly intensified; moreover, the dispersion of inclusions can be significantly increased.
- There is a substantial increase in the capacity of the heat transfer characteristics and the mass transfer process in a dispersion medium.
- During conducted experiments, inside of the central part of the reactor, it was observed the formation of floating and simultaneously rotating vapor-gas bubbles, the formation of which resembles a tornado. It is quite probable that this behavior of dispersed particles caused by the action of some rotating particles of the dispersed phase. This could be an explanation of the occurrence of motion, in which system forms a figure that look like hyperbolic. Thus, there is every reason to assume that such a distribution of dispersed particles coincides with the torsion-oriented field contours.

Fig. 2-11c. The Emergence of the Torsion-Oriented Turbulization

This research allows us to do the following:

- Take the first step in the direction of studying the physical nature of resonance cavitation.
- Make assumption that the best shape of the reactor's chamber is the single cavity hyperbolic.
- Define dependencies between the geometrical parameters of the chemical reactor filled with the dispersive medium, the rheological properties of the medium, and the amplitude–frequency characteristics of oscillation at which the torsion-oriented turbulization can occur.
- Establish conditions for the realization of the formation of dispersion systems and their stability in the batch and continuous modes.
- Establish the fact that, in the mode of vibrational cavitation, all system parameters are spontaneously and without external influence as managing factors, reconstructed in such a way that allows torsion-oriented turbulization to be achieved.
- Establish the fact that the mode of turbulization requires the minimum expenditures of energy, and only then undergoes high-intensity mixing.

Implementing the subject phenomena in industrial conditions makes it possible to offer fundamentally new and highly effective technologies.

Torsion-oriented turbulization can also be organized for processes occurring in both batch and in continuous mode, which is important for practical applications.

2.5. REACTORS FOR IMPLEMENTING OF THE SUBJECT PHENOMENON

Because most of the physicochemical technology processes are carried out continuously, I proposed chemical reactors for implementing of both batch and continuous technological processes (Fig. from 2–13 to 2–16)
To implement a continuous technological scheme, a pressurized cylindrical reactor, 4 (Fig. 2–12), was installed on a movable table, 8, of a vibrating machine, 9. The components of the mixture for forming a dispersion system of the gas-liquid type were loaded into the reactor

through the lower cover, 6, by means of flexible tubing 7, 10, and 11, into the zone with a relatively low pressure, 5. The final product was discharged from the reactor through the upper cover, 1, by means of the flexible tubing, 2, from a zone with a relatively elevated pressure, 3. The volumetric amount of components loaded into the reactor was determined by the time it takes to form the subject dispersion system. A detailed analysis of the effectiveness of the process of forming dispersion systems is discussed in CHAPTER 6.

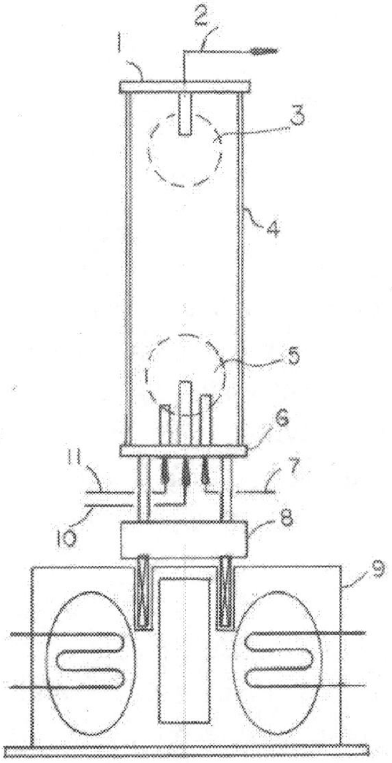

Figure 2-12. Schematic Diagram of the Cylindrical Reactor

Several reactor designs are possible [2–4]. For the sake of reactor usability, assembly, dismantling, washing and other production requirements, the reactors are constructed using interchangeable modules. Because that torsion-oriented field takes a single cavity hyperbolic shape, it would be reasonable to build a reactor's working chamber the same shape. Depending on their design, reactors for realization of torsion-oriented turbulization phenomenon could be made as cylindrical (Fig. 2–12), single cavity hyperbolic (Fig. 2–13 and 2-14), and sectional (Fig. 2–15) types.

2.6. CYLINDRICAL REACTOR

The cylindrical reactor (Fig. 2–12) is designed as a cylinder with hermetically sealed the top and bottom covers. The internal volume of the cylindrical reactor can be calculated as:

$$V = \pi r^2 h,$$

where r is the internal radius of the reactor, [m]; and h is the reactor's height, [m].

2.7. SINGLE CAVITY HYPERBOLIC REACTOR

The geometrical 3-dimensional figure corresponding to the spacial form of the torsion field is a single cavity (or one-sheet) hyperbolic. This shape is symmetrical about the coordinate planes, coordinate axes, and the origin. A one-sheet hyperboloid can be obtained by rotating the hyperbola around its real axis and then compressing it. This surface has the form of an endless pipe, "strung" on the axis OZ (Fig. 2-14) [146] and infinitely expanding when moving "up" or "down" from the XOY plane. If a one-sheet hyperboloid (Fig. 2-14) is intersected by planes parallel to the coordinate, then ellipses (if the planes are parallel to XOY) or hyperbolas can be obtained in the section. When cutting with other planes, parabolas, and pairs of intersecting straight lines, and pairs of parallel straight lines can also be obtained.

The internal volume of a single-cavity hyperboloid module can be calculated based on the definition of the single-cavity hyperboloid, which is a three-dimensional figure formed by the rotation of the hyperbola around a vertical axis, the top and bottom of which are parallel circles.

This spatial geometric figure can be described by a canonical equation:

$$\frac{x^2}{a^2}+\frac{y^2}{b^2}-\frac{z^2}{c^2}=1,$$

where a, b, and c are the half-axis of a single-cavity hyperboloid.

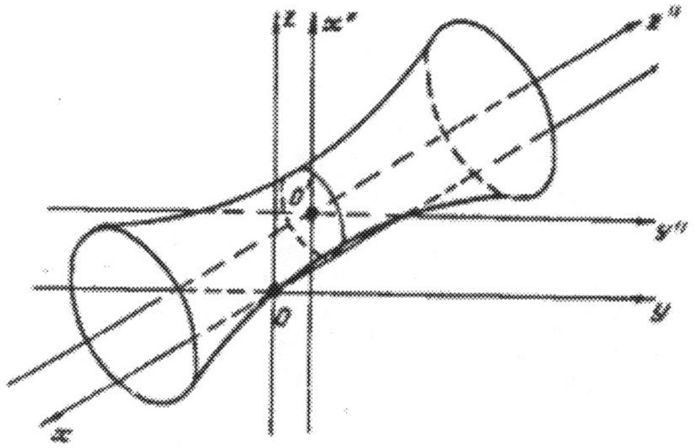

Figure 2-13. A single cavity hyperboloid [148]

The single cavity hyperbolic reactor (Fig. 2-14) can be made as a three-module structure. The central part of the reactor's, 4, is a hyperbolic module connected to the cylindrical top, 3, and bottom, 5, modules, which are sealed by covers, 1, and 6. The diameters and heights of modules differ from those of the central module. In this reactor, it is also necessary to consider the sizes and location of zones with high, 5, and low, 3, pressures.

The internal volume of the single-cavity hyperboloid can be calculated as [149]:

$$\mathcal{V}=\pi r^2 h\left(1+\frac{h^2}{12r^2}\right)=\frac{\pi h}{3}\left(2r_{min}^2+\mathcal{R}_{max}^2\right),$$

$$\mathcal{R}_{max}^2=r_{min}^2\left(1+\frac{h^2}{4r^2}\right),$$

where h is the height of an internal part of the single-cavity hyperboloid, [m]; r is the smallest radius of horizontal cross section of the single cavity hyperboloid, [m]; and $\mathcal{R}$ is the largest radius of the horizontal cross-section of the single cavity hyperbolic, [m].

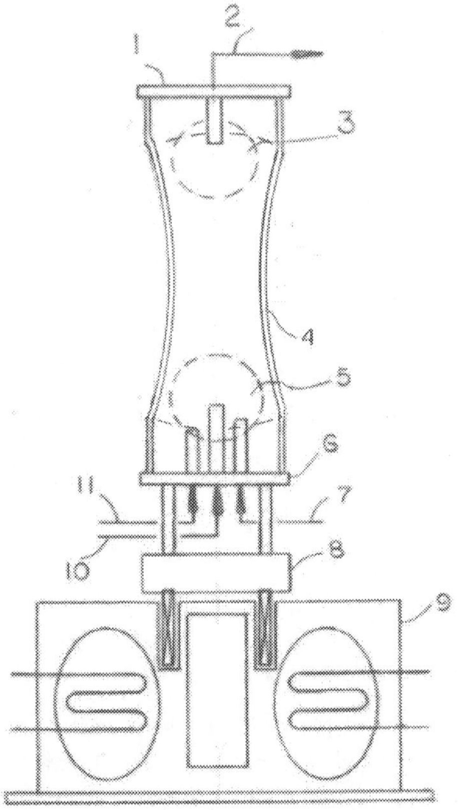

Figure 2-14. Schematic Diagram of the Hyperbolic Modular Reactor

The following should be noted. If radius $\mathcal{R} \to \infty$, then the single-cavity hyperboloid turns into a circular cylinder. Thus, to study the processes of formation of dispersion systems in the regime of torsion-oriented turbulization, it seems quite acceptable, in the first approximation, to use a cylindrical reactor's chamber with a relatively large (> 5) ratio of its height to diameter of it base.

2.8. SECTIONAL REACTOR

The sectional reactor (Fig. 2–15) contains three or more modules. The reactor's shell (the central part), 4, is made as the cylindrical module, connected to the top and bottom modules, which are sealed by covers, 1, and, 6. The diameters of the upper and lower modules can be different from that of the central part. In designing of such a reactor, it is necessary to consider the sizes of zones with high, 5, and low, 3 pressure. The design of such a reactor allows for mesh filters (screens) to be installed between the modules. Thus, parts of this reactor can be separated without changing the possibility of effective mass transfer throughout its entire volume. This type of reactor can be effectively used to carry out, for example, the processes of extraction, washing, and so on.

Figure 2-15. Three-Modular Reactor

2.9. PRACTICAL USE OF THE TORSION-ORIENTED TURBULIZATION

The practical use of the vibrational cavitation and torsion-oriented turbulization phenomena offers an opportunity to implement a new breakthrough process in the formation of dispersion systems in the batch and continuous modes. This method has practical application in the spheres of physicochemical technology and metallurgy, in automobiles, ships, aircraft, and spacecraft manufacturing, and in other areas of science and technology. To serve as a simple example, we may consider a hypothetical flow chart for the formation of a dispersion liquid–gas system.

To implement the continuous technological scheme, 100 (Fig. 2-16), the hermetic cylindrical reactor, 1, is installed on the movable table, 9, of the vibrating machine, forming a rigid "vibrator-reactor" mechanical system. The reactor is subjected to a perturbing force field, and the components of the liquid-gas mixture are supplied to the reactor separately. The fluid supply system consists of a container, 14, a valve, 13, a feed pump, 12, a control valve, 11, and an flexible tubing, 10. The fluid is supplied to the reactor through the bottom cover, 9. The gas supply system consists of a pipeline, 4, a control valve, 5, a bypass valve, 6, a vacuum pump, 7, and a feed pump, 8. The liquid is loaded through the top cover of the reactor, 3. The reactor can be ventilated through the top cover, 3, and the ventilation system can consist of a pipe, 18, and valve, 19. The finished products (foam) can be discharged from the reactor through the bottom cover, 9, by means of a system that consists of an flexible tubing, 15, a control valve, 16, and an intermediate storage tank, 17.

The resonance cavitation and torsion-oriented turbulization phenomena in question differs from most physicochemical processes in their unique development of a phase's interface. This creates new technological capabilities to produce dispersion systems that are applicable to, for example, the following:

- The processing of electronics, biochemicals, pharmaceuticals, and other branches of chemical and food technology.
- The macro–, micro–, and nanotechnological processes.
- The environmental protection processes: the dissolution and saturation of various liquids with hazardous waste, such as trapping and dissolution of carbon dioxide.
- The extraction processes in the production of herbal medicines.
- The solutions and process of etching (e.g., removing of oxides from a surface).
- The production of various food products, including the preparation of sauces, dairy products, mayonnaise, and flavors and flavorings
- The fermentation processes in the production of alcohol and alcohol beverages.

- The removal of riveting metals in diamond cutting.

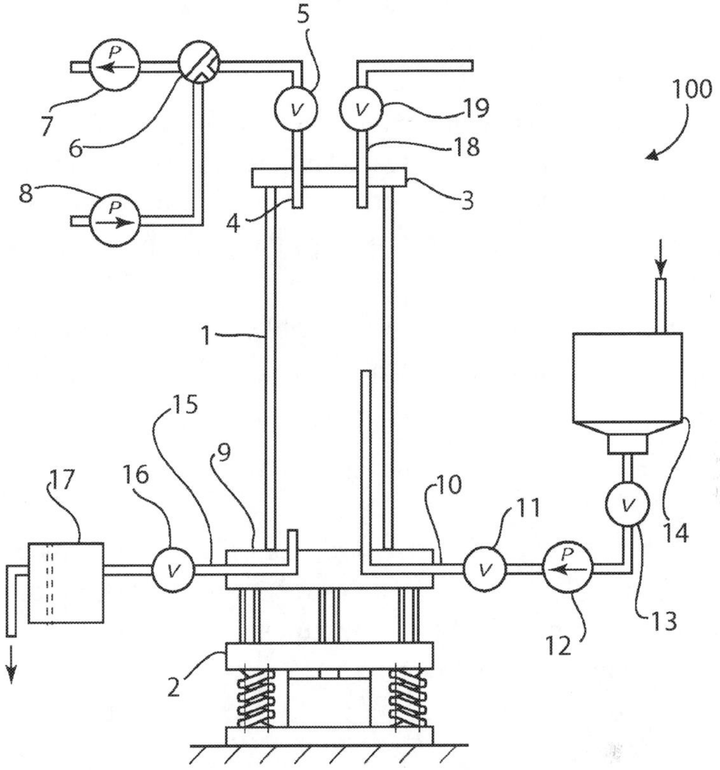

Figure 2-16. Scheme of the Formation of the Dispersion System Liquid-Gas

- The production of coatings that protect against environmental influences.

Finally, the reactors built for the torsion-oriented turbulization phenomenon can be used to produce suspensions, pastes, and creams, and in the processes of dissolution, emulsification, extraction, and homogenization, for example, either in discrete processes or continuous modes.

2.10. PROCESSING OF ALLOYS IN TURBULIZATION MODE

Another direction of the offered phenomena is the creation of multicomponent, high–performance alloys that cannot be made under terrestrial conditions. Such alloys could be processed under the acceleration of gravity acceleration from 20 to 50 times greater than terrestrial gravity acceleration. Unique alloys could possess essentially new properties that allows them to be used for special applications in hostile environments (high or low temperatures), in fossil gas and oil production, in chemical processing, and the underwater shipbuilding, in aircrafts and spacecrafts industries. There is a possibility of applying subject phenomenon in the processing of alloys (Fig. 2-17) [4].

The proposed scheme consists of a crucible, 5, installed on a moving plate, 8, of the vibration machine, 9. The crucible, 5, together with fusion, 4, is makes the reciprocating fluctuations inside the induction furnace, 11, consisting of the case, 1, and the induction coil, 2.

To create the equipment for the proposed application, it is necessary to develop and make a crucible, an induction furnace, and all additional applicable accessories, and to subsequently carry out the complex of research and development works.

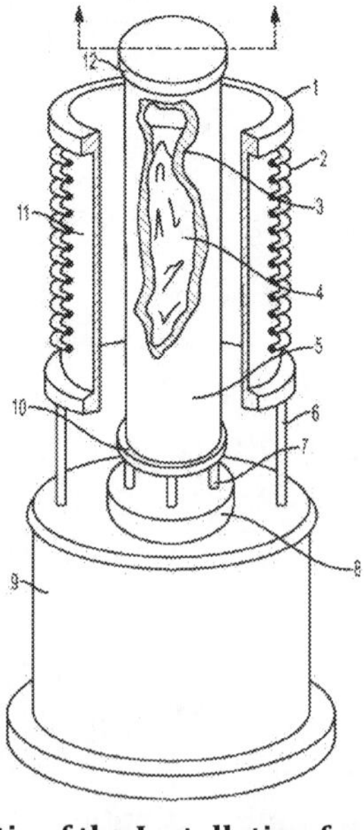

Figure 2-18. Schematic of the Installation for the Producing Alloys in Torsion-Oriented Turbulization Modes

CHAPTER 3

DYNAMICS OF THE RESONANCE CAVITATION AND TORSION-ORIENTED TURBULIZATION PHENOMENA

3.1. DYNAMICS OF THE FIRST HALF-A- CYCLE OF THE VIBRATION PRIOR TO OCCURING OF RESONANCE

The impact of external reciprocation movement on the chemical reactor is characterized by the frequency, amplitude, and dynamic forces, acting upon a rigid "vibrator-reactor" mechanical system. Then, the "vibrator-reactor" system could be considered as the material point with 1 (one) degree of freedom, where its center of inertia coincides with the center of inertia of the reactor. As stated in Chapter 1, components of a heterogeneous system—such as a mass of liquids, or liquid and gases and, sometimes, particles of solid matter—fill the internal volume of the reactor. In the essence, the space is filled with material points. The weight of a such system is:

$$G = mg, \qquad (3.1)$$

where G is the weight of the reactor and its components, [N]; g is the acceleration due to the gravity at point of measurement; h_L is the height of filling of the reactor with components of the planned dispersion system, [m]; h_R is the internal height of the reactor, [m]: $m = \pi \rho r^2 (h_L - h_R)$ is the mass of the liquid, [Kg]; π is 3,14; ρ is the liquid density, [kg/m^3];and r is the internal radius of the reactor, [m].

Using the system of equation of the fundamental law of the dynamics in the Cartesian rectangular coordinate, this condition can be described as follows:

$$\begin{aligned} F_x\, dt &= m dV_x; \\ F_y\, dt &= m dV_y; \\ F_z\, dt &= m dV_z. \end{aligned} \qquad (3.2)$$

The movement under the influence of constant force is defined as:

$$d(mV_0) = \mathcal{F}(t)\, dt = \text{const}, \qquad (3.3)$$

where mV_0 is the amount of motion of the "vibrator–reactor" system at the initial point in time t_0, at $t = 0$.

3.2. BEGINNING OF THE FIRST HALF-A-CYCLE

The force $\mathcal{F}(t)$ causes a compelled fluctuation of the "vibrator-reactor" system with components loaded inside the reactor. Thus, the kinetic energy of vibration of the considered system E_K is transferred from the vibrating machine to the mixing components loaded inside the reactor E_P via the rigid "vibrator-reactor" system.

Considering inevitable losses of energy, then $E_K = E_P + E_{Loss}$.

The internal pressure $\mathcal{P}_{In}$, acting inside of the liquid environment, can be described as follows:

$$\mathcal{P}_{In} = \frac{\rho g}{S} h = \frac{\rho g}{S} (h_L - h_R), \qquad (3.4)$$

where ρ is the specific weight of the liquid medium, [kg/m^3]; g is the acceleration due to the gravity, [m/s^2]; $h_{\mathcal{L}}$ is the height of the free surface of the liquid over the level of the ocean, [m]; h_R is the height of the reactor's bottom over the level of the ocean, [m]; and S is the area of the reactor cross-section, [m^2].

The "vibrator-reactor" system moves by simple harmonic motion. The displacement x from the equilibrium position is a function of time, given by the equation:

$$x(t) = A\cos(\omega t + \varphi),$$

where $\mathcal{A}$ is the amplitude of oscillation [m]; t is the time of one cycle, [s]; w is the vibration frequency, [Hz = 1/s]; and φ is the initial phase of oscillation, [rad];

The quantity $(\omega t + \varphi)$ is called: the phase of oscillation. The speed of oscillation is $v(t)$:

$$v(t) = -\ \omega A\ sin(\omega t + \varphi).$$

The maximum speed of the "vibrator-reactor" system v_{max} and the maximum speed of the mixing components inside of the reactor v_{VR} are:

$$v_{max} = v_{VR} = \mathcal{A}w.$$

The process of vibration is a constant reciprocation movement. When the reactor goes downward, all components move into the same direction. However, when the reactor moves upwards, the liquid component aspires to move in the opposite direction. As a result, inside the reactor elementary volumes with different internal pressures develop. This is so the liquid component has a chance to come off the reactor's upper cover. As a result, the separation zone is developed. The internal pressure in this zone must be equal to the maximum pressure under compression (without considering energy losses) and must exceed the internal pressure in the rest of the liquid component.

To understand the dynamics of the discussed process, the very last half cycle of oscillation shall be considered as occurring immediately ***before*** the occurrence of mechanical resonance. The duration of this half cycle is equal to half of the oscillation frequency. That is in the range of 1/60 to 1/120 fractions of a second. There are several periods in this process.

3.3. 1-st PERIOD: THE BEGINNING OF THE FIRST HALF-A-CYCLE

When the cyclic frequency of the indignant force comes closer to the frequency of the natural oscillation of the mixture, loaded in the reactor, it become “excited”. The processing mixture moves upward and, suddenly, meets an obstacle—the reactor’s top cover— and strikes it. The upper zones of the volume of the mixture has stopped, but the basic volume of the mixture, being compressed, continues to move upwards. In fact, liquids are considered incompressible only in comparison with gases.

When the liquid component tends to move in the opposite direction, a separation zone is formed so it can tear itself away from the upper cover of the reactor. The internal pressure in this zone is equal to the maximum pressure that increases during compression (without considering energy losses) and must exceed the internal pressure in other areas. Thus, it is possible to separate the liquid with the formation of a vacuum if the valid condition from the 1-st to the 5-th period, is fulfilled:

$$\Delta\mathcal{P}_{\text{Макс}} > \mathcal{P}_{\text{Abs}} + \Delta\mathcal{P}_{\hbar} + \Delta\mathcal{P}_{Loss}\,, \qquad (3.5)$$

where $\Delta\mathcal{P}_{\text{Макс}} = \mathcal{P}_{\text{Макс}} - \mathcal{P}_{In}$ is the maximum difference of internal pressure in the zone adjoining the top cover of the reactor at compression and external pressure, [N/m^2]; $\mathcal{P}_{\text{A}bs}$ is the absolute pressure inside the liquid, considered only a vacuum but not pressure over a free surface, [N/m^2]; $\Delta\mathcal{P}_{\hbar} = \mathcal{P}_{\text{Макс}} - \mathcal{P}_h$ is the difference of pressure between internal pressure in the zone adjoining the top cover of the reactor and at the reactor’s bottom, [N/m^2]; and $\Delta\mathcal{P}_{Loss}$ is the irreversible losses in the pressure in the processes of liquid compression and expansion and the loss upon the elastic deformations of the reactor’s body, [N/m^2].

3.4. CAVITATION

As stated before, the subject phenomenon occurs because of the influence of the external revolting force field from the vibrational machine upon mixed components loaded into the chemical reactor. Such a condition is characterized by the emergence in the reactor’s central part, which is filled with bubbles. Associations of bubbles in the dispersion phase made up of small vapor–gas bubbles. Such condition of the system cause homogenization and minimization of elements of the dispersed phase. This condition could be called vibrational cavitation.

From the position of physicochemical dynamics, the cavitation represents the process of dispersion caused by the violation of the liquid continuum and its transformation into a two-phase liquid–gas system while internal pressure in the liquid medium becomes equivalent to the pressure of the saturated vapor of this liquid. Meanwhile, from the perspective of hydrodynamics, the cavitation represents the process of vapor–gas bubbles formation in a volume of liquid because of the power influence of the indignant mechanical forces field.

3.5. 2-nd PERIOD: DEVELOPMENT ZONES WITH DIFFERENT INTERNAL PRESSURE

The upper portion of the volume of the mixture stops, having struck the upper cover, and generated the fluid hammer impact. Under the law of energy conservation, its kinetic energy E_k converts into the potential energy E_p of the elastic deformation of the processing mixture and structural elements of the reactor. This deformation is ***NOT*** absorbed by the upper cover and the upper part of the reactor's walls because of their rigidity.

This action still has not reached the middle and bottom zones of the reactor's internal space. However, the processing mixture keeps moving upwards. Simultaneously, the front border of the zone with elevated pressure (the shock wave) moves in the opposite direction. The kinetic energy E_k of the compressed mixture and the potential energy E_p of the elastic deformation of the reactor's elements cause of several zones with different internal pressures to develop inside of the processing mixture. At this time, the frequency of the external disturbance forces matches the natural frequency of the mixture inside the reactor. Thus, mechanical resonance emerges. The mixture's amplitude swiftly increases, and the upper volume of the mixture strikes the upper cover, causing the fluid hammer impact again.

3.6. 3-rd PERIOD: ZONES OF MAXIMUM AMD MINIMUM INTERNAL PRESSURES

From this moment onwards, mechanical resonance constantly acts jointly and simultaneously with the fluid hammer impact. When the first shock wave reaches the reactor's bottom, the shock wave is reflected from it. Forthwith, the second wave of the fluid hummer impact reaches the reactor's bottom and is reflected from it. And then the third, and the fourth, and so on. When these waves strike the bottom cover and are reflected from it, they overlap other upcoming and reflected waves. The mixture continues to strike reactor's upper cover until the dispersion system do not occupy the total volume of the reactor's chamber.

Because of the rigidity of the reactor's structure, the external border of the system does **NOT** absorb shock waves, and they, being reflected from the rigid reactor parts, move in the reactor, and are meeting other reflected shock waves. The reactor housing and covers are rigid and because of that they do not have any deformation. Thus, the external borders of the system do not change the kinetic energy of moving mixture volumes. Shock waves meet one other, imposed upon each other, and interact among themselves, finally dissipating in the mixture, sating the system with additional energy. That additional energy causes the formation of ruptures in the continuity of the liquid phase. Thus, this energy initiates bubbles formation inside a formed dispersion system.

3. 7. 4-th PERIOD: BEGINNING OF BACKWARDS MOTION

The internal pressure of the mixture close to the reactor's bottom is smaller than that the pressure in the mixture near the top. The compressed mixture tries to change the direction of its movement toward rarefaction zones, and the potential energy of elastic deformation E_p, again turns into kinetic energy E_K. However, during that time, the reactor's movement is already switched to the opposite direction. As a result, the border of the volume of the motionless mixture, being under the increased pressure, and tries to move from the reactor's bottom toward its top, creating an area of lower internal pressure at the reactor's bottom. This causes some elementary volumes of the mixture to try to move back to the bottom.

The speed of the movement of the border of the lower pressure zone is equal to the speed of the distribution of elastic deformations in the liquid, which itself is equal to the speed of a sound in the liquid. However, the difference in pressure at the border of zones with lower pressure is less than that at the point of the shock waves propagation. The reasons for this behavior are anomalies in the process of dissipation of the shock wave at the reactor's bottom during the previous period. With the change of pressure, the potential energy of the elastic deformation minus the losses is converted again into kinetic energy $E_K$of the mixture. Therefore, the speed of the "uncharged" mixture is practically equal to the speed of the mixture before it stops, with the only difference being that: the speed gradient is pointed in the opposite direction.

3.8. 5-th PPERIOD: FORMATION ZONES WITH ELEVATED INTERNAL PRESSURE

When the border of the lower–pressure zone reaches the reactor's top cover, the other elementary volumes of the mixture are under lower pressure and try to return at a speed equal to the initial speed of the first impact. The mixture moves toward the reactor's bottom, by virtue of inertia, as it attempts to separate itself from the cover. Therefore, due to the strong initial impact near the reactor's cover, a rarefaction zone is formed in the upper part of the reactor.

Because the duration of this process is approximately 1/120 fractions of a second, there is no additional source of heat T. Also, due to the rigid construction of the reactor, there is no change in the volume of the processed mixture. Thus, these are all reasons to assume that the thermodynamic process takes place without changing of the system's volume. Therefore, there are many reasons to consider this process to be ***ISOCHORIC.***

When the single parameter of the system is the volume $\mathcal{V}$, the isochoric process goes on without processing of external work and the differential of the internal energy U is equal:

$$dU = Td\mathcal{E},$$

where $\mathcal{E}$ is the entropy of the system; and $d\mathcal{E}$ is defined by the difference at the final $\mathcal{E}_2$ and initial $\mathcal{E}_1$ conditions of the system: $d\mathcal{E} = \mathcal{E}_2 - \mathcal{E}_1$.

If the process is reversible, it is defined by the difference between the final and initial internal energy of the system $dU = dQ$, and the heat of the process is defined as the difference between the final U_2 and initial U_1 internal energy of the system. The equation for an isochoric process, which connects a balance of constant C with temperature T and the thermal effect of chemical reaction $Q_{\mathcal{V}} = f(\mathcal{V})$ on the condition of constant volume ($\mathcal{V} = \text{const.}$), comes from an isotherm of the reaction of the Gibbs-Helmholtz equation of for a free energy U of the system [116]. Differentiating the equation of isothermal reaction on temperature and using a ratio:

$$U = \mathcal{E} - T\left(\frac{\delta\mathcal{E}}{\delta T}\right)_V.$$

There is:

$$\Delta U = WT^2 \frac{d \ln C}{dT}, \qquad (3.6)$$

where W is the enthalpy of the system.

On the condition of constancy of the volume $\mathcal{V} = \text{const.}$ and temperatures $T = \text{const.}$, there is:

$$\Delta U = - dQ_V \,.$$

Transforming equation (3.6) there is:

$$\frac{d\,ln\,C}{dT} = - \frac{dQ_V}{WT^2} \quad . \qquad (3.7)$$

If the process is running at rather small intervals of temperatures or at a small speed of temperature change, the integrating equation (2.5), there will be:

$$ln\,C = - \frac{dQ_V}{WT^2} + \Theta_\Sigma, \qquad (3.8)$$

where Θ_Σ – is the integration of the constant.

It is known that, when an irreversible isothermal process is proceeds at permanent volume ($\mathcal{V}$ = const.) and is followed by a reduction of free energy U of the system ($\delta U < 0$) decreases. Similarly, with a constant pressure ($\mathcal{P}$ = const.), the thermodynamic potential Φ of the system ($\delta\Phi < 0$) decreases. Respectively, the condition of the true thermodynamic balance is defined by the following conditions:

At T= const. and $\mathcal{V}$= const.: It is $U = U_{Min},$
At T= const. and $\mathcal{P}$= const.: It is $\Phi = \Phi_{Min}$

This conclusion is obtained by substituting the main inequality for irreversible processes of the $dQ = Td\mathcal{E}$, in the ratio:

$$dQ = dU + \mathcal{P}\,d\mathcal{V},$$

where Q is the heat received or returned by the system; and U is the internal energy of the system, which is a function of the condition of the system.

For the isothermal process in this system to be reversible, the following conditions must be satisfied:

- Heat exchange with the environment must occur in a reversible manner, or, in other words, the ambient temperature should be equal to the temperature of the system.
- Internal pressure must be equal to the external pressure.
- During the change, the system condition must be fair and equal:

$$\sum_i \Lambda_i d\lambda_i = 0, \tag{3.9}$$

where Λ_i are some functions of the condition of a body; and λ_i are the external parameters that define the system condition.

In the presence of such parameters of differentials in all thermodynamic potentials it is necessary to add the composed:

$$\sum_i \Lambda_i d\lambda_i. \tag{3.9a}$$

In this case, the differential of free energy $U$of systems is as follows:

$$dU = -\, U\, dT - \mathcal{P}\, dV + \sum_i \Lambda_i d\lambda_i \tag{3.10}$$

Thus, the considered system is isochoric, which characterizes by the change of the internal pressure only, and the volume of this system remains constant.

3.9. JUSTIFICATION THE POSSIBILITY TO CONSIDER A DISPERSION SYSTEM AS A SPECIAL CASE OF A THERMODYNAMIC SYSTEM

Before continuing the mathematical and physicochemical analysis of the initial stage of vibration impact on the reactor, it is necessary to consider the question: *IS IT* possible to consider a dispersion system as a thermodynamic system?

A thermodynamic system could be considered as macroscopic system (in any state: solid, liquid or gaseous, and as well as a multicomponent mix) that is in equilibrium from a thermodynamics position, or close to an equilibrium condition [150, 151]. However, such a definition does not exclude the possibility of a system condition in which one or several of its parameters within elementary volumes or points of this system differ from one another.

The condition of strength of the dispersion systems is characterized by an excess of free energy *U*. Moreover, the integration of particles of the dispersed phase occurs spontaneously, and causes the reduction of free energy *U*. Thus, in thermodynamic sense, dispersion systems by their nature, are unstable. Their temporary stability based on the existence of a power barrier, capable to prevent rapprochement and fixing of elementary volumes and particles of solid matters at rather small distances from each other (aggregation), the full association of droplets in emulsions and fogs, and the association of bubbles of gas in foams (coalescence).

In a dispersed state—but steady in coalescence— separate solid particles are united in rather large units and form a coagulative structure. They maintain an identity and are divided by layers of the dispersion medium. The destruction of the surface films of separation between phases causes the full associations of elementary volumes of the liquid phase in foams and emulsions, or the emergence of direct contacts between microscopically small solid objects in suspensions or colloidal solutions.

For instance, it is possible to assume the existence of systems in which temperature changes from one point of measurement to another; as well as systems (gas, liquid or system gas–liquid) in which the internal pressure in various elementary volumes differs from one another. It is obvious that, in these systems, the phenomena of heat exchange and a mass transfer would be observed. Such conditions do not remain invariable over time if they are not supported by an additional inflow of energy. Otherwise, after some time, a state is established in which the parameter values at all points or elementary volumes of the system remain unchanged for an arbitrarily long time if external conditions do not change and there is no influx of additional energy. Such states are considered to be in equilibrium.

The process of a thermodynamic system transition from a state of nonequilibrium to equilibrium is called a relaxation. For averaging or otherwise aligning values of each parameter in all volumes of a system, it is a characteristic time that is called a relaxation time for this parameter. The total relaxation time falls on the longest of all relaxation times. Estimations of the relaxation time for various processes cannot be made within the framework of thermodynamics. Physical kinetics deals with this issue.

Now, let us consider that a process in a thermodynamic system proceeds with a speed significantly lower than the speed of relaxation. This means that, at any point of such a process, all parameters would begin to level. Such a process represents a chain of equilibrium states indefinitely close to each other. These rather slow processes can be called equilibrium or quasi-static processes. It should be noted that, during equilibrium processes, the gradients of all parameters are equal to zero at any moment. It follows from this that, due to symmetry, the process in the system can go in both directions—any system parameters can increase or decrease. Therefore, in the direct process, alignment can be reversed in time. In this regard, equilibrium processes can be considered reversible.

Thus, at the initial stage of the formation of dispersion systems in the mode of vibrational cavitation, the system quickly goes into equilibrium upon the termination of the disturbing force. It is possible to apply standard thermodynamic methods to analyze these systems.

At the next stage of the formation of dispersion systems upon transition to the resonance turbulization mode, opposing hydraulic shocks and, consequently, multidirectional shock waves arise. This situation is complicated by the fact that hydraulic hummer shock impacts and shock waves are physically different in nature. Hydraulic shock impacts arise upon impact of the mixture components on the top cover of the reactor, whereas shock waves are the result of the collapse of the vapor–gas bubbles. This mass formation, development and rupture of vapor-gas bubbles could become irreversible.

Under such conditions, in the presence of chaotic shock waves, it is not possible to talk of the temperature of the mixture at a certain point (to consider this process as isothermal), nor about a low rate of temperature change, constant pressure, or the reversibility of an isothermal process (see Section 2.8). Under these conditions, the concepts of entropy or enthalpy, as well as thermodynamic potentials, need additional definitions—if this is even possible in principle.

Consequently, upon transition to the resonance turbulization regime, characterized by the simultaneous and combined mechanical resonance action and fluid hammer phenomena, the process of forming dispersion systems becomes irreversible. In this case, they cannot be analyzed using regular thermodynamic methods. At the same time, all dispersion systems, regardless of the method of their formation, are separated over time into constituent initial components after the termination of the action of an external perturbing force—relaxation. Therefore, for a final solution to this issue, additional research is required.

Thus, in the time period from 1/60 to 1/120 fractions of a second, the dispersion system is characterized only by a change in internal pressure and can be considered a thermodynamic system. This allows us to describe the nature of the movement of the components in the reactor from the 1st to the 5th periods of the first half cycle *ONLY*, using the Bernoulli's equation.

3. 10. THE FLUID DYNAMICS OF A MIXURE INSIDE THE REACTOR

To use the Bernoulli equation, it is necessary to represent the mixture filling in the reactor as an incompressible ideal liquid, i.e., a liquid that does not have viscosity ($\mu = 0$), or, otherwise, as a liquid that does not have internal friction (e.g., a degassed bi-distillate of water). Because of the energy conservation law for the stationary motion of an ideal incompressible fluid, the speed v and pressure $\mathcal{P}$, in general, are related per Bernoulli's equation. In this case, the equation can be written in the following form:

$$\rho g (h_L - h_R) + \frac{1}{2}\rho v_L^2 + \mathcal{P}_{Loss} =$$
$$= \mathcal{P}_{PVR} + \frac{1}{2}\mathcal{F}(t)\, v_{VR}^2 + \mathcal{P}_{VR}, \tag{3.11}$$

where ρ is the density of the liquid component, [kg/m^3]; g is the acceleration due to the gravity [m/s^2]; h_L is elevation over the level of the ocean of a free liquid's surface, [m]; h_R is the elevation over the level of the ocean at the bottom of the reactor, [m]; v_L is the speed of the liquid component inside reactor, [m/s]; $\mathcal{P}_{Loss}$ are losses of pressure inside the reactor (e.g., due to the elastic deformation of the reactor's components), [N/m^2]; $\mathcal{P}_{PVR}$ is the pressure due to action of the "vibrator-reactor" mechanical system, [N/m^2]; $\mathcal{P}(t)$ is the pressure developed by the action of the compelling force, [N/m^2]; v_{VR} is the speed of the movement of the "vibrator-reactor" system, [m/s]; and $\mathcal{P}_{PVR}$ are losses of pressure related to work of the "vibrator-reactor" system, [N/m^2].

The first term of equation (3.11), on the left, $\rho g (h_L - h_R)$, is the gravitational component, that represents the potential energy of the liquid phase of the mixture. The second term, $\frac{1}{2}\rho v_L^2$, is the dynamic component that represents the kinetic energy of the mixture located inside the reactor. The term, $\mathcal{P}_{Loss}$, is the uncertain losses of pressure. The first term of the equation (3.11), on the right side, $\mathcal{P}_{PVR}$, is the potential energy of the "vibrator-reactor" system. The second term, $\frac{1}{2}\mathcal{F}(t)\, v_{VR}^2$, is the kinetic energy of the "vibrator-reactor" system and is the function of the vibration's parameters: amplitude, frequency and revolting forces of the vibration machine. The third term, $\mathcal{P}_{VR}$, represents the uncertain losses of pressure related to the operation of the vibration machine.

Considering that $v_L = \mathcal{A} w_L$ and $v_{VR} = \mathcal{A} w_{VR}$:

$$\rho g(h_L - h_R) + \frac{1}{2}\rho(\mathcal{A}w_L)^2 + \mathcal{P}_{Loss} =$$
$$= \mathcal{P}_{PVR} + \frac{1}{2}\mathcal{F}(t)(\mathcal{A}w_{VR})^2 + \mathcal{P}_{VR}, \qquad (3.12)$$

NOTE: All components in the Bernoulli's equation are units of energy in relation to units of volume [J/m³ or N/m²].

Let us consider the gravitational term $\rho g(h_L - h_R)$ of equation (3.12). The reactor height is equal to 685,8 mm, and the internal diameter is equal to 114,3 mm. Components fill the reactor by 90% to 95%. It allows us to assume that $(h_L \cong h_R)$ the gravitational term is negligibly small.

Also, it is obvious that the "vibrator-reactor" system is rigid and that losses of pressure (that is related to the energy) $\mathcal{P}_{PVR}$ and $\mathcal{P}_{VR}$ are negligibly small. Hence, we can express Bernoulli's equation (3.12) as:

$$\mathcal{P}_0(\mathcal{A}w_L)^2 + \mathcal{P}_{Loss} = \mathcal{F}(t)\,(\mathcal{A}w_{VR})^2, \qquad (3.13)$$

where the first component on the left, $\mathcal{P}_0(\mathcal{A}w_L)$, represents the kinetic energy of the mix moving inside the reactor; $\mathcal{P}_{Loss}$ represents uncertain losses of pressure inside the reactor, and $\mathcal{F}(t)\ (\mathcal{A}w_{VR})$ is the kinetic energy of the "vibrator-reactor" mechanical system, which is a function of amplitude, frequency and the revolting force of the vibration machine.

3.11. 6-th PERIOD: THE COLLAPSE OF THE CONTINUUM OF A LIQUID MEDIUM

This period is the last chord of the external indignant forces operating upon the mixture. The heterogeneous mixture moves down toward the lower part of the reactor through inertia and tries to come off from the reactor's cover. Therefore, in the volumes of the mixture that are adjacent to the reactor's upper cover, at a strong initial impact in the rarefaction zone occurs. In this zone, the liquid phase "is absent" and, thus, the formed internal pressure aspires to zero. Thus, in the upper part of the reactor, rarefaction zones are formed.

The front of the shock wave, which results from fluid hammer impact, moves from the top of the reactor to the bottom. During its movement, a moving front of elevated pressure is developed. Hence, the kinetic energy of the compressed mixture, and the potential energy of the elastic deformation of the reactor, causes the development of zones with various internal pressures in the formed disperse system. It should be noted that the speed of the shock wave propulsion is equal to the speed of a sound wave in the subject heterogeneous mixture.

As a result of these strong impacts, violations in continuity occur inside the liquid—cavities are developed. These cavities fill instantly with saturated gas and vapors of the liquid, creating bubbles. These vapor–gas bubbles are increase the coefficient of the compressibility of the gas–liquid mixture.

In the considered half cycle, because of the simultaneous and joint actions of a fluid hammer impact and mechanical resonance, the excited mixture transforms into the dispersion system. In this system bubbles of gas, drops of liquid (that are immiscible and insoluble with the dispersion phase) and particles of the solid matter form the dispersed phase. The main liquid represents the dispersion phase. The considered dispersion system is characterized by the developed surface of separation between phases.

The phenomenon of the vibrational cavitation in the air and water systems, loaded into the considered reactor with dimensions outlined earlier, occurs at an amplitude of 1.5 mm, a frequency between 35 and 50 Hz, and an acceleration of 20 G. Thus, the pushing effort from vibration machine on the reactor is equal to approximately 3,000 kg [152].

It is obvious that frequency of the internal oscillation of the liquid–gas system is a function of the characteristics of the chemical composition; physical, mechanical, and physicochemical parameters and characteristics of liquids and gases; parameters of the vibration; the ratio between gas and liquid; the ratios between the internal dimensions of the reactor; and the quality of the internal surface of the reactor's chamber. In other words, even to change if the volume of the liquid phase (the level of the free surface) was changed, it would be possible to control the frequency of the internal oscillation of the liquid-gas system. [2–5].

3.12. A PHENOMENON OF THE RESONANCE CAVITATION

As visual observations during preliminary experiments have shown, in the periods preceding the appearance of the torsion-oriented turbulization phenomenon, there is an almost a complete absence of bubbles in the zones directly adjacent to the reactor's wall. Meanwhile, in its central part there is the chaotic appearance of bubbles, indicating the excited state of the dispersion medium. Therefore, the laminar motion of the dispersion medium is observed directly along the reactor's wall. While the change in the regime of the disturbing force exerted on the reactor containing the mixture components, the three main states of the system—bubble, mass, and aggregate—visually differ.

The bubble regime is characterized by the appearance of individual bubbles of relatively small sizes—from one millimeter to several millimeters in diameter—in the continuous liquid phase. Their size, shape and distribution spontaneously change, regardless of the frequency and amplitude of the vibration. In this state, the bubbles can be quite long.

As the frequency of the vibration exposure approaches the frequency of the natural vibrations in the mixture, the state of the system in the reactor goes through various stages—from the appearance of single bubbles to their mass emergence, development, and collapse. The size of the bubbles and their life spans also change. Then, the state of the system proceeds to unify the bubbles. They grow rapidly and move to the central part of the reactor. Bubbles are sometimes combined into aggregates and in other cases are separated among themselves and between the walls of the reactor with interlayers of the mixture's liquid component. A pattern of a chaotic mixture of large asymmetric and small bubbles is also observed. Such an excited state leads to the formation of asymmetric internal pressure fields in the formed dispersion system corresponding to cavitation. Therefore, we may call this regime a vibrational cavitation.

3.13. EQUATION FOR THE MIXTURE MOTION IN THE 6-th PERIOD

In the 6-th period, there is a difference in the amount of pressure in different reactor's zones. In the considered state of the mixture components for the 6th period in equation (3.13), it seems possible to replace the initial internal pressure $\mathcal{P}_0$ with the difference of the "before critical" internal pressure $\mathcal{P}_{BC}$ (which occurs when the liquid component collides with the top cover of the reactor) and the pressure in the cross section inside the reactor $(\mathcal{P}_{BC} - \mathcal{P}_0)$. Then, after a series of simple transformations, equation (3.13) is written in the form:

$$\rho g(h_L - h_R) + \frac{1}{2}(\mathcal{P}_{BC} - \mathcal{P}_0)[\varphi(h_L - h_R)]^2 + E_{Loss} = \\ = \frac{1}{2}\mathcal{F}(t)\,(\mathcal{A}\varphi)^2. \tag{3.14}$$

To determine the conditions of occurrence of mechanical resonance, it is necessary to determine the critical value of pressure $\mathcal{P}_{Cr}$ in the system, under condition that $\mathcal{P}_{Cr} \neq \mathcal{P}_{BC}$ and $\mathcal{P}_{Cr} \neq \mathcal{P}_0$. Given that the fraction $\frac{1}{2}$ does not affect the functional dependence between the terms of equation (3.14), there is:

$$\rho g(h_L - h_R) + \mathcal{P}_{Cr}\,[\varphi(h_L - h_R)]^2 - \mathcal{P}_0\,[\varphi(h_L - h_R)]^2 +$$

$$+ E_{Loss} = \mathcal{F}(t)\,(\mathcal{A}\varphi)^2.$$

Transferring some terms to the right side of the equation there is:

$$\mathcal{P}_{Cr}\,[\varphi(h_L - h_R)]^2 =$$

$$= \mathcal{F}(t)\,(\mathcal{A}\varphi)^2 - E_{Loss} + \mathcal{P}_0\,[(h_L - h_R)]^2 - \rho g(h_L - h_R),$$

where:

$$\mathcal{P}_{Cr} = \frac{\mathcal{F}(t)(\mathcal{A}w_{Cr})^2 - \mathcal{P}_{Loss} - \rho g(h_L - h_R)}{[w_{Cr}(h_L - h_R)]^2} + \mathcal{P}_L \qquad (3.15)$$

Given the previously accepted condition that the gravitational component $h_L - h_R$ is negligible or tends to 0:

$$\mathcal{P}_{Cr} = \mathcal{F}(t)\,(\mathcal{A}\varphi_{Cr})^2 - E_{Loss} + \mathcal{P}_0 \qquad (3.16)$$

or

$$\mathcal{P}_{Cr} - \mathcal{P}_0 = \mathcal{F}(t)\,(\mathcal{A}\varphi_{Cr})^2 - E_{Loss}\,. \qquad (3.17)$$

The physical sense in equation (2.15) is the condition of mechanical resonance occurrence, when the difference between the critical pressure $\mathcal{P}_{Cr}$, arises at the moment of collision of the upper volumes of the liquid phase with the reactor's top cover and the pressure in the internal cross section $\mathcal{P}_0$. This pressure difference is proportional to the indignant force $\mathcal{F}(t)$ and depends on the frequency w and amplitude $\mathcal{A}$ of oscillation and the dissipation of energy $\mathcal{P}_{Loss}$.

3.14. THE FLUID HAMMER IMPACT

The condition for vibrational cavitation phenomenon to occur is the simultaneous and joint action of a mechanical resonance and fluid hammer impact, which leads to the development of the indignant condition of components of the dispersion system. In general, the process of distribution of external indignations is possible to carry a fluid hammer impact happening at speed w, described by the differential equation with private derivatives called the Wave Equation [8]. For small indignations and a homogeneous isotropic environment this equation could be written as:

$$\frac{\partial^2 u}{\partial x^2}+\frac{\partial^2 u}{\partial y^2}+\frac{\partial^2 u}{\partial z^2}=\frac{1}{w^2}\frac{\partial^2 u}{\partial t^2} \tag{3.18}$$

Equation (3.18) is linear; uniform; and for the principle of superposition it is fair—any linear combination of solutions is the real solution. Thus, equation (3.18) allows for a solution in the form of the "Dispersing Spherical Wave":

$$u=\frac{f\,(t-\frac{\tau}{w})}{\tau}, \tag{3.19}$$

where f is the any arbitrary function and the $\tau=\sqrt{x^2+y^2+z^2}$.

Of special interest is the elementary solution, called the "Elementary Wave":

$$\varepsilon=\frac{\delta(t-\frac{\tau}{w})}{\tau}, \tag{3.20}$$

where δ is a so-called "delta-function", that characterizes the distribution of the indignation, produced by the instant dot source, which operates at the beginning of coordinates at $t=0$.

The "Elementary Wave" represents an "Infinite Splash" on a circle of radius $\tau=wt$, moving away from the beginning of coordinates with a speed w with gradual reduction of intensity. Superposing of "Elementary Waves" allows us to describe any indignation's process of propulsion. For example, if in an initial point of time $t=0$, in space are action instant sources with density $F(p)$ is:

$$u\,(M,t)=\iiint \psi\,(P)\,\frac{\delta(t-\frac{\tau}{w})}{4\pi\tau}\,d_\xi\, d_\lambda\, d_\zeta \;=\frac{1}{4\pi w}\iint_S \frac{\psi}{\tau}\,ds, \tag{3.21}$$

where τ is the distance between points of $M\,(xyz)$ and $P\,(\xi,\lambda,\zeta)$; and S is the sphere with the center in a point M, with the radius wt.

The solution of the Cauchy problem [153, 154] for the "Wave Equation" (2.18) consists in finding of the solution u, that meets the initial conditions:

$$u|t = 0 = \varphi(xyz), \text{ and } \frac{\partial u}{\partial t}|t = 0 = \psi(xyz).$$

The solution u is given using Poisson's formula:

$$u(M,t) = \frac{1}{4\pi w}\left\{\frac{\partial}{\partial t}\iint_S \frac{\varphi}{\tau} ds \iint_S \frac{\psi}{\tau} ds\right\} \qquad (3.22)$$

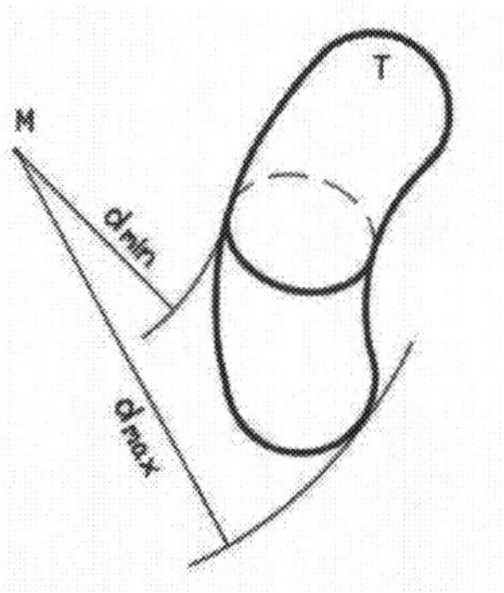

Figure 3–1.

If the initial disturbances φ and ψ were concentrated in an arbitrary selected area T (Fig. 3-1), and point M is located from it at the distance d_{min}, then in accordance with formula (3.22), the disturbance would pass the distance from area T and achieve the point M at the point of time $t = \frac{d_{min}}{w}$ (the front of the wave), which will be continued to the point of time $t = \frac{d_{max}}{w}$ (the back of the wave). It is the result of the superposition elementary waves, coming from separated points from the area of disturbances T.

Cauchy's problem is similar to the nonuniform the "Wave Equation":

$$\frac{\partial^2 u}{\partial x^2}+\frac{\partial^2 u}{\partial y^2}+\frac{\partial^2 u}{\partial z^2}-\frac{1}{w^2}\frac{\partial^2 u}{\partial t^2}=F(xyz,t) \qquad (3.23)$$

The right part of the equation (3.23) indicates the existence of the long sources of indignation that operate on area T(Fig. 3-19) since the point of time $t=0$. When initial conditions equal zero, the relevant solution can represent the superposition of elementary waves:

$$u(M,t)=\int_0^t\left(\iiint F(P,t)\frac{\delta(t-v-\frac{\tau}{w})}{4\pi v}d_\xi\, d_\lambda\, d_\zeta\right)=$$
$$=\iiint\frac{F(P,t-\frac{\tau}{w})}{\tau}dv. \qquad (3.24)$$

The solution to Cauchy's problem [153, 154] for a two-dimensional "Wave Equation" looks like:

$$\frac{\partial^2 u}{\partial x^2}+\frac{\partial^2 u}{\partial y^2}=\frac{1}{a^2}\frac{\partial^2 u}{\partial t^2}. \qquad (3.25)$$

The solution could also be formulated as:

$$\mathrm{u}\,(xyt)=\frac{C}{2\pi w}, \qquad (3.26)$$

where:

$$C=\frac{\partial}{\partial t}\iint_D\varphi(\xi,\eta)d\xi d\eta\frac{1}{\sqrt{(at)^2-(x-\xi)^2-(y-\eta)^2}}+$$
$$+\iint_D\psi(\xi,\eta)d\xi d\eta\frac{1}{\sqrt{(at)^2-(x-\xi)^2-(y-\eta)^2}},$$

where $D=2wt$ is the circle's radius wt with the center located at point $M\,(x,y)$.

Upon localization of initial indignations in a final area G, at point M, located out of area G, we will observe the sharp forward front of a wave. However, in this case, the back front of the wave is absent because of the dissipation of waves. Small, longitudinal oscillations can be generally described using a one-dimensional "Wave Equation":

$$\frac{\partial^2 u}{\partial x^2} = \frac{1}{w^2}\frac{\partial^2 u}{\partial t^2} \tag{3.27}$$

The common solution of equation (3.27) look like:

$$u = f(x - wt) + g(x + wt) \tag{3.28}$$

It represents the superposition of both straight and return waves. In this case, the solution for Cauchy's problem [154] can be introduced with D'Alembert's formula:

$$u\,(x, t) = \frac{\varphi(x-wt) + \varphi(x+wt)}{2} + \frac{1}{2w}\int_{x-wt}^{x+wt} \psi(w)\mathrm{d}w \tag{3.29}$$

The change of pressure at the fluid hammer impact for an ideal incompressible liquid (without internal friction) in the reactor can be calculated using Zhukovsky's formula [155]:

$$\Delta\mathcal{P}_{Impact} = C\rho\Delta w\ , \tag{3.30}$$

where $\Delta\mathcal{P}_{Impact} = \mathcal{P}_{Cr} - \mathcal{P}_0$ is the difference of pressure between the critical pressure $\mathcal{P}_{Cr}$, that arises at the time of impact by the top volumes of liquid components at the reactor's top cover and pressure in the cross section of the internal zones of the reactor $\mathcal{P}_0$; ρ is the specific density of the liquid components; $\Delta w = (w_2 - w_1)$ is the change of speed between adjacent volumes of liquid that are at a distance Δh ; and C is the speed of the propulsion of the shock wave.
The shock wave's speed of propulsion for the ideal incompressible liquid can be determined using the following formula:

$$C = \frac{1}{\sqrt{\frac{\rho\beta + \rho d}{\delta E}}}, \qquad (3.31)$$

where β is the coefficient of compressibility of liquid, representing change in the liquid's volume related to the change in pressure, [m²/N]; d is the reactor's internal diameter, [m]; δ is the thickness of the reactor's walls, [m]; and E is the module of elasticity of reactor's material, [m²/N]. The speed of sound in liquids is approximately 1x10 m/s to 1,5x10³ m/s range. Therefore, in a reactor with a height of 1.5 meters the process of shock wave propulsion from the bottom to the top cover or back will take approximately 1 millisecond.

The combination of formulas (3.30) and (3.31), expresses the equation for the critical value of pressure arising in an impact consequence:

$$\Delta\mathcal{P}_{Impact} = \frac{\rho\Delta w}{\sqrt{\frac{\rho\beta + \rho d}{\delta E}}}. \qquad (3.32)$$

The difference in pressure resulting from the fluid hammer impact does not depend on the initial pressure, which forces the liquid to move and depends only on the speed gained by it. As the pressure impact depends on the accumulated kinetic energy and speed of the liquid, therefore the "rigid" reactor housing and the "compressed" liquid, can accommodate a strong impact even at a rather low liquid speed. Therefore, the sharp increase in pressure in elementary volumes adjacent to the reactor's top cover, with the combined and joint influence of a resonance and a fluid hammer impact will cause to exceed the pressure in the lower zones of the reactor.

The main difference between resonance cavitation and any other kind of cavitation is that the subject cavitation occurs within the closed chamber of the reactor and simultaneously occupies its total inner space. The system of equations (3.15), (3.17) and (3.32) is a condition for the occurrence of vibrational cavitation (see 3.17):

$$\mathcal{P}_{Cr} - \mathcal{P}_L = \mathcal{F}(t)\,(\mathcal{A}w_{Cr})^2 - \mathcal{P}_{Loss},$$

where (see 3.15):

$$\mathcal{P}_{Cr} = \frac{\mathcal{F}(t)(\mathcal{A}w_{Cr})^2 - \mathcal{P}_{Loss} - \rho g(h_L - h_R)}{[w_{Cr}(h_L - h_R)]^2} + \mathcal{P}_L,$$

and

$$\Delta\mathcal{P}_{Impact} = \frac{\rho\Delta w}{\sqrt{\frac{\rho\beta+\rho d}{\delta E}}} \qquad (3.32a)$$

As a first approximation, the critical pressure $\mathcal{P}_{Cr}$ could be equal to the pressure of liquid-gas saturated steam. Thus, it is necessary to understand clearly that the occurrence of vibrational cavitation, can take place and at values of internal pressure different from the critical pressure $\mathcal{P}_{Cr}$.

Values of vibration frequency w at which a vibrational cavitation occurs, can be designated w_{Cr}. The disappearance of vibrational cavitation is defined by value w at which the phenomenon of vibrational cavitation terminates the existence with a pressure increase inside the reactor.

There are multiple reasons w_{Cr} is not a constant: the nonstationary fields of internal pressure caused by the gradient of forces of surface tension, the influence of the vapor–gas bubbles associations arising and breaking up, the geometrical dimensions, and the conditions of the reactor's chamber internal surface. It is possible that the value of w_{Cr} significantly changes from one reactor to another and that it depends on the properties of the components of the chemical composition of the liquid and gas, as well as the scale factor. As a first approximation at the present time, it seems advisable to use w_{Cr} as the characteristic of a condition of a dispersion system's movement in the vibrational cavitation mode.

3.15. FORMATION OF DISPERSION SYSTEMS

Everything that was considered at the above relates to a portion of an oscillation cycle. This event takes approximately 1/60 to 1/120 fraction of a second of the previous cycle, right before emergence of resonance. When there is no the second half of the "extreme" oscillation cycle, due to energy dissipation, the "indignant" mixture gradually comes to rest. From this moment on, every other part of each oscillation cycle begins while the liquid component just enters into the 2nd part of each subsequent cycle. Then, in the liquid, we can observe the continuous development of pressure differences between adjacent volumes.

In the first part of the extreme cycle of oscillations, the reactor moves up and now, in the second part of the "extreme" cycle, it moves down sharply. Inside the liquid medium, the phenomena corresponding to the third to sixth periods continue to occur, and the reactor has already begun to move in the opposite direction. All periods from the first to the sixth, are occurring, but in the opposite direction. It should be noted that, during the upward movement of the reactor, the gravity vector of the mixture components is targeted in the direction opposite of the movement of the reactor.

In the second part of the cycle, this vector is targeted in the same direction as the movement of the reactor, thereby complicating the asymmetry of the total process. These fluid vibrations occur in a closed r space where the components of the mixture are located, the various elementary volumes of which are moving at different speeds and in opposite directions. The collision of these volumes inhibits the movement of more speedy moving volumes of the forming dispersion system.

The elementary volumes of the mixture oscillate inside the reactor, but various volumes move at different speeds and in different directions. The collision of slow-moving volumes slows down the movement of faster-moving volumes. At the same time, together with the rarefaction zones arising under the top cover of the reactor, the disturbing force acting on the "vibrator–reactor" system again forces the components of the mixture to move deeper into the reactor, thereby repeating the movement of the first period. Thus, in the reactor there is multidirectional movement of the adjacent volumes of the dispersed system and, at the same time, the simultaneous propagation of opposing shock waves. Both processes cause the development of pressure zones and rarefaction zones. Naturally, in this case, there are energy transitions that do not coincide in time and inevitable energy losses in different volumes of liquid.

As soon as the violations of the continuity in the liquid phase are formed—that is, zones with significantly reduced pressure—the gases dissolved in the liquid diffuse in them, as well as the vapor of the liquid itself, forming vapor-gas bubbles. Due to the frequency of the vibration of the reactor (> 24 Hz), without the use of optical means of observation, this process appears to be continuous. In zones with the minimum internal pressure, there are violations of the continuity of the liquid. The secondary factors that influence the formation of dispersion systems are the violations of liquid continuity. Additional sources of concentration of internal tension include particles of solid matter, changes in viscosity between adjacent volumes, and the roughness's of reactor housing surfaces, etc. As soon as violations of continuity in the liquid occur, diffused gases and evaporations dissolved in the liquid form bubbles.

We can assume that the process of mass bubbles formation begins with differing pressure, which increases in some zones while decreasing in others to the level of its saturated steam (vapor). All these processes develop a difference in internal pressure between adjacent zones in the dispersive phase. These fields of internal tension eventually bring additional violations of continuity to some elementary volumes of the liquid. Thus, the process of bubbles formation is the result of the effect of fields of the internal tension. In such conditions, at certain parameters of vibration, repeated violations of the continuity occur in the total volume of components. This violation of continuity follows by the origination, development, and collapse of bubbles. Thus, the process of the formation of dispersion systems in the mode of torsion-oriented turbulization represents the process of the formation of a surface of separation between phases and solid particles, drops of immiscible liquid, and vapor–gas bubbles, which are separated by the film of the dispersion medium.

When each individual bubble collapses, additional shock waves are formed, which propagate inside the reactor also. Shock waves occur as the result of individual fluid hummer impacts. In front of the rapidly moving shock wave are forming areas of increased pressure, while areas of reduced pressure are formed behind the wave. These shock waves, superimposed on each other, in turn cause secondary discontinuities in the liquid dispersion medium, forming a heterogeneous dispersion system. Moreover, this process develops explosively.

Macroscopic volumes arise inside the reactor. The subject volumes characterized by the development of internal pressures in them. The values of internal pressures in each separately allocated volume, due to the difference in the density due to presents of bubbles, do not coincide with the value of the internal pressure of the adjacent allocated volume. Because of this, internal tension arises between them. The process of changing the specific density of each allocated volume changes continuously, the internal stresses between each adjacent macroscopic volumes change continuously also.

Thus, during a short period of time, measured in fraction of second, centrifugal forces develop in each selected macroscopic volume of the processing dispersion system, with continuously changing values of the modules of these forces. As a result of a complex configuration of the difference in the internal pressure between adjacent volumes, that resulting of the difference in the moments of inertia between adjacent allocated volumes. Considering the complexity of the curvature of the inner surface of a single cavity hyperbolic, it leads to a myriad of continuously changing short-lived bubbles begin to rotate in a horizontal plane around the vertical axis of the reactor's chamber, gradually enticing internal volumes in horizontal sections of the reactor.

As the indignant forces from the vibration machine continue to act upon reactor, the influence of gravitational forces in comparison with the indignant forces decreases. Finally, at some point in time, in the central part of the reactor, all bubbles begin to rotate in a vertical plane relative to the horizontal axis. A funnel is formed in the reactor, resembling a tornado. Thus, the emerging phenomenon can be represented as a torsion-oriented turbulization.

Once again, when the external indignant influence coincides in frequency with that of the natural oscillation of the mixture, it is transformed, avalanche–like, into a dispersion system. The second stage of torsion-oriented turbulization is characterized by the origination of strong vertical vortexes filled with bubbles, that get off the funneled masses. Large associations of bubbles move in the vertical direction as the sources of homogenization and minimization of the elements of a dispersed phase apply tremendous agitation.

3.16. ANALYSIS OF FORCES THAT ARE ACTING DURING FORMATION OF DISPERSION SYSTEMS

This section is devoted to the analysis of molecular–surface forces acting on the interface during the formation of dispersed systems under the joint and simultaneous actions of mechanical resonance and hydraulic shock waves.

As discussed in the previous sections, the turbulent state of a dispersion system is a phenomenon that arises as a result of the simultaneous and combined action of hydraulic shock waves and the coincidence in the frequency of harmonic oscillations of disturbing (external) forces with that of natural (internal) oscillations of the system. A necessary condition for the formation and the very existence of a dispersion system, is the appearance and cumulative development (compression and collapse) of vapor–gas mixture bubbles, leading to the development of fields of internal pressure and temperature. The heterogeneous dispersion systems that arises—wherein the dispersed phase is distributed in the form of small particles of solid matter, liquid droplets and gas bubbles in a dispersion medium—is characterized by the formation of internal pressure fields and the development of a super large surface between phases.

In research studies [155-160] on wave processes in dual-phase fluid-bubble environment, interactions of weak $(\Delta\mathcal{P}_{Cr}/\mathcal{P}_0<1)$ and medium $(\Delta\mathcal{P}_{Cr}/\mathcal{P}_0\approx1)$ fluid strikes were considered without the compressibility of the fluid medium. Publications have discussed the characteristics of fluid strikes in fluid-bubble environment in the range of pressure $(\Delta\mathcal{P}_{Cr}/\mathcal{P}_0\approx5)$ in two-dimensional approximation with considering the acoustical compressibility of the liquid phase [161, 162]. In publication [129], a mathematical model of the fluid-bubble medium to research of strong fluid strike waves in bubbled liquid was developed.

Let us consider that a three-phase dispersion system mixed of particles of solid matter-liquid-gas at an equilibrium of internal pressure in both the dispersed and dispersion phases. Thus, inside the rather small bubbles (<2 mm), the heat exchange process is significantly difficult. In such conditions, gas (vapor) in bubbles cannot be cooled down to the temperature of the liquid medium. This condition forms the basis for applying of the adiabatic model [160]. Another restriction in the considered system is the ignoring of small-scale pulsations of bubbles that are admissible for liquid-gas systems with the small gas content [160]. Under such initial conditions, this dispersion system can be considered a holonomic system, where all mechanical connections could be reduced to geometrical connections [160] that are reduced to restrictions only on possible positions of material points.

A state of equilibrium for any material point of the accepted system f_j is entered in subordination to holonomic stationary connections k, which

can be represented as:

$$f_j(x_1, y_1, z_1, x_2, y_2, z_3, \dots x_n, y_n, z_n, t) = 0 \quad (j = 1, 2, 3, \dots, k), \quad (3.33)$$

where x_i, y_i, z_i, are the projections on coordinate axes; t is the time; and k are the numbers of the imposed connections.

For the solution of the mechanical problem for holonomic systems, it is possible to use second order Lagrange equations—the differential equations of motion of mechanical systems for which a classical description is suitable, relating the kinetic energy of the system to the generalized coordinates. They are independent among themselves. In general, for holonomic systems of the second order Lagrange equations of motion:

$$\frac{d}{dt}\left(\frac{\partial T}{\partial \dot{q}}\right)_i - \left(\frac{\partial T}{\partial q}\right)_i = 0 \quad (i = 1, 2, 3, \ldots n). \qquad (3.34)$$

If nonpotential forces T are acting in a system and are incapable of performing work (e.g., an environmental resistance force), the second order Lagrange equations of motion could be assumed as:

$$\frac{d}{dt}\left(\frac{\partial T}{\partial \dot{q}}\right)_i - \left(\frac{\partial T}{\partial q}\right)_i = \mathcal{F}_i \quad (i = 1, 2, 3, \ldots n), \qquad (3.35)$$

where q_i is the generalized coordinates, whose number is equal to the number n of degrees of freedom; $\dot{q}_i$ is the generalized speeds; and $\mathcal{F}_i$ is the generalized forces.

The first term $\frac{d}{dt}\left(\frac{\partial T}{\partial \dot{q}}\right)_i$ of the equations (3.35) expresses the kinetic energy, and the second term $\left(\frac{\partial T}{\partial q}\right)_i$ expresses the potential energy.

When compiling equations (3.34) and (3.35), it is necessary to choose q_i as the generalized coordinates and to define the kinetic energy of the considered dispersion system in its movement of the rather inertial reference system and to express it through q_i —the generalized coordinates—and $\dot{q}_i$—the generalized speeds.

The function $T(q_i, \dot{q}_i, t)$ will thereby be determined. The time t enters under nonstationary connections. Values T are on the active forces, whose numbers at non–ideal connections are losses of energy, including the friction forces. From a mathematical standpoint, equations (3.34) and (3.35) represent a system of ordinary the second degree differential equations regarding coordinates q_i.

By integrating these equations and determining the integration constants through the initial conditions, $q_i(t)$, will be determined, that is the law of the movement of a system in the generalized coordinates. This considered, the system of the Lagrange's equations (considering the laws of mass conservation for each phase, and the impulse and energy for heterogeneous disperse system at the movement with one degree of freedom) could be presented in private derivatives, as follows:

1) For a two-phase dispersion system: liquid–gas, the law of mass conservation was presented in work [159] as follows:

$$\frac{\alpha_1}{\rho}\frac{\partial \rho_1{}^0}{\partial t} + \frac{\rho_1{}^0}{\rho}\frac{\partial \alpha_1}{\partial t} = -\frac{\rho_1}{\rho_0}\frac{\partial w}{\partial r} = b_1; \tag{3.36}$$

and

$$\frac{\alpha_2}{\rho}\frac{\partial \rho_2}{\partial t} + \frac{\rho_2{}^0}{\rho}\frac{\partial \alpha_1}{\partial t} = -\frac{\rho_2}{\rho_0}\frac{\partial w}{\partial r} = b_2; \tag{3.37}$$

By analogy, for a three–phase dispersion system, particles of solid matter–liquid–gas, the law of mass conservation could be presented as follows:

$$\frac{\alpha_1}{\rho}\frac{\partial \rho_1{}^0}{\partial t} + \frac{\rho_1{}^0}{\rho}\frac{\partial \alpha_1}{\partial t} = -\frac{\rho_1}{\rho_0}\frac{\partial w}{\partial r} = b_1; \tag{3.38}$$

and

$$\frac{\alpha_2}{\rho}\frac{\partial \rho_2}{\partial t} + \frac{\rho_2{}^0}{\rho}\frac{\partial \alpha_1}{\partial t} = -\frac{\rho_2}{\rho_0}\frac{\partial w}{\partial r} = b_2; \tag{3.39}$$

and $$\frac{\alpha_3}{\rho}\frac{\partial \rho_3}{\partial t} + \frac{\rho_3{}^0}{\rho}\frac{\partial \alpha_3}{\partial t} = -\frac{\rho_3}{\rho_0}\frac{\partial w}{\partial r} = b_3; \tag{3.40}$$

2) For a two–phase dispersion system, the law of impulse conservation and the law of energy conservation were presented in work [157] as:

$$\rho_0\frac{\partial w}{\partial t} = -\frac{\partial p}{\partial r}, \tag{3.41}$$

and

$$\frac{\rho_1}{\rho}\left(\frac{\partial e_1}{\partial \rho_1{}^0}\right)_T\frac{\partial \rho_1{}^0}{\partial t} + \frac{\rho_2}{\rho}\left(\frac{\partial e_2}{\partial \rho_2{}^0}\right)_T\frac{\partial \rho_2{}^0}{\partial t} + \\ + \frac{\rho_1}{\rho}\left(\frac{\partial e_1}{\partial T_1}\right)_{\rho_1{}^0}\frac{\partial T_1}{\partial t} + \frac{\rho_2}{\rho}\left(\frac{\partial e_2}{\partial T_2}\right)_{\rho_2{}^0}\frac{\partial T_2}{\partial t} = -\frac{\rho}{\rho_0}\frac{\partial w}{\partial t}, \tag{3.42}$$

By analogy, for a three-phase dispersion system, the law of impulse conservation and the law of energy conservation could be presented as:

$$\rho_0\frac{\partial w}{\partial t} = -\frac{\partial p}{\partial r}; \tag{3.43}$$

and

$$\frac{\rho_1}{\rho}\left(\frac{\partial e_1}{\partial \rho_1{}^0}\right)_T\frac{\partial \rho_1{}^0}{\partial t} + \frac{\rho_2}{\rho}\left(\frac{\partial e_2}{\partial \rho_2{}^0}\right)_T\frac{\partial \rho_2{}^0}{\partial t} + \frac{\rho_3}{\rho}\left(\frac{\partial e_3}{\partial \rho_3{}^0}\right)_T\frac{\partial \rho_3{}^0}{\partial t} + \\ + \frac{\rho_1}{\rho}\left(\frac{\partial e_1}{\partial T_1}\right)_{\rho_1{}^0}\frac{\partial T_1}{\partial t} + \frac{\rho_2}{\rho}\left(\frac{\partial e_2}{\partial T_2}\right)_{\rho_2{}^0}\frac{\partial T_2}{\partial t} + \frac{\rho_1}{\rho}\left(\frac{\partial e_3}{\partial T_3}\right)_{\rho_3{}^0}\frac{\partial T_3}{\partial t} = \\ = -\frac{\rho}{\rho_0}\frac{\partial w}{\partial t} \tag{3.44}$$

The condition of equilibrium for interphase pressure for a two–phase dispersion system could be presented in a differential form as:

$$(\frac{\partial p_1}{\partial \rho_1{}^0})_T \frac{\partial \rho_1{}^0}{\partial t} - (\frac{\partial p_2}{\partial \rho_2{}^0})_T \frac{\partial \rho_2{}^0}{\partial t} + (\frac{\partial p_1}{\partial T_1})_{\rho_1{}^0} \frac{\partial T_1}{\partial t} - (\frac{\partial p_2}{\partial T_2})_{\rho_2{}^0} \frac{\partial T_2}{\partial t} = 0. \quad (3.45)$$

By analogy, the equilibrium for interphase pressure for a three-phase dispersion system could be presented as:

$$(\frac{\partial p_1}{\partial \rho_1{}^0})_T \frac{\partial \rho_1{}^0}{\partial t} - (\frac{\partial p_2}{\partial \rho_2{}^0})_T \frac{\partial \rho_2{}^0}{\partial t} - (\frac{\partial p_3}{\partial \rho_3{}^0})_T \frac{\partial \rho_3{}^0}{\partial t} + \\ + (\frac{\partial p_1}{\partial T_1})_{\rho_1{}^0} \frac{\partial T_1}{\partial t} - (\frac{\partial p_2}{\partial T_2})_{\rho_2{}^0} \frac{\partial T_2}{\partial t} - (\frac{\partial p_3}{\partial T_3})_{\rho_3{}^0} \frac{\partial T_3}{\partial t} = 0. \quad (3.46)$$

For a vapor–gas bubbles phase, the adiabatic condition is accepted as:

$$\frac{de_2}{\partial t} + p_2 \frac{d}{\partial t} (\frac{1}{\rho_2{}^0}) = 0, \quad (3.47)$$

where $\rho_i{}^0$ is the current density of the i-s phase; $\rho_i = \rho_i \cdot \alpha_i$ is the specified density of the i-s phase; ρ is the average density for $\rho = \rho_1{}^0 + \rho_2{}^0$ (for two-phase dispersion systems) and for $\rho = \rho_1{}^0 + \rho_2{}^0 + \rho_3{}^0$ (for three-phase dispersion systems); ρ^0 is the initial average phase density; α_i is the volume concentration of a phase; T_i is the temperature of i-s phase, where ($i=1$ is the liquid phase, $i=2$ is the gas, and $i = 3$ is the solid matter particles); r is the Lagrange's coordinate; w is the mass speed; and $p_i(\rho_i{}^0, T)$ and $e_i(\rho_i{}^0, T)$ are the pressure and the internal energy, respectively, of the phases defined by the state equation.

3.17. PHENOMENON OF TORSION-ORIENTED TURBULIZATION

There are three phases in the life span of an individual gas bubble: origination, expansion, and collapse. These phases are forming a full thermodynamic cycle. The pressure of saturated vapor of the liquid, in which the development of bubbles begins, is significantly depends on the physical condition of said liquid. If in this liquid there is a consequential amount of the dissolved gas, the decrease of pressure leads to the release of this gas from the liquid. This is the beginning of the origination of vapor–gas cavities. In considered cavities, the pressure is higher than pressure of the saturated vapor–gas mix inside the liquid.

In the presence of microscopic bubbles inside the liquid, with a diameter smaller than $10x10^{-6}$ m, the resonance turbulization can arise when pressure is above the pressure of the saturated vapor–gas. Wherein, each arisen bubble, being formed of a core, develops to the size, that corresponds to the internal pressure inside a single bubble. This pressure is equal to the internal pressure in this zone of the dispersion medium. At the subsequent increase in the bubble's size, when the internal pressure of the saturated vapor in the bubble exceeds the critical point, the bubble bursts. This process—from bubble's origination to its collapse—takes no longer then several microseconds. Bubbles can develop, following one after another, so quickly that they can look like a single cavity (bubble).

In the absence of microscopic gas bubbles, or otherwise, in the absence of dissolved gas, the liquid can withstand differences in negative pressure or internal tensions fields of thousands of atmospheres without breaking its continuity. The difference in the internal pressure of water can range from 500 to 10,000 Atmosphere [158]. In practice, water treated with pressure up to several hundred and even thousands of atmospheres, (which corresponds to pressure in the depths of the ocean or in the production of heavy water for the needs of the nuclear industry), keeps continuity when the pressure difference is up to 300 Atmosphere. According to data [156], in the absence of bubble nuclei commensurate with the size of the molecules, water can maintain continuity with the development of a pressure difference of up to 15,000 Atmosphere.

However, according to other theoretical calculations [158], this does not exceed 1,500 Atmosphere. At the same time, in the presence of microparticles of solid matter in water that measure less than $10x10^{-6}$ m, the water continuity breaks when the difference is only several tens of atmospheres.

In contrast to vibrational cavitation, it is very difficult to determine the moment of occurrence of resonance turbulence, even when the sizes of the fields of internal stresses in the fluid are known. This is because the sizes of gas bubbles or particles of solid matter present in the dispersion medium are unknown. It can, however, be established approximately by measuring the total content of the gas phase in the dispersion liquid–gas system, when the dispersed phase is a vapor–gas mixture, because the value of the internal pressure depends on it. And yet, without a full understanding of the role of the gas and solid inclusions, it is not possible to predict the moment of formation of bubble formation.

At present, there is still no complete and clear theoretical explanation of the nature of the presence of microscopic bubbles in a liquid, which are additional centers of bubble formation. On the one hand, surface tension forces should lead to the collapse of small bubbles invisible to the eye, but, on the other hand, larger bubbles visible to the human eye would have to float and burst at the interface between the liquid and gas phases. To explain the appearance and development of bubbles in the torsion-oriented turbulization mode, it could be assumed that small bubbles can form not only from microscopic volumes of gas trapped in the liquid, but also on the surface of microscopic abnormal points that bind to the volume of the liquid phase. This is confirmed my observations that the development of turbulence centers occurs at the walls and at the bottom of reactors.

Another source of bubble formation can be the development of an internal stress state between the elementary volumes of a dispersion medium. These differ in the values of internal pressures that arise because of the difference in the pressure moduli of the vapor-gas mixture acting from within the existing bubbles.

The third source of bubble formation is internal pressure waves arising from the propagation of waves that have resulted from the hydraulic shock to the system components against the rigid top cover of a reactor. And finally, any sources of internal stresses can be centers of the nucleation of bubbles, for example, solid particles that are elements of a dispersed phase.

As it was noticed earlier, during conducted experiments, inside of the central part of the reactor, it was observed the formation of floating and simultaneously rotating vapor-gas bubbles, the formation of which resembles a tornado. It is quite probable that this behavior of dispersed particles caused by the action of some of the moments $\mathbf{M}_i$ on the rotating particles of the dispersed phase. This explains the occurrence of motion, in which the system forms a figure that look like hyperbola. Thus, there is every reason to assume that such a distribution of dispersed particles coincides with the torsion-oriented field contours.

The formed dispersion system is distinguishable by its advanced surface of separation between phases. The asymmetric condition of a dispersion system depends on the chemical composition; physical and mechanical characteristics of liquid and gas, parameters of vibration, reactor's internal dimensions, and the character of the reactor's surface. This leads to the formation of asymmetric fields of internal pressure tensions, which could be called torsion-oriented turbulization. The intensity of fields of internal pressure is caused by continuous but unevenly origination, development, and collapse of gas bubbles. Also, in the considered dispersion systems, a special role is assigned to the surface phenomena, characterized by molecular interaction forces, including capillary–surface tension forces.

3.18. FORMATION OF DISPERSION SYSTEMS (Continue)

In the two-phase system, the dispersed phase is gas and the dispersion phase – liquid. In the three-phase system, the dispersed phase is gas and particles of solid matter or drops of the liquid immiscible and insoluble with the main liquid, and the dispersion phase is the liquid.

Considering the practical usage of the process of formation of dispersion systems, composite materials, and alloys, it is necessary to spend more time to stress the point, that formed dispersion systems are distinguished by two features. The first one is an ultra–developed the size in the surface of separation between different phases, and the second is the development of fields of internal pressure between adjacent elementary volumes of the dispersion medium. The tension of internal pressure fields develops between elementary volumes of the dispersion medium, due to the continuous and uneven occurrence, development, and bursting of gas bubbles. This phenomenon is the cause of the intensive homogenization and minimization of components of the dispersed phase. Distinguished in this process is the surface phenomena, which are characterized by the forces of the intermolecular interaction.

It is known that physicochemical technological processes are proceeding because of the movement of the viscous (both compressible and incompressible) natural liquids and the liquids formed during the movement of the interphase separation surface. In addition, the processes of heat exchange and a mass transfer also occur through the interphase separation surface. Therefore, the mathematical analysis of torsion-oriented turbulization, the fluid dynamics, and diffusive and thermal similarity is of particular importance.

3.19. TURBULIZATION MOTION OF THE DISPERSION PHASE

As already noted, the phenomenon of torsion-oriented turbulization is characterized by the components of the planned dispersion system located in the reactor, at certain parameters of the low frequency vibrational force, experience continuous ruptures in some elementary volumes of the liquid and caverns are formed. They are filled with a gas–vapor mixture, forming bubbles. It is the appearance, development and bursting of bubbles that lead to the formation of a dispersion system that fills up the entire internal chamber of the reactor.

It should be emphasized that the phenomenon of torsion-oriented turbulization occurs in a single cavity hyperbolic reactor under the vibrational influence of a field of disturbing forces. As a result, only an unsteady motion is constant in the liquid inside the dispersion system.

It should also be noted that, inside of each individual bubble the process occurs at constant temperatures but during rapidly changing pressure and elementary volume of the vapor–gas mixture. In thermodynamics, such processes are usually called *isothermal*. Because the dispersion system itself occupies the entire internal space of the reactor, its internal surface (considering the rigidity of the reactor's structure), represents the external boundaries of the dispersion system. Thus, the processes occurring in the reactor do not change the volume of the considered system. In thermodynamics, such processes are usually called *isochoric*.

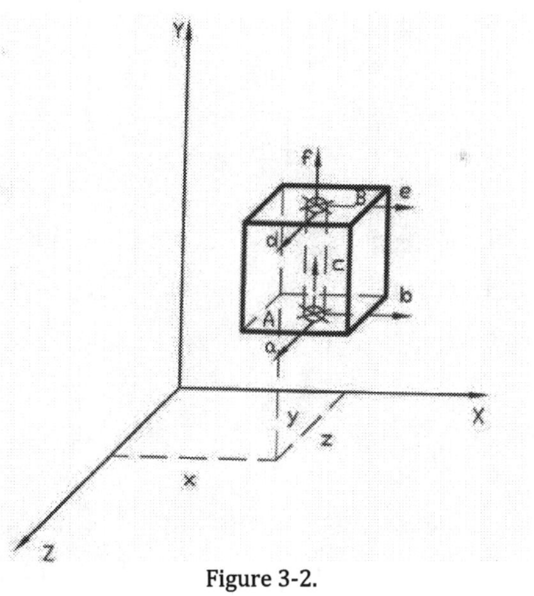

Figure 3-2.

Let us consider the unsteady motion of the dispersion medium at which in each elementary volume the speed of the motion and the internal pressure are changing continuously. For this purpose, let us allocate in the elementary parallelepiped with edges of dx, dy, and dz (Fig. 3-2) in the elementary volume of continuously moving liquid medium.

Because of the continuity of the liquid phase, the entire internal volume of the allocated parallelepiped despite the turbulent condition of the dispersion system, will always be completely filled with liquid, which is in the constant motion. Thus, the mass of the compressed liquid that proceeds out of the volume of the allocated elementary parallelepiped and the mass of the same liquid that comes that into this volume are generally not considered equal. This is because of the inconstancy of the speed w and the liquid density ρ.

Through the left face A, which is parallel the plane YOZ, liquid moves at the speed w_x parallel to OX axis. Let us consider this component and liquid density ρ as constant at all points of this side and equal to their values in A. Then:

$$w_x = F_1\,(x, y, z, t), \tag{3.48}$$

and

$$\rho = F_2\,(x, y, z, t), \tag{3.49}$$

where x, y, z are the projections on coordinate axes; and t is the time. At the same point in time, on the opposite (right) face B, those dimensions will be equal to:

$$w_x + \left(\frac{\partial w_x}{\partial x}\right) dx \text{ and } \rho + \left(\frac{\partial \rho}{\partial x}\right) dx. \tag{3.50}$$

The amount of liquid expressed in units of mass moves through an elementary platform $dy\,dz$ of the left face of A for a unit in time t and is equal:

$$dM_{x1} = \rho w_x\, dy\, dz. \tag{3.51}$$

At the same point of time, the mass of liquid that is moving through the opposite face B is equal:

$$dM_{x2} = \left[\rho w_x + \frac{\partial}{\partial x}(\rho w_x)\,dx\right] dy\,dz\,. \qquad (3.52)$$

Thus, the increment in the liquid mass during a unit of time t in the allocated elementary parallelepiped caused by the distinction of values w_x and ρ on faces of A and B is equal:

$$\Delta M_x = \frac{\partial}{\partial x}(\rho w_x)\,dx\,dy\,dz\,. \qquad (3.53)$$

It is not too difficult to see, that in the directions of perpendicular to axes OY and OZ, it would be fair to similar expressions ΔM_y and ΔM_z. The full increment of the mass of liquid in the elementary parallelepiped in the unit of time will be equal:

$$\Delta M = \left[\frac{\partial}{\partial x}(\rho w_x) + \frac{\partial}{\partial y}(\rho w_y) + \frac{\partial}{\partial z}(\rho w_x)\right] dx\,dy\,dz. \qquad (3.54)$$

At the continuity of the flow of a liquid, which forms the dispersion phase, the mass change in the volume of $dx\,dy\,dz$ is caused by the change in the liquid density ρ in this volume. Therefore:

$$\Delta M = \frac{\partial \rho}{\partial t}\,dx\,dy\,dz. \qquad (3.55)$$

Equalizing the received expressions (3.54) and (3.55), we get:

$$\left[\frac{\partial}{\partial x}(\rho w_x) + \frac{\partial}{\partial y}(\rho w_y) + \frac{\partial}{\partial z}(\rho w_z)\right] dx\,dy\,dz =$$

$$= -\frac{\partial \rho}{\partial t}\,dx\,dy\,dz. \qquad (3.56)$$

By dividing both sides of the equation into the product $dx\,dy\,dz$ and transferring terms to the left, it will be:

$$\frac{\partial \rho}{\partial t} + \frac{\partial}{\partial x}(\rho w_x) + \frac{\partial}{\partial y}(\rho w_y) + \frac{\partial}{\partial z}(\rho w_z) = 0. \qquad (3.57)$$

Expression (3.57) is an equation of continuity of the dispersive phase. In special cases, the equation of continuity assumes the following:

1. For the dropping liquid, when $\rho_o = \text{const.}$:

$$\left(\frac{\partial w_x}{\partial x}\right)_x + \left(\frac{\partial w_y}{\partial y}\right)_y + \left(\frac{\partial w_z}{\partial z}\right)_z = 0. \qquad (3.58)$$

In a vector's form expression of continuity assumes:

$$\text{div}\, \overrightarrow{\mathfrak{B}} = 0, \qquad (3.59)$$

where $\overrightarrow{\mathfrak{B}}$ is the vector's expression of the speed of the flow.

From equilibrium (3.57), it follows that: with the constant motion of the liquid, while the liquid volumes flow into and out of the same allocated volume of space, and at the same period of time, are equal.

2. For a uniform gas (disperse phase), when $\rho_o = F_2(t)$:

$$\frac{\partial \rho}{\partial t} + \rho\left[\frac{\partial w_x}{\partial x} + \frac{\partial w_y}{\partial y} + \frac{\partial w_z}{\partial z}\right] = 0. \qquad (3.60)$$

or

$$\frac{\partial \rho}{\partial t} + \rho\, \text{div}\, \overrightarrow{\mathfrak{B}} = 0. \qquad (3.61)$$

3. For the steady movement, when:

$$\frac{\partial \rho}{\partial t} = 0, \qquad (3.62)$$

then:

$$\frac{\partial}{\partial x}(\rho w_x) + \frac{\partial}{\partial y}(\rho w_y) + \frac{\partial}{\partial z}(\rho w_z) = 0. \qquad (3.63)$$

or

$$\frac{\partial \rho}{\partial t} + \rho \operatorname{div} \overrightarrow{\mathfrak{B}} = 0. \tag{3.64}$$

From equation (3.57) at condition (3.62), it follows that, at the condition of the steady movement, the liquid does not change its mass, that is, the mass of the liquid flowing into and out of the allocated part of the space are equal.

The fundamental law of mechanics is applicable for concluding the equation of the movement: the force is equal to the mass multiplied by acceleration.

At any point of a continuously moving fluid, there should be an equilibrium of forces that determines a motion. Such forces are gravitational forces, external indignant forces, and friction forces. As mentioned above, the external indignant forces act on the reactor containing the components of the planned dispersion system and under the condition of simultaneous and joint action of mechanical resonance and fluid hammer impacts. This leads to the formation of a dispersion system.

In the liquid phase that is in the movement, let us allocate an elementary parallelepiped with volume dV and edges dx, dy, dz. Also, let us allocate projections to an axis OX of the forces of gravity, pressure and friction operating on this elementary volume (Fig. 3-3). For the gravity applied to the center of the elementary volume dV, is:

$$g_x \rho \, dV = g_x \rho \, dx \, dy \, dz, \tag{3.65}$$

where g_x is the projection of gravity acceleration to the axis OX.

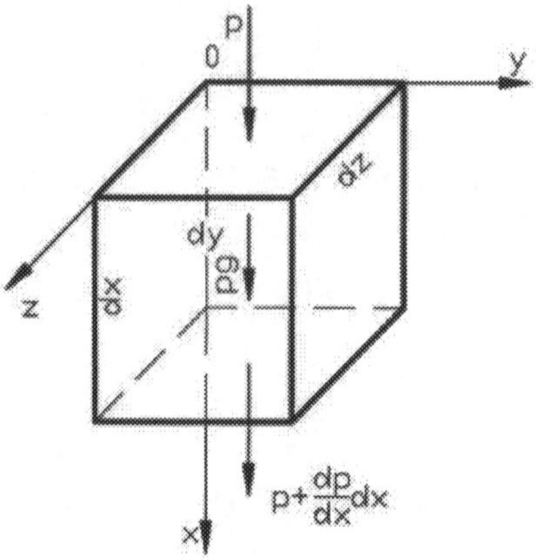

Figure 3-3.

Let us designate the specific pressure $\mathcal{P}$ of a liquid. Then, the force of pressure on a vertical face of elementary volume will be equal to $\mathcal{P}\,dy\,dz$. On the lower face the acting force is:

$$-(\mathcal{P}+\frac{\partial \mathcal{P}}{\partial x}\,dx)\,dy\,dz. \qquad (3.66)$$

where $\frac{\partial \mathcal{P}}{\partial x}dx$ is the change of hydrostatic pressure in the direction of axis OXon the entire length of the edge dx.

This force acts in the direction opposite to that of the liquid's movement.

The projection of those resultant forces of the pressure is equal:

$$\mathcal{P}\,dy\,dz-(\mathcal{P}+\frac{\partial \mathcal{P}}{\partial x}dx)\,dy\,dz=-\frac{\partial \mathcal{P}}{\partial x}\,dxdydz. \qquad (3.67)$$

The action of the internal friction force can be considered through the example of the motion of a flat laminar flow, where the projection of speed w_x depends only on y. In the case under consideration, the friction force arises only on the lateral face of the allocated elementary volume. The directions and sizes of friction forces are shown in Fig. 3-4. In section y, there is friction force: $Sdxdz$, which is directed against the movement, as the speed of the liquid movement on the sides of an elementary parallelepiped and is less than that inside of the elementary volume. In the section $y + dy$, the friction force is equal:

$$(S + \frac{\partial S}{\partial y} dy)\, dxdz. \tag{3.68}$$

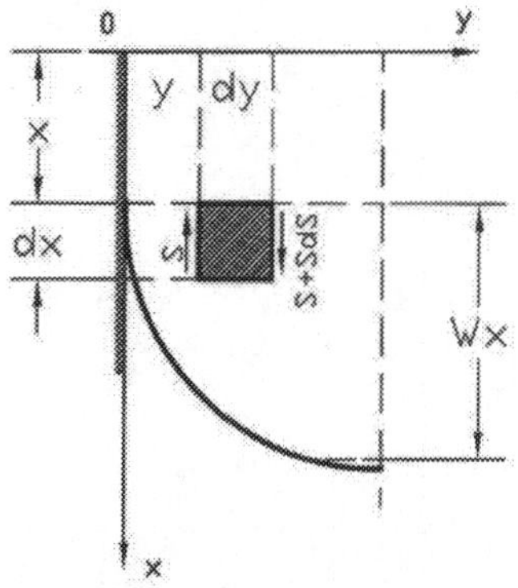

Figure 3-4.

The friction force S is directed towards the movement. Thus, in this case, the speed of the liquid's movement is faster that inside the elementary volume. The projection of these resultant forces is:

$$(S + \frac{\partial S}{\partial y} dy)\, dxdz - S\, dxdz = \frac{\partial S}{\partial y}\, dxdydz. \tag{3.69}$$

where: S is the friction force, related to the surface unit, [N/m^2].

In compliance with Newton's Law: $S = \mu \frac{dw_x}{dy}$, where μ is the viscosity of the liquid, substituting value S in the equation (3.69), will result in:

$$\frac{\partial S}{\partial y} dV = \mu \frac{d^2 w_x}{dy^2} dV. \tag{3.70}$$

Generally, when the speed w_x changes in all three coordinates, the projection of the equally resultant friction force to the axis OX will be:

$$\mu\left[\frac{\partial^2 w_x}{\partial x^2}+\frac{\partial^2 w_x}{\partial y^2}+\frac{\partial^2 w_x}{\partial z^2}\right] dV=\mu\nabla^2\, w_x dV. \qquad (3.71)$$

where $\Delta = \nabla^2$ is the symbol called a Laplace's Operator [161, 162], symbolizing the sum of the second private derivative of a speed projection to the OX axis:

$$\nabla^2 = \Delta = \frac{\partial^2}{\partial x^2}+\frac{\partial^2}{\partial y^2}+\frac{\partial^2}{\partial z^2}.$$

By adding projections (3.65), (3.67), and (3.69), we receive the projection of the resultant actions, which applies for the elementary volume of dV on the OX axis:

$$\left\{g_x \rho - \frac{\partial P}{\partial x} + \mu\left[\frac{\partial^2 w_x}{\partial x^2}+\frac{\partial^2 w_x}{\partial y^2}+\frac{\partial^2 w_x}{\partial z^2}\right]\right\} dV. \qquad (3.72)$$

This resultant force is equal to the multiplication of the mass of an element of volume dV upon its acceleration $\frac{Dw_x}{Dt}$. This expression (3.70) could be presented as:

$$\rho\frac{Dw_x}{Dt}dV=\rho\left[\frac{\partial w_x}{\partial t}+w_x\frac{\partial w_x}{\partial x}+w_y\frac{\partial w_y}{\partial y}+w_z\frac{\partial w_z}{\partial z}\right]dV. \qquad (3.73)$$

The symbol $\frac{Dw_x}{Dt}$ is a full or substantial derivative w_x upon t. This derivative represents the change of speed w_x at this point of the dispersion phase and is characterized by a private derivative w_x upon t:

$$\frac{d^2 w_x}{dt^2} = \lim_{\Delta t \to 0} \frac{w_x(\mathbb{K},t+\Delta t)-w_x(\mathbb{K},t)}{\Delta t}, \qquad (3.74)$$

where $\mathbb{K}$ denotes any constant geometric point inside the dispersive medium.

A substantial derivative, that is also known as Lagrange's derivative [130], is a derivative taken as a function of the coordinate system, which moves with at a speed of w_x. It is determined using scalar's function $\phi(\vec{r}, t)$, coordinates, time, and the vector's function $\vec{u}\ (\vec{r}\ , t)$:

$$\frac{D\phi}{Dt} = \frac{\partial \phi}{\partial t} + (\mathrm{u} \cdot \nabla)\ \phi; \qquad \text{(a)}$$

$$\frac{D\mathrm{v}}{Dt} = \frac{\partial \mathrm{v}}{\partial t} + (\mathrm{u} \cdot \nabla)\ \mathrm{v} \cdot\ \vec{u}. \qquad \text{(b)}$$

where ∇ is Laplace's operator.

In equalities (a) and (b) the first term represents a private derivative of time t. The second term is a convective derivative of this function from the vector or the scalar function at point $\mathbb{K}$ at time t [162]. This derivative defines a change of parameters of the function $\mathbb{K}$ at time t at convective flow of the liquid at the determined speed.

The convective derivative is defined by an action of the operator $(\vec{u} \cdot \nabla)$ on the scalar or vector function. In the most general case, the material derivative could be expressed as [162]:

$$\frac{DA_{ij}}{Dt} = \frac{DA_{ij}}{Dt} - A_{ik} \cdot \frac{\partial w_k}{\partial x_j} - \frac{\partial w_i}{\partial x_k} \cdot A_{kj} + \propto_1 \cdot A_{kj} \cdot \frac{\partial w_i}{\partial x_k} +$$

$$+ \propto_2 \cdot A_{ik} \cdot \frac{\partial w_j}{\partial x_k} + \propto_3 \cdot A_{ij} \frac{\partial w_k}{\partial x_k}.$$

To describe any possible changes w_x for this elementary volume of the dispersive phase during the interval of time Δt, it is necessary to express the increment w_x as the difference between values of function w_x at the moment of time $t + \Delta t$. This has to be done at the point of space $\mathbb{K}^*$, where this volume is exactly at this point in time, and the value of function w_x at time t has to be at its initial location $\mathbb{K}_0$. The limit of the relation of this increment to Δt [aspire to zero $(\Delta t \longrightarrow 0)$] is the Lagrange's derivative.

The relationship between the partial and total derivatives is that, when the total derivative of the function $w = f(x, y, z, t)$ is compiled, then x, y, z are considered functions of t because the elementary volume at time t and the coordinates x, y, z, during time Δt, will move along a certain trajectory.

Considering $w = f(x,y, z, t)$ as a composite function from t, we get:

$$\frac{Dw_x}{Dt} = \frac{\partial w_x}{\partial t} + \frac{\partial w_x}{\partial x} \cdot \frac{\partial x}{\partial t} + \frac{\partial w_x}{\partial y} \cdot \frac{\partial y}{\partial t} + \frac{\partial w_x}{\partial z} \cdot \frac{\partial z}{\partial t} =$$

$$= \frac{\partial w_x}{\partial t} + w_x \frac{\partial w_x}{\partial x} + w_y \frac{\partial w_x}{\partial y} + w_z \frac{\partial w_x}{\partial z}, \qquad (3.75)$$

which is the expression in square brackets of formula (3.73). By comparing formulas (3.73) and (3.74), we get:

$$\rho \frac{\partial w_x}{\partial t} + \rho \left[w_x \frac{\partial w_x}{\partial x} + w_y \frac{\partial w_x}{\partial y} + w_z \frac{\partial w_x}{\partial z} \right] =$$

$$= g_x \rho - \frac{\partial P}{\partial x} + \mu \left[\frac{\partial^2 w_x}{\partial x^2} + \frac{\partial^2 w_x}{\partial y^2} + \frac{\partial^2 w_x}{\partial z^2} \right] \qquad (3.76)$$

In the same algorithm, the equations for equally effective projections of forces to axes of OY and OZ would be received:

$$\rho \frac{\partial w_y}{\partial t} + \rho \left[w_x \frac{\partial w_y}{\partial x} + w_y \frac{\partial w_y}{\partial y} + w_z \frac{\partial w_y}{\partial z} \right] =$$

$$= g_y \rho - \frac{\partial P}{\partial y} + \mu \left[\frac{\partial^2 w_y}{\partial x^2} + \frac{\partial^2 w_y}{\partial y^2} + \frac{\partial^2 w_y}{\partial z^2} \right], \qquad (3.77)$$

$$\rho \frac{\partial w_z}{\partial t} + \rho \left[w_x \frac{\partial w_z}{\partial x} + w_y \frac{\partial w_z}{\partial y} + w_z \frac{\partial w_z}{\partial z}\right] =$$

$$= g_z \rho - \frac{\partial \mathcal{P}}{\partial x} + \mu\left[\frac{\partial^2 w_z}{\partial x^2} + \frac{\partial^2 w_z}{\partial y^2} + \frac{\partial^2 w_z}{\partial z^2}\right]. \qquad (3.78)$$

Equations (3.76), (3.77), and (3.78) form a system of the differential equations of the movement of incompressible liquid. These equations are called Navier–Stokes equations. This system of equations is fair for both laminar and turbulence flows.

When the viscosity of the liquid phase μ is permanent, the system of equations (3.76), (3.77), and (3.78) can be replaced with one vector's equation:

$$\frac{\overrightarrow{\partial w}}{\partial t} + \rho\,(\overrightarrow{w}, \text{grad})\overrightarrow{w} = \overrightarrow{g\rho} - \text{grad}\,\rho + \mu\nabla^2\overrightarrow{w}. \qquad (3.79)$$

Considering that $\xi = \frac{\mu}{\rho}$ is the coefficient of kinematic viscosity, [m^2/s]; μ is the coefficient of dynamic viscosity, [Ns/m^2]; and ρ is the specific density, [kg/m^3]:

$$\frac{\overrightarrow{\partial w}}{\partial t} + (\overrightarrow{w}, \text{grad})\overrightarrow{w} = \vec{g} - \frac{1}{\rho}\text{grad}\,\rho + \xi\nabla^2\overrightarrow{w}. \qquad (3.80)$$

Applying the "whirlwind" vector operation to each member of the equation (3.76) can make this equation simple.

Operation "whirlwind" is defined as follows, for any vector $\overrightarrow{\mathfrak{N}}$:

$$\text{rot}\,\overrightarrow{\mathfrak{N}} = \left(\frac{\partial N_y}{\partial x} - \frac{\partial N_x}{\partial y}\right)\overrightarrow{\mathfrak{K}} + \left(\frac{\partial N_z}{\partial y} - \frac{\partial N_y}{\partial z}\right)\overrightarrow{\mathfrak{I}} + \left(\frac{\partial N_x}{\partial z} - \frac{\partial N_z}{\partial x}\right)\overrightarrow{\mathfrak{J}}, \qquad (3.81)$$

where $\overrightarrow{\mathfrak{K}}$, $\overrightarrow{\mathfrak{I}}$ and $\overrightarrow{\mathfrak{J}}$ are vectors, directed on axes of coordinates x, y, z.

Equation (3.80), $\vec{g}$ is gravity acceleration. As a constant vector, we get:

$$\text{rot}\,\vec{g} = 0, \tag{3.82}$$

and

$$\text{grad}\,\vec{\rho} = \frac{\partial p}{\partial x}\vec{\mathfrak{I}} + \frac{\partial p}{\partial x}\vec{\mathfrak{I}} + \frac{\partial p}{\partial x}\vec{\mathfrak{K}}. \tag{3.83}$$

After performing operation "whirlwind" over grad $\vec{\rho}$, there is:

$$\text{rot grad}\,\vec{\rho} = \left(\frac{\partial^2 \rho}{\partial y \partial x} - \frac{\partial^2 \rho}{\partial y \partial x}\right)\vec{\mathfrak{K}} + \ldots = 0. \tag{3.84}$$

Vector $\vec{g}$ is the gravity acceleration and, within the height of the reactor. Vector $\vec{g}$ is constant. Thus rot $\vec{g} = 0$. As a result of operation of "whirlwind", the component in equation (3.80) is:

$$\left(\vec{g} - \frac{1}{\rho}\,\text{grad}\,\vec{\rho}\right), \tag{3.85}$$

Term (3.80) could be excluded. Therefore, the equation (2.80) could be expressed as follows:

$$\text{rot}\,\frac{\overrightarrow{\partial w}}{\partial t} + \text{rot}\,(\vec{w}, \text{grad})\vec{w} = \xi\,\text{rot}\,\nabla^2\vec{w}. \tag{3.86}$$

Also, a Navier's–Stokes equation could be composed for the compressible liquids. Then, equation (3.74), relating to the OX axis, assumes the following:

$$\rho\left[w_x\frac{\partial w_x}{\partial x} + w_y\frac{\partial w_x}{\partial y} + w_z\frac{\partial w_x}{\partial z}\right] = g_x\rho - \frac{\partial P}{\partial x} + \tag{3.87}$$

$$+\mu\left[\frac{1}{3}\frac{\partial}{\partial x}\left(\frac{\partial w_x}{\partial x} + \frac{\partial w_y}{\partial y} + \frac{\partial w_z}{\partial z}\right) + \frac{\partial^2 w_x}{\partial x^2} + \frac{\partial^2 w_x}{\partial y^2} + \frac{\partial^2 w_x}{\partial z^2}\right];$$

Similarly, for axes of OY and OZ:

$$\rho\left[w_x\frac{\partial w_y}{\partial x}+w_y\frac{\partial w_y}{\partial y}+w_z\frac{\partial w_y}{\partial z}\right]=g_y\rho-\frac{\partial P}{\partial y}+ \qquad (3.88)$$

$$+\mu\left[\frac{1}{3}\frac{\partial}{\partial y}\left(\frac{\partial w_x}{\partial x}+\frac{\partial w_y}{\partial y}+\frac{\partial w_z}{\partial z}\right)+\frac{\partial^2 w_y}{\partial x^2}+\frac{\partial^2 w_y}{\partial y^2}+\frac{\partial^2 w_y}{\partial z^2}\right];$$

$$\rho\left[w_x\frac{\partial w_z}{\partial x}+w_y\frac{\partial w_z}{\partial y}+w_z\frac{\partial w_z}{\partial z}\right]=g_z\rho-\frac{\partial P}{\partial z}+ \qquad (3.89)$$

$$+\mu\left[\frac{1}{3}\frac{\partial}{\partial z}\left(\frac{\partial w_x}{\partial x}+\frac{\partial w_y}{\partial y}+\frac{\partial w_z}{\partial z}\right)+\frac{\partial^2 w_z}{\partial x^2}+\frac{\partial^2 w_z}{\partial y^2}+\frac{\partial^2 w_z}{\partial z^2}\right].$$

At a continuity condition in which ρ is constant, for incompressible liquids equations (3.76) and (3.87) could be converted into:

$$\frac{\partial w_x}{\partial x}+\frac{\partial w_y}{\partial y}+\frac{\partial w_z}{\partial z}=0. \qquad (3.90)$$

3.20 THE EQUATION OF HEAT BALANCE FOR THE TORSION-ORIENTED TURBULIZATION

Considering that, in Bernoulli's equation (3.15) there is a dissipative component and, as a result, in the mode of resonant turbulization, the energy dissipation takes place. This energy dissipation is spent on, among other things, on the change of temperature inside the reactor.

Let us compose the heat balance equation for the resonance turbulization regime. Suppose that the heat entering the elementary volume of liquid in question at a steady thermodynamic state is equal to that of the same amount of waste heat. To this volume, as in equation (3.76), heat is supplied due to thermal conductivity and with the help of material volumes of the dispersion medium flowing through this elementary volume while it is simultaneously cooled. If the temperature of this volume remains constant in time, then the total amount of heat supplied must be zero.

Some physicochemical processes require having an external source of heat. When considering the existence of such a source of heat flux of intensity of Q_i, the following equality takes place:

$$C\rho\,(w_x\frac{\partial t}{\partial x}+w_y\frac{\partial t}{\partial y}+w_z\frac{\partial t}{\partial z})=\lambda\,(\frac{\partial^2 t}{\partial x^2}+\frac{\partial^2 t}{\partial y^2}+\frac{\partial^2 t}{\partial z^2})+q_i. \qquad (3.91)$$

where C is the thermal capacity, [J/1⁰K]; Q_i is the heat flux, [W]; ρ is the surface heat flux density, [W/m^2]; and λ is the coefficient of the heat conductivity, [W/m 1⁰K];

Note: [W/m^2 = J/m^{2}s], [W = J/s], and [W/m 1⁰K = J/m s 1⁰K]

In terms on the left side of equation (3.91), the amount of heat in the elementary volume—which is used for heating the dt of the elementary volumes—proceeds through an elementary parallelepiped with edges dx, dy and dz. This heat gets covered at the expense of the heat supply from the environment—which is the first component on the right side of equation (2.91) —and at the expense of the heat source Q_i. By dividing both sides of the equation into $C\rho$, we get:

$$w_x\frac{\partial t}{\partial x}+w_y\frac{\partial t}{\partial y}+w_z\frac{\partial t}{\partial z}=\frac{\lambda}{C\rho}(\frac{\partial^2 t}{\partial x^2}+\frac{\partial^2 t}{\partial y^2}+\frac{\partial^2 t}{\partial z^2})+Q_i/C\rho. \qquad (3.92)$$

Or, in a vector form:

$$(\vec{w}, \text{grad}\ t)=a\,\nabla^2 t+Q_i/C\rho, \qquad (3.93)$$

where $a=\frac{1}{C}$ is the coefficient of thermal diffusivity, [W/m 1⁰K].

Equations (3.57), (3.76), (3.77), (3.78) and (3.92) are forming a system of five differential equations with private derivatives. These equations together with boundary conditions completely describe the process of the movement of viscous liquid movement—the substance of the dispersive phase of the disperse system formed in the mode of resonance turbulization.

Near the reactor wall, the movement of the liquid phase is laminar in nature; therefore, heat transfer occurs because of heat conduction. According to the well-known equation it is:

$$dQ = -\lambda \left(\frac{\partial t}{\partial n}\right)_S dS, \tag{3.94}$$

where $\left(\frac{\partial t}{\partial n}\right)_S$ is the temperature gradient of the liquid phase directly at the wall of the reactor, [1⁰K/m]; n is the normal to dS; and S is the surface of heat exchange, [m^2];

Using Newton's formula:

$$Q = \propto (t_S - t_0)\, S t, \tag{3.95}$$

where $\propto$ is the coefficient of thermal diffusivity, [$W/m^2\ 1^0K$].

Or

$$\frac{Q}{t} = \propto (t_S - t_0)\, S, \tag{3.96}$$

the differentiated equation (3.96) is:

$$dq = \propto (t_S - t_0) dS = -\lambda \left(\frac{\partial t}{\partial n}\right)_S dS, \tag{3.97}$$

Thus:

$$\propto = -\frac{\lambda \left(\frac{\partial t}{\partial n}\right) dS}{t_S - t_0}, \tag{3.98}$$

where t_S is the temperature of the reactor's walls, [^0K]; and t_0 is the temperature of the dispersion phase, [^0K].

This formula allows the coefficient of thermal diffusivity $\propto$ to be introduced into the system of differential equations for convective heat transfer. Because the temperature gradient $(\frac{\partial t}{\partial n})_S$ in formula (3.98) depends on the temperature of the reactor wall, the temperature of the liquid phase, and the thickness of the boundary layer (i.e., the nature of the mode of motion), the coefficient $\propto$ is a function of all quantities contained in the equations from (3.55) to (3.92) inclusive.

3.21. VECTOR ANALYSIS OF THE MOTION OF THE MEDIUM OF DISPERSION SYSTEMS

Let us consider the movement of the dispersion medium within the dispersion system, which is formed under the influence of an external force field in the mode of torsion-oriented turbulization. This formation of the dispersion system is followed by an emergence, development, and a collapse of vapor-gas bubbles. The density of the dispersion environment $\rho(x, y, z, t)$ changes over time. The vector of speed of this environment's movement can be designated through $\overrightarrow{\mathfrak{W}}$.

In the flow of the dispersion phase, let us allocate the motionless elementary volume $\mathcal{V}$, limited by a surface S. The liquid flows through an allocated surface on an elementary platform dS. As this occurs, the amount of liquid and the mass of this liquid is equal:

$$\rho \overrightarrow{\mathfrak{W}}_n dS. \tag{3.99}$$

During the same period of time, the amount of mass of this liquid Q flows through the total surface S:

$$Q = \iint_S \rho \overrightarrow{\mathfrak{W}}_n dS. \tag{3.100}$$

On the other hand, the mass of liquid contained in volume $\mathcal{V}$ is equal:

$$\iiint_V \rho \, dV . \qquad (3.101)$$

During the considered unit of time the mass of the liquid will change to:

$$\iiint_V \frac{\partial \rho}{\partial t} \, dV. \qquad (3.102)$$

Therefore, during a period of time, an amount of liquid will flow from the considered volume that is equal to:

$$Q = -\iiint_V \frac{\partial \rho}{\partial t} \, dV. \qquad (3.103)$$

After the equilibrium of the right parts of expressions (3.98) and (3.101), we get:

$$\iint_S \rho \overrightarrow{\mathfrak{W}}_n dS = -\iiint_V \frac{\partial \rho}{\partial t} \, dV. \qquad (3.104)$$

Applying Ostrogradsky's formula [153] to the integral standing in the left part of equality (2.93), we get:

$$\iiint_V [\frac{\partial \rho}{\partial t} + \text{div} \, (\rho \overrightarrow{\mathfrak{W}})] \, dV. \qquad (3.105)$$

As the volume $\mathcal{V}$ is taken randomly, it follows that:

$$\frac{\partial \rho}{\partial t} + \nabla \cdot (\rho \overrightarrow{\mathfrak{W}}) = 0. \qquad (3.106)$$

Expression (3.106) is the main equation of the fluid dynamics. Its physical meaning is the condition of the dispersion phase continuity.

For incompressible liquid, when density $\rho = \text{const.}$, the: $\frac{\partial \rho}{\partial t} = 0$, and:

$$\rho(\nabla \cdot \overrightarrow{\mathfrak{W}}) = 0. \tag{3.107}$$

If the flow of liquid moves forward without rotation, then $\nabla \cdot \overrightarrow{\mathfrak{W}} = 0.$

In this case, vector $\overrightarrow{\mathfrak{W}}$ is a gradient of a scalar function $\varphi(x, y, z)$, and:

$$\overrightarrow{\mathfrak{W}} = \nabla\varphi.$$

From the equation (3.107), for the incompressible liquid, it will be:

$$\nabla \cdot \overrightarrow{\mathfrak{W}} = 0. \tag{3.108}$$

Therefore, function φ must satisfy the equation:

$$\nabla \cdot \nabla\varphi = 0, \tag{3.109}$$

or

$$\text{div grad } \varphi = 0. \tag{3.110}$$

Expression (3.110) is a so-called Laplace's equation. It determines the speed potential for moving the incompressible liquid.

In physics, the concept of speed is usually associated with the movement of a material point. In the case in question—the movement of a compressible dispersion system—the separate adjacent elementary volumes move at different speeds. Thus, instead of linear speed, it is more appropriate to consider the *gradient* of linear speed. For the gradient of linear speed for moving in a dispersion system in which various layers (zones, volumes) are moving at different speeds, it is acceptable to define the change of linear speed related to the unit of the distance between different layers (zones, volumes) as:

$$\text{grad } \overrightarrow{\mathfrak{W}} = \frac{d\mathfrak{w}}{dh}.$$

If there is a uniform change in speed in the unit of the thickness of the film of a dispersion system's cross section, then:

$$\text{grad}\ \overrightarrow{\mathfrak{W}} = \frac{1}{h}(w_2 - w_1),$$

where grad $\overrightarrow{\mathfrak{W}}$ is the gradient of linear speed; dW is the infinitely small change in speed; dh is the infinitely small distance between layers (films), which corresponds to changes in speed dW; and $(w_2 - w_1)$ is the change in speed in two layers of a dispersion system that are at distance h from each other.

Similarly, instead of linear acceleration, it would be correct to consider the acceleration gradient, as the change of linear acceleration upon the distance between the layers (zones, volumes) of a dispersion system:

$$\text{grad}\ \mathcal{A} = \frac{dw}{dh},$$

$$\text{grad}\ \mathcal{A} = \frac{1}{h}(a_2 - a_1),$$

where grad $\mathcal{A}$ is the gradient of linear acceleration; $d\mathcal{A}$ is the infinitely small change in acceleration; dh is the infinitely small distance h between layers relating to changes in acceleration $d\mathcal{A}$; and $(a_2 - a_1)$ is the change in acceleration in two layers of a dispersion system that are at distance dh from each other.

3.22. SURFACE TENSION AND INTERFACE BETWEEN PHASES

In classical understanding the surface tension σ represents the thermodynamic characteristic of the interface between two phases that are in balance. This is determined by the work of isothermal A (at the temperature T) reversible formation of the unit of the area S_{12} under the conditions that the temperature, volume, and chemical potentials of all components in both phases of the system are remain constant:

$$\sigma_{12} = \left(\frac{A}{S_{12}}\right)_T .$$

The chemical potential represents the thermodynamic function, used to describe the condition of a system with a variable number of particles. It defines the change of thermodynamic potentials, such as enthalpies and internal energy. It also represents the energy of bringing one particle into the system without commissioning of work.

Surface tension has different meanings in energy and power. Its energy (thermodynamic) definition is surface tension is the specific work of increasing a surface when it is stretched under conditions of constant temperature. Its power (mechanical) definition is surface tension is the force acting on a unit length of a line that limits the surface of a liquid.

The force of surface tension is directed on a tangent to the surface of the liquid, which is perpendicular to the site of a contour and is proportional to the length of the counter of this surface. The force acting on this counter per unit of the length is called "the coefficient of a surface tension" σ. Upon a rupture of the unit of the surface [m^2], it is better to provide the definition of the surface tension as a unit of energy [J]. In this case, there is a clear physical sense of the concept of the surface tension.

Surface tension acts on the perimeter of separation between phases—liquids, gases, and solid matters. In the case in question, surface tension could be the force, acting per unit of the length of the counter of the surface and aspiring to reduce this surface to a minimum at the set volumes of phases.

The free surface of liquid is connected to the concept of free energy U:

$$U\,Sr = \sigma\,S,$$

where σ is the coefficient of the surface tension, [N/m = J/m^2]; and S is the full surface area of liquid [m^2].

As the free energy U of the isolated system aspires to a minimum, the liquid (for lack of external force fields) seeks to take the form with the smallest possible surface area. Thus, the task of forming the liquid comes down to the solution of the isoperimetric task of finding the three-dimensional geometric object that has the largest volume among all bodies with the same surface area. This object is, as we know, the sphere.

Let us consider the full free surface that arises when forming a dispersion system using torsion-oriented turbulization.

In Euclidean geometry, the concept of a surface is accepted as a two-dimensional topological variety. In real life, in three-dimensional space, the concept of a surface is accepted as an external perimeter of a system. In mathematics the concept of a function assumes the existence of a point at which the mathematical object that is a mathematical function is disputable. That is, there is a point at which the function loses its continuity; in other words: the function becomes undifferentiated or singular.

Usually, a surface can be presented as several material points with the coordinates satisfying the following:

$$S\,(xyz) = 0. \qquad (3.111)$$

If at some point of time function $S(xyz)$ is continuous and occur in continuous private derivatives—at least one of which is not equal to zero—near this point the surface satisfying equation (3.109) is considered to be the correct one.

The most important attribute of a surface is an area that can be determined

by a formula:

$$S = \iint [r_u \times r_v]\, du\, dv. \qquad (3.112)$$

where $r_u = \{\frac{dx}{du}, \frac{dy}{du}, \frac{dz}{du}\}$ and $r_v = \{\frac{dx}{dv}, \frac{dy}{dv}, \frac{dz}{dv}\}$.

Transforming the expression (3.112) for defining a surface, we get:

$$S = \iint \sqrt{(\frac{df}{dx})^2 + (\frac{df}{dy})^2 + dxdy}\,. \qquad (3.113)$$

The formula for defining a surface that is accepted as the solution for a parametrical task looks like:

$$S = \iint \sqrt{(\frac{D(x,y)}{D(u,v)})^2 + (\frac{D(y,z)}{D(u,v)})^2 + (\frac{D(z,x)}{D(u,v)})^2 dudv}\,. \qquad (3.114)$$

Substituting the value S from (3.114) in an expression for the free energy of U_{Sr}, the general meaning of free energy in a dispersion system is:

$$U_{Sr} = \sigma \iint \sqrt{(\frac{D(x,y)}{D(u,v)})^2 + (\frac{D(y,z)}{D(u,v)})^2 + (\frac{D(z,x)}{D(u,v)})^2 dudv}\,.$$

(3.115)

The free vapor–gas bubble takes a spherical form, however, under complicated conditions the task of forming the surface of a bubble becomes very difficult.

Let us consider a thin liquid film whose thickness can be disregarded. Seeking to minimize the free energy, the film creates a difference in pressure on both of its sides. The film shrinks until the pressure inside the bubble does not exceed the atmospheric pressure, at the amount of the additional pressure from this film. The additional pressure at the surface point depends on the average surface curvature at this point and is defined using Laplace's formula:

$$\Delta\mathcal{P}_S = \sigma k = \sigma \left(\frac{1}{r_1} + \frac{1}{r_2}\right). \tag{3.116}$$

where r_1 and r_2 are the radiuses of the main curvature at the point.

If the relevant centers of curvature lie on one side of the tangent plane in the considered point, then the radiuses have an identical sign. The opposite is also true: radiuses have the different signs if they located on the different sides of the tangent plane. For example, in a sphere, the centers of curvature at any point coincide with the center of the sphere.

Therefore, $r_1 = r_2 = r$, is:

$$\Delta\mathcal{P}_S = \frac{2\sigma}{r}. \tag{3.117}$$

In the case of the surface of a bubble, when the film limits this surface, an increment of surface pressure $\Delta\mathcal{P}_S$ serves as the continuous function on the film surface because choosing the "positive" side of the film unambiguously sets a positive side of a surface in its rather close points of proximity.

3.23. DISSIPATION OF ENERGY DURING TORSION-ORIENTED TURBULIZATION

In the mode of torsion-oriented turbulization, the times of pressure changes inside a single bubble are quite comparable with the times of pressure changes during explosions. Dispersion systems are very compressed. Contracting like a spring, the dispersion system "will amortize" the blow. The greater the distance from the epicenter of a rupture of a separate bubble, the slower the rate of increase in the pressure change resulting from this gap it would in close proximity to the torn bubble. However, because there is the simultaneous action of mechanical resonance and fluid hammer phenomena and because of the rather small compressibility of the dispersion medium and the rigidity of the reactor, such a rapid increase in pressure impacts the entire internal volume of the reactor.

This sharp pressure increase corresponds to large values of acceleration and the braking of elementary volumes of substance braking when the front of a shock wave passes through them. The avalanche-like increase of pressure happens within nanoseconds. Therefore, the general shift in the size of the elementary volume in a dispersion environment is rather small because of its small compressibility. The shift in the size of the elementary volume is most likely to be measurable in micrometers or nanometers. Nevertheless, in comparison with the sizes of atoms and molecules, these shifts are very large, as are the forces arising from them. Thus, it is impossible to exclude the assumption that these phenomena, occurring at the microscopic level can become the reason for some abnormal manifestations.

The torsion-oriented turbulization arising from the simultaneous action of a mechanical resonance and fluid hammer phenomena should not be considered only from "traditional" mechanistic positions. In the experiments, it was noticed that the torsion-oriented turbulization was also followed also by other physical phenomena: at the time of the collapse of bubbles, their weak luminescence could be observed.

P. Jarmen's work [163] shows that the high internal pressure that develops upon the collapse of bubbles is the reason of for the luminescence of a gas bubble. The flash of luminescent light lasts from 1/20 to 1/1000 fraction of a seconds. The intensity of the luminescent flashing depends on the volume of the gas. Luminescent flashing is very weak when it arises from the collapse of a single bubble. But there are a lot of such bubbles, and, consequently, the luminescence becomes noticeable even with the naked eye.

Let us consider the physicochemical dynamics of the process of the luminescent flashing. Let us also recall that the bubble represents a vapor–gas mix. Thus, the molecules of the gas component, consisting of the evaporation of the substance of the dispersed phase, diffuse from the bubble, and dissolve in the liquid, representing the dispersion medium.

It is known for physics that the gas ionization is observed in the small volume of a bubble in the vapor–gas mix under the influence of the high pressure that results from the collapse of said bubble. This happens when the pressure is in the hundreds and thousands of the atmospheres (however, acting in microscopic volumes!) in the small volume of the bubble in a steam-gas mix. Thus, a positive and equal quantity of negative ions is formed in the gas environment of the bubble.

As the positive and negative ions interconnect, among their total number tends to zero. From the total quantity of positive ions n during period of time t, some part of them disappears in quantities proportional to n^2. The paired connection of ions proceeds as an irreversible bimolecular reaction. The differential equation of this process can be presented as:

$$\frac{dn}{dt} = q - \propto n^2.$$

The coefficient of proportionality $\propto$ depence significantly upon the nature and conditions of the steam-gas mix forming a bubble. The solution of this equation represents a functional dependence between the quantity of ions of n and time t.

After defining variables and after integration, we get:

$$t = \int \frac{dn}{q - \propto n^2} = \frac{1}{\propto} \int \frac{dn}{\frac{q}{\propto} - n^2}. \qquad (3.118)$$

Designating $\frac{q}{\propto} = k^2$,

$$t = \frac{1}{\propto} \int \frac{dn}{k^2 - n^2}. \qquad (3.119)$$

Having spread out the sub-integral expression:

$$\frac{1}{k^2-n^2}=\frac{1}{(k+n)(k-n)}$$

to the partial fractions, we get:

$$\frac{1}{(k+n)(k-n)}=\frac{1}{2k(k+n)}+\frac{1}{2k(k-n)}, \qquad (3.120)$$

Having substituted expression (3.120) in the integral (3.119), we receive:

$$t=\frac{1}{2\propto k}[\int\frac{dn}{k+n}+\int\frac{dn}{k-n}]=\frac{1}{2\propto k}\ln\frac{k+n}{k-n}+C. \qquad (3.121)$$

If $t=0$ and $n=0$, then $C=0$. Thus:

$$\frac{k+n}{k-n}=e^{2\propto kt}. \qquad (3.122)$$

Therefore, the total number of ions at each timepoint, is equal:

$$n=k\frac{e^{2\propto kt}-1}{e^{2\propto kt}+1}. \qquad (3.123)$$

It should be noted that, acting simultaneously (though during a very short time, from 1/20 to 1/1,000 fraction of a second), the mechanical resonance and fluid hammer impact create maximum extreme conditions for the substance when the internal pressure in a dispersion system can increase by hundreds and thousands of times (within a very small space!). This corresponds to conditions at ocean depths where substances gain exotic properties and undergo unusual transformations (e.g., solid substances showing fluidity, and graphite turning into diamond).

But even, if the pressure does not significantly increase, **the speed of change of the gradient of pressure** for each part of the substance is very high: the **10^{12} Pascal/second** and above.

3.24. SUMMARY OF THE CHAPTER 3

The conditions for the occurrence of a state of resonance cavitation are the validity of statements (3.17) and (3.32):

$$\mathcal{P}_{Cr} - \mathcal{P}_0 = \mathcal{F}(t)\,(\mathcal{A}\varphi_{Cr})^2 - E_{Loss} \quad (3.17)$$

$$\Delta\mathcal{P}_{Impact} = \frac{\rho \Delta w}{\sqrt{\frac{\rho\beta + \rho d}{\delta E}}} \quad (3.32)$$

where $\Delta\mathcal{P}_{Impact} = \mathcal{P}_{Cr} - \mathcal{P}_0$ is the pressure drop between the critical pressure $\mathcal{P}_{Cr}$ (which occurs when the upper volumes of the liquid component hit the top cover of the reactor) and the pressure in the cross section of the inner zones of the reactor is $\mathcal{P}_0$—where the centers of mass of the elementary volumes of liquid are located; ρ is the specific gravity of the liquid component; $\Delta w = (w_2 - w_1)$ is the change in velocity between adjacent volumes of liquid located at a distance Δh from each other (in the case of the liquid completely stopping or being at a flow velocity for an instant before it stops); and C is the shock wave propagation velocity.

In a first approximation, $\mathcal{P}_{Cr}$ can be taken equal to the pressure of the saturated vapor of the liquid. It should be understood, the appearance of torsion-oriented turbulization can also occur at internal pressures other than $\mathcal{P}_{Cr}$. The value of the vibration frequency φ, at which torsion-oriented turbulization occurs, can be denoted as φ_{Cr}. From formula (3.17) it follows that the disappearance of torsion-oriented turbulization is determined by the value of φ, where the torsion-oriented turbulization phenomenon ceases to exist with increasing pressure inside the reactor.

The nonstationary nature of the internal pressure fields (due to the gradient of surface tension forces, the influence of emerging and decaying associations of vapor-gas bubbles, and the geometric dimensions and the state of the inner surface of the reactor) is the reasons that φ_{cr} is not a constant value. It is highly likely that the value of φ_{cr} varies significantly from reactor to reactor and depends on the chemical composition of the liquid and gas, scale factors. However, despite this, in a first approximation, the use of φ_{cr} as a characteristic of the state of motion of a dispersion system in the torsion-oriented turbulization regime is currently advisable.

The influence of the geometric dimensions of the reactor on the possibility of a torsion-oriented turbulization state should also be considered.

CHAPTER 4

THE RESEARCH OF INFLUENCE OF THE EXTERNAL VIBRATION FIELD ON THE RESONANCE CAVITATION AND THE TORSION-ORIENTED TURBULIZATION PHENOMENA

4.1. THE WORKING MODEL OF VIBRATING MACHINE

In a course of the subject research the working model (pre-prototype) of vibration machine for realization of resonance cavitation and torsion-oriented turbulization phenomena.

As noted in the previous chapters, homogeneous and heterogeneous materials (as a special case—dispersion systems) could be formed in the modes of resonance cavitation and torsion-oriented turbulization. These modes are the result of the actions of low frequency, vertically directed reciprocating sinusoidal disturbing influence of external vibration force fields. Those forces are applied by the vibrator-reactor system to the components of dispersion system. The intensity of interaction between elementary volumes of the formed dispersion systems is defined by the intensity of the fields of external forces and internal forces, including fields of chemical potential, mechanical, rheological, physical, and chemical characteristics [2–5].

The source of the external revolting influence that makes the uniform vibrator-reactor system, as a rule, is a vibration machine. There are three types of vibration facilities that can be used for the purpose of the formation of dispersion systems: electrodynamic, electrohydraulic, and mechanical installations.

Electrodynamic vibrating machines use a magnetic field to create a force field for the movement of the vibration table. An advantage of such devices is the stability of oscillation parameters that could be controlled by a computer.

Electrohydraulic vibrating machines constitute another type of vibrational device. These use four-way valves to control the flow of hydraulic fluid from a pump to a hydraulic actuator connected to a vibrating platform. These powerful facilities are used for testing on products such as airplanes, helicopters, etc.

Both electrodynamic and electrohydraulic vibrating machines are very large in size and relatively expensive and thus cannot be used as a source of vibration for the subject application.

Mechanical vibration machines, as a rule, include an eccentric or rotary mechanism with a displaced center of rotation. This mechanism connects with various pistons that push a moving plate of the vibrator's machine. These devices can create mechanical oscillations from 1 Hz to 3,000 Hz. In theory these machines must be capable of creating invariable pusher efforts and generate constant frequencies and amplitudes, but because of elastic deformations of some components of vibration machine, frequencies and amplitudes of the vibration could not be sustainable. In addition, these devices experience fast wear of the contacting elements. However, this is not a serious obstacle in the inexpensive mechanical vibrators that use electric motors as their source of rotation.

The other reason why mechanical vibration devices cannot be used in the mode of torsion-oriented turbulence is that vibration machines are sensitive of to their own mechanical resonance. This makes it is necessary to anchor the vibration machine to a massive foundation. Second, the increase in amplitude results in additional wear on the machine's components.

Unfortunately, existing vibration machines cannot be used to process homogeneous and heterogeneous materials in the mode of resonance cavitation and torsion-oriented turbulization phenomena. So, it was a time to build a vibration machine exactly for the subject application.

Based upon previously conducted experiments and theoretical analysis, the pre-prototype of the mechanical vibrating machine was developed (Fig. 4-1). The availability of recently developed of standard components create the opportunity to design, develop and built a pre-prototype of a mechanical vibration machine at a reasonable cost that meet all requirements for equipment to be used for the application in question.

Fig. 4-1. Vibrating Machine with Experimental Reactor.

This machine consists of a frame, electrical closure box, control panel), variable speed electric motor, a variable frequency motor speed controller, eccentric mechanism for transforming rotary motion into linear motion, clavis, and movable plate on which the reactor is installed (Fig. 4-2).

Fig. 4-2. Vibrating Machine / Driving Assembly.

The massive frame was made from combination of structural channels, beams, round tubing, and plates to guarantee the required mechanical strength of the machine. A variable speed 3-phase 7-1/2 HP electrical motor: 230/460 VAC, suitable for 208 VAC at 60 Hz, 3600 RPM was selected as a power source. The variable frequency drive controller 5.5KW 7.5 HP inverter is uses for a spindle motor speed control. This inverter has 220 single phase input and an 208 VAC 3 phase output.

An eccentric as a rotating element with 1" Dia. Mechanical shaft assembly is used to generate power with smooth reciprocating motion of power from electric motor. The eccentrics ranged in size from 1 to 4 millimeters.

Fig. 4-3. Vibrating Machine / Moving Plate and Reactor.

4.2. FLUCTUATION OF THE MATERIAL POINT

For the purpose of an analysis of the physical nature of the processes connected with the formation of dispersion systems, we have to consider several types of behavior of material points dispersed in a dispersion medium. These dispersion systems can be formed because of vibrational impact on the chemical reactor. The reactor makes strictly vertical reciprocating movements, (i.e., movements that possessing a single degree of freedom) that is affected by the external revolting force of a certain frequency and amplitude. Furthermore, the size of the revolting force also depends on the acceleration of gravity.

In physics, it is acceptable to define a fluctuation as the process of repeatable changes in time of the varying degree of a system's conditions at a chosen point of equilibrium [164–166]. In mechanics, as a rule, fluctuations are directly connected to the mechanical oscillations exerting notable impact on a mechanical system. In physicochemical technological processes, it is used for the minimization of solid matters (their transformation into powders of various degrees of dispersion) and for the formation emulsions, suspensions, colloidal solutions, and foams.

Fluctuations are always connected with an alternate transformation of one type of energy into another. The nature of the interaction with the environment of fluctuation can be subdivided as follows:

- Compelled fluctuations which proceed in a system under the influence of external periodic exposure. At the coincidence of external oscillatory influence with the own frequency of system fluctuations, resonance could arise.
- Own (natural) fluctuations, which act in a system that is under the influence of internal forces, as a rule, of forces of intermolecular interaction.
- Self-oscillations, where the system has a stock of potential energy that is spent for the commission of fluctuations (for example, the mechanical clock). The characteristic difference between self-oscillations and compelled fluctuations is that their amplitude is defined by properties of the system, but not by entry conditions.
- Periodic fluctuations that arise if values of the physical quantities that change during the fluctuations repeat at regular intervals. They arise the at the change of any parameter of the oscillatory system as a result of the influence of the field of external force.
- Casual fluctuations for which external or parametrical loading is a casual process.

In real life all vibration processes are result from the action of the revolting force of a certain frequency and amplitude. The vibration is transferred from the vibration machine to a devices or materials. In this particular case, the vibration impacts applied upon a dispersion system processing inside a reactor.

Vibrating machines, as a rule, have a mechanical effect in the form of harmonic oscillations described by the equation:

$$x = x_m \cos(\omega t + \varphi_0), \qquad (4.1)$$

where x is the deviation of a material point, a vibration platform, a reactor, etc., from a position of equilibrium, [m]; $\mathcal{A} = x_m$ is the amplitude of fluctuations, (i.e., the maximum deviation from the position of balance), [m]; ω is the cyclic or circular frequency of fluctuations, [Hz = 1/s]; t is the time, [s]; $(\omega t + \varphi_0) = \varphi$ is the phase of the harmonious process; and φ_0 is the an initial phase.

The minimum interval of time through in which there is a repetition of the movement is called the period of fluctuations T. The physical unit, which is the opposite of the period of fluctuations is called the frequency of fluctuations f:

$$f = \frac{1}{T}, \text{ [Hz]}.$$

The frequency of fluctuations f defines the number of fluctuations made per a second. A frequency unit is Hertz (Hz). The frequency of fluctuations is connected to the cyclic frequency ω and the period of fluctuations of T as follows:

$$\omega = 2\pi f = \frac{2\pi}{T}.$$

The material point is considered to be the spherical element of a dispersed phase. To determine the nature of the movement in a dispersion system that is in a reactor, it must be considered separately from the material point. As a material point, is considered to be a gas bubble, a particle of the solid matter, or a drop of liquid that is immiscible and insoluble with the liquid forming the dispersion phase.

4.3. TASK No.1: FLUCTUATION OF A SINGLE MATERIAL POINT

Let us consider the movement of a spherical material point, that can make only reciprocating fluctuations in the direction of a vertical axis of coordinates. For this task, as the dispersive environment should be considered a virtual incompressible liquid in which there is no internal friction and that has the viscosity $\mu = 0$, and the coefficient of heat conductivity $\lambda = 0$.

The element of a dispersed phase is kept in a suspended state by surface tension forces that are connected to the dispersion system by elastic connections, which are formed by forces of molecular interaction. In other words, the subject of consideration is the fluctuations of a material point with one degree of freedom in relation to a center of equilibrium. In this case, it is possible to disregard the ability of the material point to rotate relative to the center of balance due to its insignificant influence on the nature of the considered movement.

Such nature of the movement corresponds to fluctuations of the sphere suspended on an elastic spring, that has a certain weight and slides inside of a vertical tube. In this task, the mass of this spring, all the forces resulting from friction of the sphere along the tube's wall, and the resistance of the dispersive environment could be disregard also. The considered material point is brought out of the state of equilibrium by the external revolting force and oscillates relative to the center of the equilibrium.

Let us consider the system of coordinates whose center coincides with the center of the fluctuation of a material point. Also, let us direct an axis of coordinates OX from the center of coordinates down along a vertical line. The material point moves goes along this line. During the oscillating motion of the material point along axis OX, the vector of the speed is also directed along this straight line as well. If the increments of time aspire to zero ($\Delta t \to 0$), then the speed of this point is defined by the expression:

$$v = \frac{\Delta x}{\Delta t}, \qquad (4.2)$$

Determining the limit of the fraction $\frac{\Delta x}{\Delta t}$ at $\Delta t \to 0$ comes down to the calculating of the first derivative function $x(t)$ on the time and indicates as with one point up above, $\dot{x}(t) = \frac{dx(t)}{dt}$.

From the prospective of equation (3.1), $x = x_m \cos(\omega t + \varphi_0)$, so that the calculation of the derivative looks like:

$$v = \dot{x}(t) = -\omega x_m \sin(\omega t + \varphi_0) = \omega x_m \cos(\omega t + \varphi_0 + \frac{\pi}{2}). \qquad (4.3)$$

The emergence of the term $\frac{\pi}{2}$ in the cosine's argument indicates a change in the initial phase. The maximum value (on the module) of the speed, when $v = \omega x_m$ reaches at the point of time, when the material point passes through the equilibrium ($x = 0$).

If $\Delta t \to 0$, the acceleration a of a material point that is in harmonic oscillations could be defined in the same way:

$$a = \frac{\Delta v}{\Delta t}. \qquad (4.4)$$

Therefore, the acceleration of a fluctuation of a material point, is equal to the derivative function $v(t)$ on time t and indicates as with one point above, $\dot{v}(t) = \frac{dv(t)}{dt}$ or the second derivative function $x(t)$ on time t indicates with one point above $\ddot{x}(t)$. Calculating this will get:

$$a = \dot{v}(t) = \ddot{x}(t) = -\omega^2 x_m \cos(\omega t + \varphi_0) = -\omega^2 x(t). \qquad (4.5)$$

The minus sign in the above expression (4.5) means that the acceleration of the material point $a(t)$ is always has the sign opposite to the sign of deviation $x(t)$. Thus, under the Newton's second law, the force applied to a material point to make harmonic oscillations is directed towards the position of equilibrium position ($x = 0$).

Based on the Newton's second law, the differential equation of the movement, is:

$$\mathcal{F} = ma \qquad (4.6)$$

where m is the mass of a material point, [kg]; a is the acceleration of the movement, [m/s^2]; and $\mathcal{F}$ is a total component of all forces operating on a material point, [N = kg m /s^2].

At the position of equilibrium the total component of all forces operating on the material point having the mass m and being projected to axis OX is equal to mg and g is the acceleration due to gravity.

The gravitational term can be compensated for by the elastic force of the virtual spring. In this case, the balance of a material point is equalized by the elastic force of a spring that, according to Hooke's law, is proportional to the lengthening of a spring λ. Thus, the condition of balance can be expressed as:

$$m = g - k\lambda, \qquad (4.7)$$

where k is the coefficient of spring's rigidity.

In principle, in relation to the considered dispersion systems, k is the coefficient of proportionality of the joint action of molecular forces acting upon the considered material point from the dispersion phase. In other words, the compelled force is acting in the opposite direction of forces of gravitation.

Let us designate the deviation of the material point from the position of the equilibrium as $x(t)$. Thus, at this point in time t, the considered material point would be affected by two forces: mg, the force of gravity, which is acting downward, and the elastic force of a spring $k(\lambda +$

$+ x)$, which is acting in the opposite direction. Thus, the co-acting of these forces would be equal to their difference:

$$\mathcal{F} = mg - k(\lambda + x). \tag{4.8}$$

Proceeding from the equation (4.7), it is:

$$\mathcal{F} = -kx. \tag{4.9}$$

In compliance with Newton's second law (4.6):

$$ma = -kx. \tag{4.10}$$

For rectilinear movement along axis OX, the acceleration a is equal to:

$$a = \frac{\partial^2 x}{\partial t^2} = \ddot{x}(t).$$

Therefore, the equality (4.10) can be written down as:

$$m = \ddot{x} - kx, \qquad \text{or} \qquad \ddot{x} + k^2 x = 0. \tag{4.11}$$

where $\omega^2 = \frac{k}{m} > 0$.

Equation (4.11) represents the differential equation of the movement of the considered material point. It is a linear uniform equation of the second order with constant coefficients [165].

The roots of this characteristic equation $r^2 + \omega^2 = 0$ are:

$$r_1 = \omega i \text{ and } r_2 = -\omega i.$$

Therefore, the solution of the equation (4.11) takes the following form:

$$x = C_1 \cos \omega t + C_2 \sin \omega t. \tag{4.12}$$

To clarify the physical meaning of the obtained solution (3.12), let us multiply and divide the right side of this equation by the same number $\mathcal{A}$.

If $$\mathcal{A} = \sqrt{C_1^2 + C_2^2},$$

then:

$$x = \mathcal{A}\left(\frac{C_1 \cos \omega t}{\mathcal{A}} + \frac{C_2 \sin \omega t}{\mathcal{A}}\right), \quad (4.13)$$

as

$$\left(\frac{C_1}{\sqrt{C_1^2 + C_2^2}}\right)^2 + \left(\frac{C_2}{\sqrt{C_1^2 + C_2^2}}\right)^2 = 1. \quad (4.14)$$

It is known that $\cos^2 \omega t + \sin^2 \omega t = 1$. Therefore:

$$\frac{C_1}{\sqrt{C_1^2 + C_2^2}} = \sin \omega t \text{ and } \frac{C_2}{\sqrt{C_1^2 + C_2^2}} = \cos \omega t. \quad (4.15)$$

Thus, the common solution for equation (4.12), could be written as:

$$x = \mathcal{A}(\sin \cos \alpha\ \omega t + \cos \sin \alpha \omega t),$$

or

$$x = \mathcal{A} \sin(\omega t + \varphi), \quad (4.16)$$

where $\mathcal{A}$ and φ are new arbitrary constants.

The physical meaning of the constant $\mathcal{A}$ is the amplitude and the argument $(\omega t + \varphi)$ is the phase of oscillation. The value φ at $t = 0$ represents the initial phase and designates φ_0. At the same time ω is the frequency of oscillation.

Let us assume that at the initial moment of time is $t = 0$, the deviation of a material point from the position of balance is x_0, then the speed of the movement is equal to $\frac{\partial x}{\partial t} = \dot{x}_0$. Or alternatively:

$$x_{(0)} = x_0 \text{ and } \dot{x}_{(0)} = \dot{x}_0.$$

Upon these designated entry conditions, it is possible to find the amplitude and the initial phase. At $t = 0$, considering $\dot{x}(t) = \mathcal{A}\ \omega\, cox(\omega t + \varphi)$, it is:

$$\mathcal{A} sin\, \omega t = x_0 \text{ and } \mathcal{A}\omega\, cox\, \omega t = \dot{x}_0. \qquad (4.17)$$

Thus:

$$\mathcal{A} = \sqrt{x_0^2 + \frac{\dot{x}_0^2}{\omega^2}}, \text{ and } \omega t = arctg\frac{\omega x_0}{\dot{x}_0}. \qquad (4.18)$$

By substituting values $\mathcal{A}$ and ωt from (4.18) into (4.17), it will be:

$$x = \sqrt{x_0^2 + \frac{\dot{x}_0^2}{\omega^2}}\ sin\,(\omega t + arctg\frac{\omega x_0}{\dot{x}_0}). \qquad (4.19)$$

Equality (4.19) expresses the law of the movement of the material point.

From (4.19), it follows that the material point with the mass m, performs harmonic oscillations around the equilibrium position. The frequency ω and the period T of oscillations are equal:

$$\omega = \sqrt{\frac{k}{m}} \text{ and } T = \frac{2\pi}{\omega} = 2\pi\sqrt{\frac{m}{k}}. \qquad (4.20)$$

From (4.20), it follows that the frequency ω and the period T of oscillation depends only upon the rigidity of a virtual spring. This means that it depends on the power of interaction of the molecular connections and, first of all, on the surface tension that is acting in dispersion systems and on the mass of the material point. In other words, the frequency ω and the period T of fluctuations are defined by the physical and physicochemical properties of the forming dispersion system. The amplitude of fluctuations $\mathcal{A}$ and the initial phase φ depend on entry conditions x_0 and $\dot{x}_0$ being equal:

$$\mathcal{A} = \sqrt{x_0^2 + \frac{\dot{x}_0^2}{\omega^2}} \text{ and } \varphi = arctg\frac{\omega x_0}{\dot{x}_0}, \qquad (4.21)$$

4.4. Task No. 2: FLUCTUATION OF A MATERIAL POINT WITH CONSIDERATION OF THE RESISTANCE A DISPERSION MEDIUM

In this task, the nature of the movement of a material point is considered under conditions similar to those of **Task No.1**. However, the resistance of the dispersive environment is also considered here, where there is some spherical elementary volume, and which is proportional to the speed of the movement of the considered material point. This nature of the movement corresponds to oscillations of, for example, of the sphere hanging on an elastic spring coefficient of rigidity k and having a certain weight. The sphere slides inside the vertical tube filled with liquid of viscosity μ.

Dynamic viscosity ($-\mu$), or rather the coefficient of dynamic viscosity in other words, is the property of liquids that characterize their resistance to sliding or shearing. A minus sign in front of the coefficient of viscosity indicates that the resistance force of the medium is directed opposite the direction of the speed of movement of the material point.

As conditions of **Task No. 2,** let us introduce the parameters that characterize the internal friction arising between elements of the dispersed phase and the dispersion environment. The quantitatively viscosity—or the coefficient of internal friction—is defined by the size of the tangent force that is applied to the unit of the area of the deviated layer to support a laminar current in this layer. In this case, the dynamic viscosity can be determined using Newton's formula for a laminar flow, where linear speed in the direction perpendicular to the deviate plane is equal to zero. The coefficient of dynamic viscosity could be represented as:

$$\mu = \frac{F}{S\, grad\, v}, \qquad (4.22)$$

where $\mathcal{P} = \frac{\mathcal{F}}{\mathcal{S}}$ is the tension of deviation, [N/m²]; $\mathcal{F}$ is the deviation force (force of external influence), [N]; $\mathcal{S}$ is the contact surface area, [m²]; $\mathcal{v}_{\sigma} = \frac{\partial \varepsilon}{\partial t}$ is the speed of relative deviation, [m/s]; $\varepsilon = \frac{\Delta x_0}{h}$ is the unit of the gradient of the speed, $\frac{d\mathcal{v}}{dx} = \frac{\mathcal{v}_0}{h}$, as: $\frac{\partial \varepsilon}{\partial t} = \frac{1}{h}\frac{d\Delta x_0}{dt} = \frac{\mathcal{v}_0}{h}$; and h is the thickness of the film of the dispersive medium, [m].

A different interpretation of the physical nature of the coefficient of viscosity μ proceeds from a Bachinsky's empirical ratio [168]. He defines the coefficient of viscosity is defined by the intermolecular forces depending on the average distance between molecules determined by the molar volume of the substance of the dispersion environment V_m:

$$\mu = \frac{C}{V_m - b},$$

where C and b are constants, selected empirically for each substance of the dispersion environment.

It is known that the dynamic viscosity μ increases with an increase in pressure and decreases with an increase in temperature [168].

The role of kinematic viscosity ξ is no less important:

$$\xi = \frac{\mu}{\rho},$$

where ρ is the density of the liquid, that forms the dispersion phase, [kg/m³]; and μ is the coefficient of dynamic viscosity, [N s/m²].

Thus, in this task, some elementary volume of the considered dispersed phase is considered represents a spherical particle—either of a particle of solid matter, bubble of gas or drop of liquid that is immiscible and insoluble with the liquid that forms the dispersion environment. The following affects the considered spherical volume:

a) The gravitation force $\mathcal{F}_g$:

$$\mathcal{F}_g = mg = \frac{\pi}{6}\rho_{df} g D^3, \qquad (4.23)$$

where m is the mass of a spherical particle, [kg]; g is the acceleration of gravity, [m/s^2]; ρ_{df} is the density of the materials of elementary volume, [kg/m^3]; and D is the diameter of a particle, [m].

b) The Archimedes force (buoyancy force) $\mathcal{F}_A$:

$$\mathcal{F}_A = \frac{\pi}{6}\rho_{ds} g D^3, \qquad (4.24)$$

where ρ_{ds} is the density of the liquid forming the dispersion medium; and D is the diameter of volume of the dispersion medium that is forced out by a spherical particle.

c) The environment resistance force determined by Stokes's law $\mathcal{F}_\xi$:

$$\mathcal{F}_\eta = 3\pi v \xi D, \qquad (4.25)$$

where ξ is the kinematic viscosity of the liquid forming the dispersion environment, [m^2/s]; v is the speed of the movement of a spherical particle, [m/s]; and D is the diameter of a spherical particle, [m].

If the considered elementary volume is affected by no other forces and it is in a state of equilibrium, then:

$$\mathcal{F}_g + \mathcal{F}_A + \mathcal{F}_\eta = 0. \qquad (4.26)$$

If in scalar form (4.26), we consider the direction of the action of forces substituting the corresponding expressions (4.23, 4.24 and 4.25) for acting forces (4.26) is taking into account, then:

$$\frac{\pi}{6}\rho_{ds} g D^3 - \frac{\pi}{6}\rho_{ds} g D^3 - 3\pi v \xi D = 0 \qquad (4.27)$$

After some simplifications, we get:

$$v = \frac{gD^2}{18\xi}(\rho_{df} - \rho_{ds}).$$

Considering that speed v can be presented as $\dot{x}(t)$ and $\xi = \frac{\mu}{\rho_{ds}}$, then:

$$\dot{x}(t) = \frac{gD^2}{18\mu}(\rho_{df} - \rho_{ds})\,\rho_{ds}.$$

Based on the given value of dynamic viscosity $\mu = -j\dot{x}(t)$, the coefficient of the environment resistance j, can be defined as:

$$j = -\frac{\dot{x}(t)}{\mu}.$$

The equation of the movement for the question of Task No. 2 can be expressed as:

$$\mathrm{m} = \ddot{x} - j\dot{x} - kx, \tag{4.28}$$

or

$$\ddot{x} + 2k\dot{x} + \omega^2 x = 0, \tag{4.29}$$

In this case:

$$2k = \frac{j}{m} \text{ and } \omega^2 = \frac{k}{m},$$

where j is the coefficient of resistance of the environment; and k is the coefficient of the rigidity of the spring.

Equation (4.29) is a linear uniform equation of the second order with constant coefficients. The solution of this characteristic equation, is:

$$r^2 + 2jr + \omega^2 = 0,$$

with numbers: $r_{1+2} = -j \pm \sqrt{j^2 - \omega^2}$.

Three solutions are possible, as outlined below:

Task No. 2: Solution 1

If $j < \omega$, then $j^2 - \omega^2 < 0$:

$$r_{1+2} = -j \pm \sqrt{-(\omega^2 - j^2)} = -j \pm i\sqrt{-(\omega^2 - j^2)}\,,$$

then:

$$x = e^{-jt}(C_i\, cos\sqrt{\omega^2 - j^2} \cdot t + C_i\, sin\sqrt{\omega^2 - j^2} \cdot t\,) =$$

$$= \mathcal{A}e^{-jt}\; sin\,(\sqrt{\omega^2 - j^2} \cdot t + \varphi). \qquad (4.30)$$

where $\sqrt{\omega^2 - j^2}$ is the frequency of fluctuations; and φ is the initial phase.

The multiplier $\mathcal{A}e^{-jt}$ is monotonously to tend to zero at $t \to \infty$. Setting entry conditions $x_{(0)} = x_0$ and $\dot{x}_{(0)} = \dot{x}_0$, it is possible to define $\mathcal{A}, \omega$ and φ.

Task No. 2: Solution 2

If $j > k$, the coefficient of the environment's resistance j is larger than the rigidity of a spring k. The roots r_1 and r_2 are real negative numbers, and:

$$x = C_1 e^{tr_1} + C_2 e^{tr_2}, \qquad (4.31)$$

where $r_1 < 0$ and $r_2 < 0$.

Moreover, eventually over the time $x \to 0$.

Task No. 2: Solution 3

When $j = \omega,\ r_1 = r_2 = -k,$ then:

$$x = (C_1 + C_2 t)\, e^{-jt} = \frac{C_1 + tt}{e^{jt}}. \tag{4.32}$$

Per L'Hopital's rule [154], the limit of the ratio $\frac{C_1 + tC_2}{e^{jt}}$ is equal:

$$\lim_{t \to +\infty} \frac{C_1 + tC_2}{e^{jt}} = \lim_{t \to +\infty} \frac{C_2}{e^{jt}} = 0. \tag{4.33}$$

Thus, in this case: $\lim_{t \to +\infty} = 0.$

At the substantial resistance of the environment, when the dispersive phase has a relatively high viscosity **(Solution 2 and Solution 3)**, the functions obtained have no more than one extremum. Therefore, at the considerable resistance of the environment, the movement of a material point is not oscillatory. Since some point in time, the deviation of the material point from the position of balance tends to zero. At the relatively small resistance of the environment, when the dispersive phase has a rather low viscosity **(Solution 1)** the frequency of fluctuations decreases as:

$$-k > \sqrt{\omega^2 - j^2},$$

and amplitude of such fluctuations eventually also tends to zero. These fluctuations are called ***Fading Harmonic Oscillations***.

4.5. Task No. 3: FLUCTUATION OF THE MATERIAL POINT THAT IS UNDER THE INFLUENCE OF AN EXTERNAL REVOLTING FORCE, BUT WITHOUT CONSIDERATION OF THE RESISTANCE OF THE DISPERSION MEDIUM

In **Tasks No. 1** and **No. 2**, the action of the external revolting force was not considered. Fluctuations of the material point were caused by the action of elastic connections. Such fluctuations are called free or own (natural) oscillations. When the influence of the revolting force is applied upon the material point, a forced vibration occurs.

Let us define the character of the movement of the material point, that was considered in the **Task No. 2: Solution 1**. The revolting force (i.e., the compelled fluctuations) was taking into consideration, but without the resistance of the dispersive environment:

$$F = f(t).$$

In this case, it is necessary to add the revolting force $f_1 = (t)$ to the forces operating upon the material point from formula (4.10). Then:

$$m\ddot{x} = -\,kx + f_1(t), \tag{4.34}$$

and

$$\ddot{x} + \omega^2 x = f(t), \tag{4.35}$$

where:

$$\omega^2 = \frac{k}{m}, \text{ and } f(t) = \frac{f_1(t)}{m}.$$

Thus, the solution of the equation (4.35), could be defined as the law of the movement of the material point under the entry conditions of **Task No. 3**.

Equation (4.35) is a linear non-uniform equation of the second order with constant coefficients and coincides with the uniform equation (4.11). Therefore, to define the common solution of the nonuniform equation (3.35), it is necessary to find its private solution. It is quite obvious, that this type of equation depends on the right term of equation (4.35).

4.6. Task No. 4: FLUCTUATION OF THE MATERIAL POINT THAT IS UNDER THE INFLUENCE OF AN EXTERNAL SINUSOIDAL FORCE, BUT WITHOUT CONSIDERATION OF THE RESISTANCE OF THE DISPERSION MEDIUM

As noted, the revolting force that was developed by the vibration machine is the sinusoidal function. Therefore, for this task it is necessary to define the nature of the movement of the material point considered in **Task No. 3: Solution 3**, accepting the additional condition that the revolting force is equal $\mathcal{B} = \mathcal{B}\sin\beta t$, where both $\mathcal{B}$ and β are constants. By utilizing results arrived at earlier for **Task No. 3: Solution 3** equation (4.35) could have like:

$$\ddot{x} + \omega^2 x = \frac{1}{m}\,\mathcal{B}\sin\beta t\,. \tag{4.36}$$

Or, when $\mathcal{B}_1 = \dfrac{\mathcal{B}}{m}$, then:

$$\ddot{x} + \omega^2 x = \mathcal{B}_1 \sin\beta t\,. \tag{4.37}$$

The corresponding uniform equation is:

$$\ddot{x} + \omega^2 x = 0. \tag{4.38}$$

The common solution for equation (4.38) looks like (4.17):

$$x = \mathcal{B}\sin(\omega t + \varphi).$$

Let us now define below private solutions to the nonuniform equation (4.35) under two conditions:

4.7. Task No. 5: Solution 1

If the frequency of the external revolting force does not coincide with the internal frequency, or own (natural) fluctuations, then the private solution can be written down as:

$$\mathcal{Y} = M\cos\beta t + N\sin\beta t, \tag{4.39}$$

where M and N are coefficients, that need to be defined.

Carrying out certain transformations and calculations, there are:

$$M = 0 \text{ and } N = \frac{\mathcal{B}_1}{\omega^2 - \beta^2}.$$

At the same time:

$$\mathcal{Y} = \frac{\mathcal{B}_1}{\omega^2 - \beta^2}\sin\beta t. \tag{4.40}$$

Thus, under condition No 1, the character of the movement of the material point is expressed by the common solution for equation (4.35):

$$x = X + \mathcal{Y} = \mathcal{A} \sin(\omega t + \varphi) + \frac{\mathcal{B}}{m(\omega^2 - \beta^2)} \sin \beta t. \quad (4.41)$$

The first term in the equation (4.41) defines own fluctuations of the material point caused by the rigidity of the intermolecular connections. This depends upon the forces of surface tension (that acting in the considered dispersion system) and upon the mass of the material point. The second term in the equation (4.41) defines the compelled fluctuations of the material point caused by the revolting force acting upon the reactor.

4.7a. Task No. 5: Solution 2

If_$\omega = \beta$, then the equation (3.37) takes the following form:

$$\ddot{x} + \omega^2 x = \mathcal{B}_1 \sin \omega t. \quad (4.42)$$

In this case, the private solution should be:

$$\mathcal{Y} = (M \cos \omega t + N \sin \omega t), \quad (4.43)$$

After transformations: $M = -\frac{\mathcal{B}}{2m\omega}$ and $N = 0$. Therefore, the private solution, that defines the character of fluctuations is:

$$\mathcal{Y} = -\frac{\mathcal{B}}{2m\omega} \cos \omega t. \quad (4.44)$$

From equation (3.44), it follows that the amplitude of the forced vibrations could turned out relatively large, even at small constant $\mathcal{B}$ values. This phenomenon of sharp increase in the amplitude of oscillation under the influence of relatively small revolting forces is called a resonance.

4.8. Task No. 6: FLUCTUATION OF THE MATERIAL POINT THAT IS UNDER THE INFLUENCE OF AN EXTERNAL SINUSOIDAL FORCE, AND A FORCE OF THE RESISTANCE OF THE DISPERSION ENVIRONMENT, PROPORTIONAL TO THE SPEED OF THE MOTION

Let us define the character of the material point's movement at the action of the revolting sinusoidal force and the force of resistance of the dispersion environment proportional to the speed of the movement. To do that, let's assume that the revolting force is equal:

$$F(t) = \mathcal{B}\sin\beta \neq 0.$$

Under this condition the resistance of the dispersive medium is equal to $j = -\frac{\dot{x}(t)}{\xi}$, where j is the coefficient of the environmental resistance. This depends on the speed of the movement, which is the function of kinematic viscosity. The vector of forces of the environmental resistance looks in the direction opposite to the movement. It is clear, that the solution to this task is the synthesis of solutions of **Tasks No. 2 and No. 4.**

The differential equation of the movement of a material point is equal:

$$m\ddot{x} = -kx - j\dot{x} + \mathcal{B}\sin\beta t \qquad (4.45)$$

or

$$\ddot{x} + 2k\dot{x} + \omega^2 x = \mathcal{B}\sin\beta t, \qquad (4.46)$$

where $2k = \frac{j}{m}, \omega^2 = \frac{k}{m}$ and $\mathcal{B}_1 = \frac{1}{m}\mathcal{B}; j = -\frac{\dot{x}(t)}{\xi}$ is the coefficient of resistance of the dispersive environment, which functionally depends upon the speed of the movement of the material point (i.e., upon the coefficient of kinematic viscosity ξ of the substance of the dispersive medium); and k is the coefficient of proportionality of the combined action of the molecular forces, operating upon the considered material point from the dispersive environment.

In practice, the resistance of the dispersion medium is relatively small:

$$k^2 - \omega^2 < 0.$$

The common decision of the corresponding uniform equation was found in **Task No. 2: Solution 1:**

$$x = \mathcal{A}e^{-kt}\ sin\,(\beta_1 t + \varphi), \qquad (4.47)$$

where: $\beta_1 = \sqrt{\omega^2 - k^2}$.

The private solution to the nonuniform equation (4.46) can be found as in (4.39):

$$x = M\cos\beta t + N\sin\beta t,$$

if

$$\mathcal{B} = \frac{\mathcal{A}_1}{\sqrt{(\omega^2 - k^2)^2 + 4k^2\beta^2}} \quad \text{and} \quad \gamma = \text{arctg}\frac{2k\beta}{\omega^2 - k^2}.$$

The analysis shows that: $x = \mathcal{B}\sin(\beta t - \gamma)$. Thus, the common solution for **Task No. 5** is:

$$x = \mathcal{A}e^{-kt}\,sin\,(\beta_1 t + \varphi) + \mathcal{B}\ sin\,(\beta t - \gamma), \quad (3.48)$$

where $\mathcal{A}$ is the amplitude of own fluctuations; and $\mathcal{B}$ is the amplitude of forced fluctuations.

By analogy with the solution for **Task No. 4**, the first term in equation (3.48), the fading harmonic oscillations and the amplitude of the compelled fluctuations $\mathcal{B}$, are defined without depending on the time t.

The amplitude $\mathcal{B}$ has the maximum values at $\beta = \sqrt{\omega^2 - 2k^2}$. At such value β the amplitude of fluctuations $\mathcal{B}$ becomes equal:

$$\mathcal{B} = \frac{\mathcal{A}_1}{2k\sqrt{(\omega^2 - k^2)}} . \qquad (4.49)$$

The amplitude of fluctuations of the material point could achieved the great values with a relatively small amount of the coefficient of resistance of the dispersive environment j. At the same time, the frequency of the forced fluctuations β is close to the frequency of the own fluctuations ω. Therefore, at a small resistance of the dispersion medium and under the condition of the frequency of the compelled fluctuations approaching the own frequency, the amplitude of the compelled fluctuations increases promptly, that is, the resonance occurs in the dispersion system.

4.9. Task No. 7: FLUCTUATION OF THE MATERIAL POINT THAT IS UNDER THE INFLUENCE OF AN EXTERNAL SINUSOIDAL FORCE AND FORCE OF THE RESISTANCE OF THE DISPERSION MEDIUM

Let us define the character of the movement of the material point at simultaneous action of the external revolting sinusoidal force and internal forces of the resistance of the dispersive environment.

For this purpose, let us consider the cylindrical reactor that is installed vertically on the vibration machine with an open upper lid. The reactor is loaded up to 90 % of its height with two immiscible and insoluble liquids that differing from each other in terms of specific weight, the viscosity, the coefficient of a surface tension coefficient, and others physical and chemical characteristics. The energy balance of this liquid–gas–liquid system can be composed of the potential energy acting in the gravitational field E_p, and the average value refers to the time of kinetic energy through E_k. The total energy of the system in question is determined by the height h, which is equal to:

$$E_{(h)} = E_{p\,(h)} + E_{k\,(h)} \qquad (4.50)$$

Let us designate m as the mass of elementary volume, [m]; g as the acceleration due to the gravity, [m/s^2]; Δd as the diameter of the elementary volume, [m]; Δh is the height of the elementary volume, [m]; ρ_1 as the specific density of the liquid # 1, [kg/m^3]; ρ_2 as the specific density of the liquid # 2, [kg/m^3]; h as the internal height of the reactor, that is coinciding with the level of the volume of the disperse system, [m]; S as the internal cross-sectional area of the reactor, which coincides with the internal cross-section of the dispersion system, [m^2]; and $v^2_{(h)}$ as the average value of the speed of harmonic oscillations at the level of the considered elementary volume, [m/s].

The potential energy $E_{p\,(h)}$ could then be represented as follows:

$$E_{p\,(h)} = mg\left(h + \frac{\Delta h}{2}\right) - Sh\rho g \Delta h + C_g \; .$$

where $C_g = \frac{1}{2}\,\rho g S\,(H^2 - \Delta h^2)$.

The average value of kinetic energy $E_{k\,(h)}$ could be determined as:

$$E_{k\,(h)} = \frac{1}{2}\; m v_{(h)}^2 - \rho S \int_{h}^{h+\Delta h} \frac{1}{2} v_{(h)}^2 dh + C_k,$$

where $C_k = \rho S \int_{0}^{H} \frac{1}{2} v_{(h)}^2 dh$.

It is known that the influence of the energy field decreases as the distance from the energy source resulting from dissipation increases.

An elementary mathematical model of the energy dissipation process can be represented as:

$$v_{(h)}^2 = v_{(0)}^2 \exp\left(-\varepsilon h\right), \qquad (4.51)$$

where ε is the coefficient of the dissipation of energy and $\varepsilon = \text{const}$.

The attenuation of the intensity of harmonic oscillations depends on the physical properties of the dispersed phase and the dispersion medium, the ratio of the reactor's interior diameter to its height, and the degree of the dispersion—the sizes of the spherical drops of liquid or the particles of solid matter of the dispersed phase.

The change in the particles of solid matter or drops of the liquid of the dispersed phase is equivalent to the replacement of the considered particle or a drop of liquid that the equal to the volume of the mass of the dispersion medium. At the rather small dimension of components of a dispersed phase, when $\Delta h \ll \varepsilon^{-1}$, the change in the energy of the system could be described without integration. If $m > m_0$, (i.e., under conditions, when the density of the dispersed phase exceeds the density of the dispersion phase), the considered particle moves in the vertical direction from the initial level $h = 0$, upwards to the level h, and the increment of the system's energy is equal:

$$\Delta m_{(h)} = (m - m_0)\left\{gh + \frac{1}{2}\left[v_{(h)}^2 - v_{(h=0)}^2\right]\right\}, \quad (4.52)$$

where $v_0^2 = v^2_{(0)} \geq v_{(h)}^2$ corresponds to the condition where the source of fluctuations is at the level $h = 0$. That is, when the reactor is installed vertically on the vibration machine. At the same time, index "0" designates the level of the reference height of the dispersive medium.

If $$v_0^2 \geq v_{(h=0)}^2 + 2gh, \quad (4.53)$$

then occurs the situation of the increment of total energy $\Delta E < 0$ occurs. That is, the system's total energy, ***decreases***.

A similar situation occurs when the density of the dispersed phase is higher than that of the dispersion phase; then, the movement occurs from top to bottom:

$$\Delta m_{(H)} = (m - m_0)\left\{gh + \frac{1}{2}\left[v_{(h)}^2 - v_{(H)}^2\right]\right\}, \quad (4.54)$$

where h is the maximum level of the dispersion system inside the reactor.

In this case, the dissipation of energy $\Delta E < 0$ arises under the condition, when:

$$v_0^2 < v_{(h)}^2 + 2gh. \quad (4.55)$$

Thus, emersion in the dispersion environment of particles of: (1) a dispersed phase with a higher density, than the density of the dispersive medium and, on the contrary, (2) a dispersed phase with a lower density, than the dispersion medium reduces the general energy of system that is influenced by the vibration field.

4.10. TASK No 8: ANALYSIS OF THE MOVEMENT OF ELEMENTS OF THE DISPERSED PHASE IN THE VIBRATION FIELD

Let us use a concept of mechanochemical potential [93,169] to describe the character of the movement in the vibrational and gravitational fields of the elements of the dispersed phase that containing particles of different density. That typically takes place in physicochemical processes, such as extraction, crushing, emulsions, suspensions, fabricating composite materials, in processing of alloys, and producing magnetic and electronic liquids and so on:

$$\mu_{i(h)} = \mu_i^0 + \rho_i V_i \left\{gh + \frac{1}{2} v_{(h)}^2 + \mathcal{P}_{(h)} V_i + \theta \ln[n_{i(h)}]\right\}, \quad (4.56)$$

where $\mu_{i(h)}$ is the mechanochemical potential of the dispersed phase designated by the index i; ρ_i is the density (per mole) of the components of the dispersed phase; V_i is the specific volume (per mole) of the components of the dispersed phase; $n_{i(h)}$ is the share of particles of a dispersed phase; and $\mathcal{P}_{(h)}$ is the hydrostatic pressure.

Note: Chemistry, physical chemistry, and thermodynamics, for example often use the concept of individual mass: the mole. The mole refers to the mass of a substance in grams, numerically equal to its relative molecular weight.

For the indissoluble and incompressible dispersion medium, both amounts $v_{(h)}$ and $p_{(h)}$ are equal to all components. In the equation (4.56) use molar characteristics of components when $\theta = RT$ and use the individual characteristics when $\theta = kT$.

It had been shown [93, 169] that, under thermodynamic equilibrium, the mechanochemical potentials of the components are invariant. The invariancy is the property of a class of mathematical objects used to remain invariable when transforming a certain type. Under the condition of invariancy in the equilibrium system, $\mu_{(h)} = \text{const}$.

If the concentration of the substance forming the dispersed phase is substantially low compared to the substance forming the dispersion medium $n_i \ll n_0 \cong 1$, then from equation (3.56), as well as with $\mu_{0(h)} = \mu_{0(h=0)} = \text{const.}$, there is:

$$\mathcal{P}_{(h)} = \mathcal{P}_{(h=0)} - \rho_0 gh\left\{1 - \frac{1}{2}\left[v_{(h=0)}{}^2 - v_{(h)}{}^2\right]\right\}. \quad (4.57)$$

The concentration of components of the dispersed phase that is weighed in the dispersion phase can be defined by substituting of $\rho_0 h$ into equation (4.56). Let us to write down this equation as it is received from the condition of invariancy of the mechanochemical potential in the state of equilibrium, when $\mu_i(h) = \mu_i(0) = \text{const.}$:

$$n_{i(h)} = n_{i(0)} \exp\left\{-\frac{M_i gh}{\theta}\left(1 - \frac{\rho_0}{\rho_i}\right)\frac{1}{2gh}\left[v_{(0)}{}^2 - v_{(h)}{}^2\right]\right\}. \quad (4.58)$$

Distribution (4.57) has an extremum if $v_{(0)}{}^2 > 2\text{gh} > \left[v_{(0)}{}^2 - v_{(H)}{}^2\right]$.

For the law of ordinary attenuation of fluctuations (4.51), the extremum will be located at the level:

$$h = \varepsilon^{-1}\ln\frac{2g}{\varepsilon v_0^2}. \quad (4.59)$$

From the so-called hypsometric distribution, considered in [4.59], which describes the case of diffusion—sedimentation equilibrium in a gravitational field—expression (4.58) differs by the last factor [91- 93].

For the elementary volumes of liquid or solid particles forming a dispersed phase, whose density ***exceeds*** the density of the substance of the dispersion phase, equation (3.59) determines the height of the layer in the reactor at which these volumes of liquid or particles are forming ***the maximum*** concentration. For the volumes of liquid or solid particles forming a dispersed phase whose density is ***lower*** that the density of the substance of the dispersive phase, the equation (4.59) determines the height of the layer of the chemical reactor at which these volumes or particles form ***minimum*** concentration in the lower or upper part of the chemical reactor. In other words, a dispersion system that occurs in a chemical reactor because of the phenomenon of low-frequency vibrational resonance is distinguished by the development of zones with a different distribution structure to the dispersed phase in the dispersion medium. Thus, is determined by the ratio of the density of the components of the dispersion system.

Thus, in the considered model, the stratification of the formed layers does not depend on the physical characteristics of the substance(s) forming dispersed phase. The density and degree of dispersion affect only the layer thickness—their number. In accordance with equation (4.58), an increase in the density of elements of the dispersed phase reduces the thickness of the layer of their concentration.

Naturally, it is not difficult to assume that if the density components of the dispersed phase are close to the dispersion medium, the distribution of the dispersed phase will be uniform over the entire height of the reactor.

4.11. Task No. 9: FLUCTUATION OF THE MATERIAL POINT THAT IS UNDER THE INFLUENCE OF AN EXTERNAL SINUSOIDAL FORCE INCLUDING THE ELASTIC COMPONENT OF THE DISPERSION PHASE

In all previous tasks, the existence of an elastic component of a dispersed phase was not considered. For the consideration the influence of elastic properties of the components of the dispersed phase in expression of mechanochemical potential, it is necessary to add elastic energy of particles of solid matter: $\sigma_{(h)}{}^2 \frac{V_i}{2\gamma_i}$, and for the liquid and gas components to add $\mathcal{P}_{(h)}{}^2 \frac{V_i}{2\gamma_i}$, where γ_i is the module of elasticity. The module of volume elasticity for liquid and gas is equal to the inverse value of the coefficient of compressibility β, that is $\gamma_i = \beta_i^{-1}$.

Task No. 9: Solution 1

The ratio of concentration of the dispersed phase to dispersion environment is significantly large: $n_0 \cong 1 \gg n_i$. At the same time, the elementary volumes of liquid or solid particles that forming a dispersed phase do not have any physical contacts to each other. So, it is obviously possible, to consider that the elastic (internal) tension acting inside them equates to the hydrostatic pressure of the dispersion environment $\sigma_{(h)} = \mathcal{P}_{(h)}$.

The mechanochemical potential of the dispersion environment (liquid) μ_0 [92] is:

$$\mu_{0(h)} = \mu_0^0 + \rho_0 V_0 \left\{gh + \tfrac{1}{2}\left[v_{(h)}{}^2\right]\right\} +$$

$$+\mathcal{P}_{(h)} V_0\left[1 + \frac{\mathcal{P}(h)}{2\gamma_0}\right] = \text{const.} \qquad (4.60)$$

For components of the dispersion phase μ_i:

$$\mu_{i(h)} = \mu_i^0 + \rho_i V_i \{gh + \tfrac{1}{2}[v_{(h)}{}^2]\} +$$

$$+ \mathcal{P}_{(h)} V_i [1 + \frac{p(h)}{2\gamma_i}] + \theta \ln[n_{i(h)}] = \text{const.} \qquad (4.61)$$

For the incompressible dispersion environment (when the coefficient of compressibility of the liquid phase $\beta \to 0$) the distribution of hydrostatic (internal) pressure could be determined using formula (4.57). For the compressed environment the condition of invariancy $\mu_{0(h)} = \mu_{0(0)} = \mu_{0(H)}$ allows us to express the distribution of internal pressure in the dispersion environment could be expressed as the solution to a quadratic equation:

$$\mathcal{P}_{(h)}{}^2 + 2\text{p}\,\gamma_{0\,(h)2} + C\gamma_0 = 0 \text{ and } \mathcal{P}_{(h)} = \gamma_0(1) - \pm\sqrt{1-2C}, \qquad (4.62)$$

where parameter C could be expressed through a condition of the system at any reactor's level. The pressure $\mathcal{P}_{(0)}$ at the bottom of the reactor inside the vibrating dispersion environment, is unknown. However, the pressure at the top level $\mathcal{P}_{(h)}$ is equal to the external pressure, that is, in proportion to the external revolting field of forces.

$$C = \rho_0 \{gh + \tfrac{1}{2} v_{(h)}{}^2 - v_0^2\} - \mathcal{P}_{(0)} - \frac{p_{(0)}^2}{2\gamma_0} =$$

$$= \rho_0 \{gh + \tfrac{1}{2}[v(h)^2 - v(H)^2 - g(H-h)]\} - \mathcal{P}_{(H)} - \frac{p_{(H)}^2}{2\gamma_0}. \qquad (4.63)$$

In accordance with equation (4.62), there could be the negative values for both $\mathcal{P}_{(0)}$ and $\mathcal{P}_{(H)}$.

The physical meaning of the negative values of internal pressure is that: in the compressed environment, they are identified with the zones of negative pressure, where formation of cavities occurs. That is, the break in the continuity of the dispersion environment develops. This phenomenon is described in detail in [156].

Thus, based on equation (4.62), it is quite obvious that zones with various internal pressures are formed in the considered dispersion system. This leads to the development of fields of the internal pressure (tension). It is easy to assume that, in such zones the mass transfer and heat exchange are also different, in the same measure, as the internal pressure developing in various zones.

According to the condition of invariancy $\mu_{i(h)} = \mu_{i(h=0)} = \text{const.}$ of the mechanochemical potentials for elementary volumes of the dispersed phase of the equilibrium of the distribution of particles on reactor's height, it is possible to present it hypsometrically as [91-93]:

$$n_{i(h)} = n_{i(0)} \exp\left\{-\frac{ghM_i}{\theta}\left[1 - \frac{1+\frac{\mathcal{P}_{(h)}+\mathcal{P}_{(0)}}{2\gamma_i}}{1+\frac{\mathcal{P}_{(h)}+\mathcal{P}_{(0)}}{2\gamma_0}}\frac{\rho_0}{\rho_i}\right] \text{x}\right.$$

$$\left.\text{x}\left[1-\frac{v_0^2}{2gh}-\frac{v_{(h)}^2}{2gh}\right]\right\}. \qquad (4.64)$$

If $\gamma_i \gg \mathcal{P}_{(h)}$ and/or $\gamma_i = \gamma_0$, the distribution comes down to equation (4.37), when elastic components do not influence upon their distribution in the internal volume of the reactor.

Unlike equation (4.58), the extremum of distribution (4.64) essentially depends on the properties of elementary volumes of liquid or vapor–gas bubbles, which possess various elasticities and has the extremums at the different reactor's levels. This leads to the formation of multilayered structures. In addition, rather elastic particles at which $\gamma_i < \gamma_0$, behave in a way that makes the influence of the external vibration field reduces their density. This effect, so-called "vibrational fluidity" [168]. It is fully used during filling forms with cement during the fabrication of concrete products. On the contrary, for systems with more rigid particles at which

$\gamma_i > \gamma_0$, seem to have structures with higher density. Considering the compressibility of components of dispersion systems, the external pressure $\mathcal{P}_{(H)}$, the atmospheric pressure and pressure from other reactor's layers become relevant.

The analysis of equations (4.58) and (4.64) indicates one more regularity of influence of the oscillatory process on hypsometric distributions. As the intensity of fluctuations increases, under the conditions of the gravitational field, particles layers at $v_0^2 - v_{(h)}{}^2 > 4gh$ will become thinner. They get thicker at $v_0^2 - v_{(h)}{}^2 < 4gh$ (rather than in the absence of the vibration field). Under the condition of $v_0^2 - v_{(h)}{}^2 = 2gh$, particles reach a condition of weightlessness as though at " zero gravity".

A similar condition of weightlessness arises when in an exponential part of expression (3.64) when the right bracket becomes equal to zero. This takes place when:

$$[\mathcal{P}_{(h)} + \mathcal{P}_{(0)}]\,(\rho_0\gamma_0 - \rho_i\gamma_i) = 2\,\gamma_0\gamma_i(\rho_i - \rho_0)\,. \qquad (4.65)$$

Usually, when components of the dispersed phase and the dispersion environment have approximately equal density and modules of elasticity, a component of the dispersed phase is led to uniform distribution along the entire height of the reactor. For macroscopic particles when concentrations at the lower level $n_i = 0$, they can become disappearing small, so, that the calculation of the function evaluation of distribution (4.58) and (4.64) loses any physical meaning in the entire volume of the reactor. Quantitative calculations under such circumstances can be executed when to presenting both functions (4.58) and (4.64) at their maximum distributions [92]:

$$\frac{n_{i\,(h)}}{n_{i\,(h*)}} = \exp\left\{\frac{M_i g_{(h-h*)}}{\theta}\left[1 - \frac{1+\frac{\mathcal{P}_{(h)}+\mathcal{P}_{(h*)}}{2\gamma_i}}{1+\frac{\mathcal{P}_{(h)}+\mathcal{P}_{(h*)}}{2\gamma_0}}\,\frac{\rho_0}{\rho_i}\right] \times \right.$$

$$\left. \times\left[1 - \frac{v_0^2}{2gh} - \frac{v_{(h)}^2}{2gh*}\right]\right\}. \qquad (4.66)$$

Equation (4.66) allows for a description of layers of thin particles h^*, out of which functions of distribution lose their meaning. For distribution (4.58) the level h^* for particles with rather large density can be determined using ratio (4.59). However, for particles with a small density, the level of distribution is at the top or lower levels of the reactor. If the function of distribution is expressed by equation (4.64), the problem of calculating the level of distribution is connected to macroscopic particles when the ratio is fair:

$$\frac{M_i g h}{\theta} \gg 1.$$

The research of height h^*should begin with areas for the condition when the value of multipliers in brackets is equal to zero or close to zero, which corresponds to the state of weightlessness.

The fair assumption is that more complicated levels of distribution arise for multicomponent dispersion systems. For these the structure and density of the dispersion environment are under the influence of the external revolting forces and are functionally connected to the size of the internal pressure, that is determined by roots of the equation (4.62) [92].

4.12. SUMMARY OF CHAPTER 4

For dispersion systems the nature of the distribution of the dispersed phase in the dispersion environment essentially depends on the field of the internal pressure, which develops in the system under the influence of the external revolting force. Therefore, to analyze the processes of the formation of the dispersion systems, it is necessary to measure and compare values of the internal pressure in various zones of the system. The arising and developing the tension (difference) in the measurements of the internal pressure in conjugated (adjacent) zones allows for research into the emergence and development of fields of internal tension between the adjacent zones of the formed dispersion system, composite materials, and alloys.

CHAPTER 5

PHYSICOCHEMICAL DYNAMICS OF DISPERSION SYSTEMS

5.1. DEVELOPMENT OF MOLECULAR-SURFACE FORCES DURING FORMATION OF A DISPERSION SYSTEM UNDER MODES OF RESONANCE CAVITATION AND TORSION-ORIENTED TURBULIZATION

During formation of dispersion systems, processes connected to the emergence of interaction among phases play a special role. The value of interaction between separate elements of dispersion systems is defined by the intensity of the fields of forces of external influence and internal forces, including fields of chemical potential and their thermodynamic characteristics. At the same time, as in [167, 1168], the field of forces that results from the influence of the external field exerts an impact on the external field from within. The results of this interaction are shown through the interfaces of phases, where the key role is allocated to the activation of the action of molecular and superficial forces.

The structural parameters of dispersion systems, characterized by the development of interfaces between phases, have a level of their dispersion is measured by the size of a specific surface S_0. For nano-dispersion and thin-dispersion systems that are consisting of particles (volumes) of, approximately, identical forms and, approximately, equal sizes, the volume of the specific surface is equal to [167]:

$$S_0 = \frac{k}{V} \int_{a_{min}}^{a_{max}} \vartheta(a)\, da$$

where k is the coefficient, depending on the forms of the dispersed particles; a_{min} and a_{max} are the minimum and maximum sizes of dispersed particles; V is the volume of the dispersed phase within dispersion system; and $\vartheta_{(a)}$ is the relative content of the particles of the dispersed phase having the chosen size a.

Let us consider some surface phenomena caused by the influence of the fields of external forces during formation of the dispersion systems representing the particles of the dispersed phase distributed in the dispersion environment. It is known, that the attraction forces act on the surface of separation between phases, arising between different atoms and molecules. These forces are called Van der Waals forces. They arise in the following situation:

- The crushed particles of solid matter are distributed in volume of liquid, solutions, or mixture of several liquids, that forms suspensions or colloidal solutions.
- The dispersed volumes of liquids are distributed in the volume of the liquid or the mixture of several immiscible and insoluble liquids that forms emulsions.
- The dispersed volumes of gas or vapor–gas mixtures are distributed in the volume of liquid or the mixture of several immiscible and insoluble liquids that forms foams.

When the dispersion systems form in the mode of resonance cavitation or torsion-oriented turbulization, vapor–gas bubbles occur in the system, and capillary meniscuses form on the surface of separation between phases. The curvature of films located on the border between the liquid and gas border corresponds to these meniscuses, which correspond to some value of surface free energy [171-172].

Surface free energy U represents the excess of the energy of molecules on a surface of the dispersed phase in comparison with energy of molecules in volume of the dispersion environment. This energy can be considered the total energy of uncompensated molecular forces relating to the unit of the surface of separation between phases or a measure of surplus of the specific superficial energy [173]. The superficial free energy acting on the gas–liquid border is called a superficial tension. The size of free surface energy is determined by the formula:

$$dU = \sigma dS, \qquad (5.1)$$

where $\mathcal{U}$ is the free surface energy, [J=Nm]; σ is the coefficient of the surface tension, [J/m^2]; and $\mathcal{S}$ is the free surface, [m^2].

The borders of separation of double (liquid–gas) and threefold (solid particles–liquid–gas) systems have the surface the curvature that corresponds to the maximum values of saturation of molecular-surface forces, the density of the energy field of these forces, and the density of the dispersed phase. A change in the form of the interface between phases leads to a reduction in energy density and weight, which reduces the internal pressure in the dispersion environment. Therefore, in the case of the concave surface of a meniscus, liquid is under negative pressure in comparison with a flat surface [174].

The molecular-surface forces determinate a negative pressure. They are directed to the center of the curvature of the meniscus. The size of Laplace's pressure $\mathcal{P}_L$ depends on the coefficient of the surface tension σ and the radiuses of the main curvature of the surface r_1 and r_2 :

$$\mathcal{P}_L = \sigma \left(\frac{1}{r_1} + \frac{1}{r_2}\right). \tag{5.2}$$

The inaccuracy of the ratio (5.2) was discovered and corrected [175] as:

$$\mathcal{M} = \mathcal{M}_0 - 2\varepsilon\mathcal{H} - \frac{\partial\mathcal{H}}{\partial(\frac{1}{\mathcal{H}})}; \tag{5.3}$$

$$\mathcal{P} = \mathcal{P}_0 - 2\sigma\mathcal{H} - \frac{\partial\mathcal{H}}{\partial(\frac{1}{\mathcal{H}})}. \tag{5.4}$$

where $\mathcal{H} = r_1 + r_2$ is the average curvature of a surface defining change of molecular $\mathcal{M}$ and hydrostatic $\mathcal{P}$ pressure of the dispersion medium with development of its mobility; $\mathcal{E}$ is the function depending on surface energy and the coefficient of a surface tension σ; and $\mathcal{T}$ is the temperature of the dispersion system.

$$\mathcal{E} = \sigma - \mathcal{T}\frac{\partial U}{\partial \mathcal{T}}. \tag{5.5}$$

Equation (5.3) is different from the classical Laplace's formula (5.2) using a negative sign in the front of the second term and the introduction of the third term considering the dependence of the function on the radius of gas-vapor bubbles or drops of the liquid dispersed in the dispersion environment.

5.2. FORMATION AND STABILITY OF DISPERSION SYSTEMS

The interaction of the components of a dispersed phase (crushed solid particles, the minimized drops of immiscible and insoluble liquids, and vapor-gas bubbles) with macro-surfaces made of films from the dispersion environment defines the formation process, stability, and rheological characteristics of dispersion systems. Because of the spread in the environment and consumption by the industry of the dispersion systems, it is worth considering their physical and chemical nature and process of their formation in the modes of resonance cavitation or torsion-oriented turbulization. At the same time, it is necessary to recognize the difference between these phenomena and mechanical, thermal, and ultrasonic cavitation—however similar they may appear upon first glance.

The influence of modes on the formation of different kinds of dispersion systems and on their stability is especially important. The primary feature of the systems in question is the existence of a highly determined border of separation among elements of the dispersed phase and the dispersion phase with the coefficient of surface tension σ. The main contribution to the change of free energy U caused by minimization of substances of system components comes from the atoms located on the surface of the interphase. The number of atoms is quite comparable to their number in the volume of the substance that forms the dispersion environment.

As noted previously, the strength condition of the dispersion systems is characterized by an excess of free energy U. Moreover, the integration of particles of the dispersed phase happens spontaneously, causing the reduction of free energy U. Thus, dispersion systems are unstable in a thermodynamic sense. Their temporary stability depends on the existence of the power barrier to prevent rapprochement and the fixing of elementary volumes and particles at rather small distances from each other (aggregation), the full association of droplets in emulsions and fogs, or the association of bubbles of gas in foams (coalescence). In a dispersed state, although steady for coalescence, separate solid particles are united in somewhat large units and form a so-called coagulative structure. They keep their identity because of layers of the dispersion environment. Destruction of the films of surface separation causes the full associations of elementary volumes of the liquid phase in foams and emulsions or the emergence of direct contacts between microscopically small solid objects in suspensions or colloidal solutions.

5.3. ELECTRIC DOUBLE LAYER

The condition of dispersion systems depends substantially upon the distribution of ions around elements of the dispersed phase. As a result of the interaction between the dispersed phase and the dispersion phase, there is a transition of electricity carriers. The elements of the dispersed phase receive an excess of surface charge in the form of electrons or the adsorbed ions. This charge is compensated for by a charge that is equal in size but of an opposite sign, coming from the dispersion medium. This charge is formed by the so-called anti-ions and by some quantity of counter-ions (ions charged by the same sign), which have the identical charge sign with the charge of the surface of separation between phases. Presumably, the concentration of counter-ion and anti-ions can be determined separately using the thermodynamic method [176].

Counter-ions are ions of a double electric adsorption layer, having a charge opposite to the charge of potential-determining ions (PDI), and located between the layer of PDI and the diffuse layer. A double electric layer is a thin surface layer of spatially divided electric charges of the opposite sign, which is formed at the phase boundary. Because spatial distribution of charges is always preceding the emergence of electric potential difference, the double electric layer can be considered as a peculiar micro-condenser, where distance between facings is defined by the sizes of molecules.

Because of electrostatic attraction, the counterions are in close proximity to the elements of the dispersed phase—some of them are located in the form of a fixed layer similar to one of the plates of a flat capacitor, and the rest are distributed diffusely under the influence of the thermal motion. The distribution of counterions in the diffuse part of the double layer depends on the nature in the concentration of electrolytes and, as a rule, is determined using three equations [176]:

1. Poisson's equations:

$$\mathrm{Div}\ [\theta\ (x)\ \mathrm{Grad}\ \psi\ (x)] = 4\pi\rho\ (x); \qquad (5.6)$$

2. Boltzmann's equations:

$$n_i(x)\ = n_i(\infty)\ \exp\left[-\frac{w_i\ (x)}{kT}\right]; \qquad (5.7)$$

3. The equations for the volume density charges:

$$\rho\ (x) = \sum_i z_i e n_i(x) \qquad (5.8)$$

where θ is the dielectric constant in volume of the dispersion medium; ψ is the potential; ρ is the charge's volume density; n_i is the number of ions of i-grades per 10^{-2} m; x is the distance to the phase surface separation; $W_i\ (x)$ is the work necessary for the movement of a single ion from the inside of the dispersion medium for a distance x; k is the Boltzmann's constant; T is the absolute temperature, $[^0K]$; z_i is the ion's valency; and e is the electron's charge.

For the solution of Poisson's equation (5.6), found by [176], some simplifications were stipulated [177 – 179}:

- A double layer must be considered as a flat surface.

- The dielectric constant in volume of the dispersive environment θ does not depend on coordinate x.
- The own volume of ions equals 0, meaning that the double layer is considered to be a system of dotted charges.
- For the translation of ions from the volume of the dispersion environment into a double layer, it must work against forces of electrostatic interaction only—that is $W_i(x) = z_i e\psi(x)$.

Under these circumstances, equations (5.6) and (5.7) could look like:

$$\frac{d^2\psi(x)}{dx^2} = \frac{4\pi\rho(x)}{\varepsilon}; \tag{5.9}$$

$$n_i(x) = n_i(\infty)\exp\left[-\frac{z_i e\psi(x)}{kT}\right]. \tag{5.10}$$

Equations (5.6), (5.7) and (5.9) in common set Poisson-Boltsman's ratio:

$$\frac{d^2\psi(x)}{dx^2} = -\frac{4\pi}{\varepsilon}\sum_i z_i e n_i(\infty)\exp\left[-\frac{z_i e\psi(x)}{kT}\right]. \tag{5.11}$$

The first integration of expression (5.11) was carried out in [174]:

$$x \to \infty,\ \psi = 0 \text{ and } \frac{d\psi}{dx} = 0.$$

For a symmetrical electrolyte with a valency of ions z:

$$\frac{d\psi(x)}{dx} = -\sqrt{\frac{8\pi n_i(\infty)kT}{\varepsilon}}\left[\exp\left(\frac{ze\psi}{2kT}\right) - \exp\left(-\frac{ze\psi}{2kT}\right)\right]. \tag{5.12}$$

It was accepted that $x = 0$ and $\psi = \psi_0$ at the second integration [176]. The formula that characterizes the dependence of the potential upon the distance to the boundary of phase separation is:

$$\chi x = \ln \frac{[\exp\left(\frac{ze\psi}{2kT}\right)+1]}{\left[\exp\left(\frac{ze\psi}{2kT}\right)-1\right]} \frac{[\exp\left(\frac{ze\psi_0}{2kT}\right)-1]}{[\exp\left(\frac{ze\psi_0}{2kT}\right)+1]}. \qquad (5.13)$$

where χ is the parameter opposite to the thickness of the diffusive electric double layer:

$$\chi = \sqrt{\frac{4\pi e^2 \sum_i n_i z_i^2}{\varepsilon kT}}. \qquad (5.14)$$

Because the value of parameter χ is in direct proportional to the square root of the concentration of the electrolyte, the content of ions in the solution (5.13) defines the change of potential in a double layer. The introduction of indifferent electrolytes in the dispersion phase reduces potential. It has an essential influence for the coagulation of colloidal systems.

For low potentials, it is enough to consider only the first two members of decomposition in a row of exponential functions, from expression (5.13). It is not hard to see:

$$\chi x = \ln \frac{\psi_0}{\psi}. \qquad (5.15)$$

It is quite obvious that, when the distance to the boundary of a phase's separation increases, under the exponential law, the potential moves toward zero. If $x = \frac{1}{\chi}$, the value ψ decreases by e times by comparison with ψ_0.

On the other hand, for high potentials and long distances to the boundary of the phase's separation, when $\frac{ze\psi_0}{kT} \gg 1$ and $\frac{ze\psi}{kT} \ll 1$, then:

$$\frac{ze\psi}{kT} = 4 \exp(-\chi x) \frac{\exp\left(\frac{ze\psi_0}{2kT}\right)-1}{\exp\left(\frac{ze\psi_0}{2kT}\right)-1}. \qquad (5.16)$$

Using the expression (5.10) and in view of:

$$\sigma_0 = -\frac{\varepsilon}{4\pi} \times \frac{d\psi}{dx}. \quad (5.17)$$

When $x = 0$, the ratio between the area's density of charges σ_0 and the potential is the following:

$$\sigma_0 = \sqrt{\frac{\varepsilon n_i kT}{2\pi}} \left[\exp\left(\frac{ze\psi}{2kT}\right) - \exp\left(-\frac{ze\psi}{2kT}\right)\right]. \quad (5.18)$$

The boundary conditions adopted when solving the problem of a flat double layer are applicable only when the radius of curvature of the particles significantly exceeds the thickness of the double layer. For spherical symmetric particles, the Poisson–Boltzmann equation in an approximation formulated in [177–179] takes the form [180]:

$$\frac{1}{r^2} \cdot \frac{d}{dr}\left(r^2 \frac{d\psi}{dr}\right) = -\frac{4\pi e}{\varepsilon} \cdot \sum_i z_i n_i(\infty) \exp\left(-\frac{z_i e\psi}{kT}\right), \quad (5.19)$$

where r is the distance measured from center of a particle.

5.4. ELECTROSTATIC REPULSIVE FORCES OF DISPERSED PARTICLES

Furthermore, it is necessary to consider issues related to the electrostatic repulsive forces of dispersed particles resulting from their identical charge. However, because the particles are surrounded by counterions that compensate for their charge, and outside of the double layer the electric field strength is zero, it is impossible to calculate the repulsive forces using the Coulomb's Law. The interaction of two particles is detected only when their diffusion electric layers overlap. The interaction of two particles is found only when their diffusive electric layers are blocked. The calculation of energy of electrostatic repulsive forces was carried out in [181–187].

Provided that the thermodynamic equilibrium is maintained when particles approach each other, accompanied by overlapping double layers, there is no change in potential at the phase boundaries; moreover, the surface charge density decreases [176]. An analysis of the reasons for repulsion is given in works [180-186]. When the double layers overlap, the forces acting on the side of the inner shells of both dispersed particles on the ions located between the adjacent surfaces would not be completely shielded by the outer shells. Such a change in forces violates the static equilibrium that existed before the ionic shells were superimposed upon each other and caused a redistribution of charges.

As a result, the concentration of the electrolyte in the film of the liquid separating the particles transpires to be different from the concentration of the electrolyte in the uncoated double layer, so to speak. Thus, we can conclude that when the double layers overlap, forces of both an osmotic and an electrostatic nature can connect. Moreover, their simultaneous accounting is the basis for evaluating the ion–electrostatic interaction.

There are two ways to assess the energy of the ion-electrostatic interaction: the first is to define changes of free energy of the double layer upon transition from infinitely distant particles to particles that are blocked by double layers, and the second is to receive a formula for energy, having carried out integration of expression for repulsive forces of two equally loaded surfaces as functions of distance between those surfaces.

At the same time, as noted in work [188], the quantity of forces that are found under conditions of potential constancy and surface charge practically coincide with each other in that there are rather long distances between particles: $\hbar$ $(\chi\hbar \gg 1$. However, when $\hbar \rightarrow 0$, then the distinction increases sharply. At ψ_0 = const. and σ_0 = const., the ion-electrostatic repulsive forces are always varying in quantity. They grow indefinitely as particles approach.

5.5. ENERGY OF THE INTERACTION OF DISPERSED PARTICLES

The question of determining the interaction energy that develops when rapprochement of dispersed particles occurs can be modeled by two plane-parallel plates. Moreover, as was considered [180-182], the size of the dispersed particles significantly exceeds the thickness of the diffusion part of the double layer. Until the particles interact with each other (Fig. 5-1a), the change in potential in the double layer obeys equation (5.12) and $\psi = 0$, $\frac{d\psi}{dx} = 0$ at $x \to \infty$. When two particles are so close that their double layers overlap, then one can assume the change in potential is the same as in an uncoated double layer in areas that lie in the immediate vicinity of the particle surface, (Fig. 5–1b).

For determining the dependence of the potential between two interacting particles as a function of distance, the Poisson–Boltsman's equation (5.9) is usually used. However, the nonblocked double layer boundary conditions for integration are different:

$$\psi = \psi_0 \text{ at } x = 0, \text{ and } \psi = \psi_d \text{ at } x = \frac{h}{2},$$

where ψ_d is the potential in the symmetry plane between dispersed particles.

Because ψ_d represents the minimum value of the potential (Fig. 5–1a), for $x = \frac{h}{2}$ the derivative potential upon distance is $\frac{d\psi}{dx} = 0$.

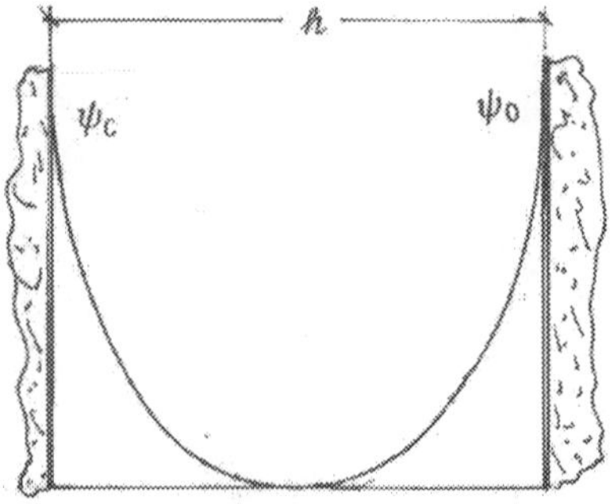

Figure 5-1a

The first integration of the equation (5.9) under the changed boundary conditions is:

$$\frac{d\psi}{dx} = -\sqrt{\frac{8\pi kT}{\varepsilon}\,K}\,, \qquad (5.20)$$

where :

$$K = \Big[n_i^-(\infty)\exp\Big(\frac{z^- e\psi}{kT}\Big) + n_i^+(\infty)\exp\Big(-\frac{z^+ e\psi}{kT}\Big) -$$

$$- n_i^-(\infty)\exp\Big(-\frac{z^- e\psi_d}{kT}\Big) + n_i^+(\infty)\exp\Big(-\frac{z^+ e\psi_d}{kT}\Big)\Big],$$

and a large number of independent variables $[z^+, z^-, n_i^-(\infty), \psi_d, h]$ is considered.

The second integration can be executed only graphically. Therefore, it is advisable to limit the consideration of symmetric electrolyte with valency of ions are as follows: $z^+ = z^- = z$.

Let us enter designations: $\frac{ze\psi}{kT} = u$, $\frac{ze\psi_0}{kT} = u_0$, $\frac{ze\psi_d}{kT} = u_d$. In addition, in view of that hyperbolic functions are defined as follows:

$$\exp(u) + \exp(-u) = 2\mathrm{ch}(u),$$
$$\exp(u) - \exp(-u) = 2\mathrm{sh}(u).$$

The integration of the equation (4.19) under boundary conditions $\psi = \psi_0$ at $x = 0$, and $\psi = \psi_d$ at $x = \frac{h}{2}$ leads to a formula that establishes a connection among values ψ, ψ_d and χ_h:

$$\chi h = \sqrt{2}\int_{u_d}^{u_0} \frac{du}{\sqrt{chu - chu_d}}\,. \qquad (5.21)$$

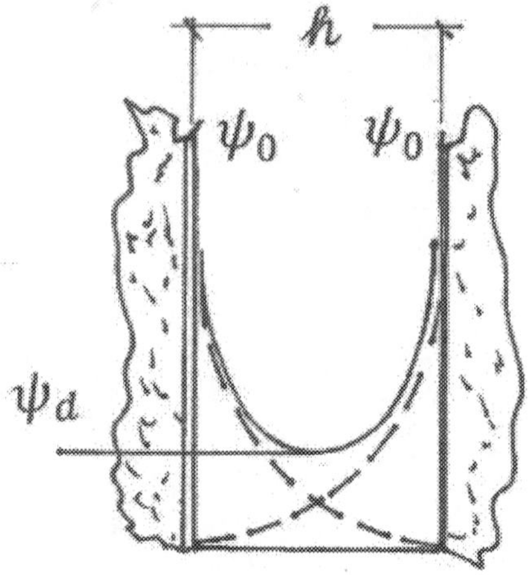

Figure 5-1b

The calculation of this elliptic integral of the first order allows us to present the potential for various quantities as the function of the distance between parallel plates (Fig. 5–2). Considering expression (5.18) for the charge of a diffusive part of a double layer when there are overlapping double layers, the equation is:

$$\sigma_0 = -\frac{\varepsilon}{4\pi}\cdot\left(\frac{d\psi}{dx}\right)_{x=0} = \sqrt{\frac{n\varepsilon kT}{2\pi}\,\mathrm{B}}\ , \qquad (5.22)$$

where:

$$\mathrm{B} = \left[\exp\left(\frac{ze\psi_0}{kT}\right) - \exp\left(-\frac{ze\psi_0}{kT}\right) - \exp\left(\frac{ze\psi_d}{2kT}\right) - \exp\left(-\frac{ze\psi_d}{2kT}\right)\right].$$

As it follows from the equation (5.21) with the increase in potential ψ_d, i.e., when the interaction is strengthening—the charge of a surface decreases. In the limit, at the contact of interphase borders, $\sigma_0 = 0$.

The free energy of a double layer $\mathcal{F}_{ds}$ is proportional to the quantity of the charge of the area's density [180–183]:

$$\mathcal{F}_{ds} = -\int_0^{\psi_0} \sigma d\,\psi\ . \qquad (5.23)$$

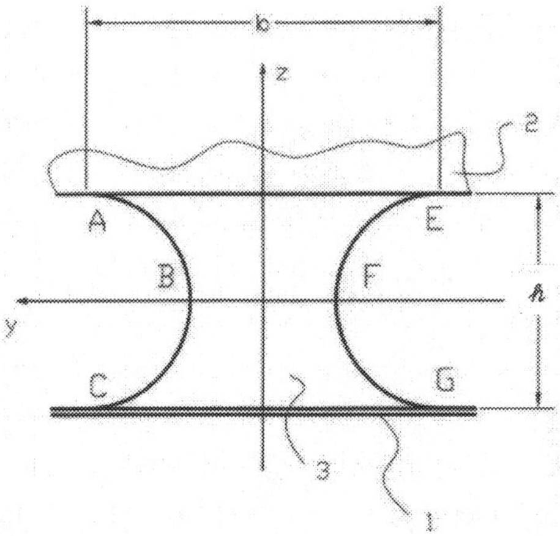

Figure 5-2. Model of the Cell of Dispersion System's Elements [1]

By comparison with equations (5.19) and (5.22), we get:

$$\mathcal{F}_{ds} = -\int_0^{\psi_0} \sqrt{\frac{n\varepsilon kT}{2\pi}} \cdot \left[\exp\left(\frac{ze\psi}{2kT}\right) - \exp\left(-\frac{ze\psi}{2kT}\right)\right] d\psi. \quad (5.23)$$

After the integration of (5.19) and the introduction of Debye-Guekkelj's parameter $\frac{1}{\chi}$ [176]:

$$\mathcal{F}_{ds} = \frac{4nkT}{\chi}\left\{\left[\exp\left(\frac{ze\psi_0}{2kT}\right)-1\right] + \right.$$
$$\left. + \left[\exp\left(-\frac{ze\psi_0}{2kT}\right)-1\right]\right\} \equiv \frac{8\pi kT}{\chi}\left(\mathrm{ch}\,\frac{u_0}{2}-1\right), \quad (5.24)$$

where $\chi = \sqrt{\left[\frac{4\pi e^2}{\varepsilon kT}\sum_i n_i z_i^2\right]}$.

The repulsion energy V_i of two particles can be determined by calculating the change in free energy during the transition of two particles from a state with undisturbed double layers, characterized by free energy $\mathcal{F}_{ds}$, to the state corresponding to the overlapping of diffuse layers, using the method for determining the interaction energy of double ion layers proposed in [187]:

$$\mathcal{V}_i = 2\,(\mathcal{F} - \mathcal{F}_{ds}). \qquad (5.25)$$

The expression for free energy $\mathcal{F}$ of the blocked double layers is defined as for quantity $\mathcal{F}_{ds}$. Substituting the equations (5.21) with (5.22), there is:

$$\mathcal{F} = -\frac{nkT}{\chi}\left[\chi h\Psi + 2\sqrt{\Phi} + \Omega\right], \qquad (5.26)$$

where:

$\Psi = \left(\mathrm{ch}\,\frac{u_d}{2} - 1\right).$

$\Phi = s\; sh^2\,\frac{u_0}{2} - h^2\,\frac{u_d}{2}.$

$\Omega = \chi h \mathrm{sh}\; 4\exp\frac{u_d}{2} - E_{(\psi_0, u_d)}\;\frac{u_d}{2}.$

$E_{(\psi_0, u_d)} = \int_{\psi_1}^{\pi/2} \sqrt{\Theta}\cdot d\text{–}\psi_1$ is the elliptic integral of the second order.

$\Theta = 1 - \exp\left[-(u - u_d)\right].$

$\psi_1 = \arcsin\,\exp\left(-\,\frac{u_0 - u_d}{2}\right).$

Thus, by defining the difference $2(\mathcal{F} - \mathcal{F}_{ds})$, it is possible to determine the quantity of the repulsive energy for two disperse particles [187]. The expression for the energy of ion-electrostatic interaction of flat particles was analytically received by V.M. Muller [188].

5.6. MOLECULAR INTERACTION OF DISPERSED PARTICLES

The forces of attraction that are acting between individual atoms and molecules are called Van der Waals forces. They are weaker than chemical bonding forces, cannot be saturated, and, by a first approximation, are additive. Additivity of a quantity means that the quantity related to the system as a whole is equal to the sum of the quantities related to its constituent parts. Such quantities are called extensive, as opposed to intense (e.g., temperature or density, etc.). The

Van der Waals forces can be composed of three building blocks: dipole–dipole interaction (Keesom forces), inductive interaction (Debye force) and dispersion interaction (London force). The existence of the first two types of interaction implies the presence of at least the guidance of the dipole moment in both molecules. Between nonpolar molecules, only dispersion forces act, which are caused by charge fluctuations arising from the motion of electrons.

Electronic fluctuations in atoms or molecules lead to the appearance of time–varying dipoles. The mutual influence of fluctuation dipoles causes a phase shift of the oscillations (at small distances it is 0^0) and therefore two non–polar molecules are always attracted to each other.

For a definition of the contribution of dispersion interaction to the total energy of the molecular attraction V_d, consider two atoms as connected isotropic harmonious three–dimensional oscillators [187]. For two atoms having polarizability α_{01} and α_{02} and frequencies ω_{01} and ω_{02} in the main state in work [187] the approximate equation was received:

$$V_d = -\frac{3\pi\hbar}{r^6} \cdot \frac{\omega_{01}\omega_{02}}{\omega_{01} + \omega_{02}} \alpha_{01}\alpha_{02} , \qquad (5.27)$$

where V_d is the energy of dispersive interaction; r is the interatomic distance; and $\hbar$ is the Plank's Constant ($\hbar = \frac{h}{2\pi}$).

By consideration of two identical atoms: where $\alpha_{01} = \alpha_{02} = \alpha_0$ and $\omega_{01} = \omega_{02} = \omega_0$, the equation looks like:

$$V_d = -\frac{3\pi\hbar}{2r^6} \cdot \omega_0 \alpha_0^2 . \qquad (5.28)$$

For two identical molecules, each of which has s of electronic oscillators, the equation in [187] agrees:

$$\mathcal{V}_d = -\frac{3\pi\hbar}{2r^6} \cdot \omega_0\, \alpha_0^2 \sqrt{s}\,, \qquad (5.29)$$

where $\omega_0 \sqrt{s} = \omega_v$ is the characteristic frequency.

Usually, the frequency of atoms depends on the charge of an electron e and its mass m_e:

$$\omega_0 = \frac{1}{2\pi} \sqrt{\frac{e^2}{m_e \alpha_0}}. \qquad (5.30)$$

Therefore:

$$\mathcal{V}_d = \frac{3e\alpha_0^{3/2}\hbar}{4r^6} \sqrt{\frac{s}{m_e}}\,. \qquad (5.31)$$

This form of writing is convenient, given that in formula (5.30), there is no hard to determine quantity $\mathcal{V}_d$.

5.7. SPHERICAL PARTICLES

As it is known [189], the molecular attraction energy $\mathcal{V}_m$ for two spherical particles with radiuses a_1 and a_2, each of which contains a set of atoms in 10^{-2} meters, is formulated as such:

$$\mathcal{V}_m = -\int_{u_1} du_1 \int_{u_2} \frac{q^2\beta}{r^6}\, du_2, \qquad (5.32)$$

where u_1 and u_2 are volumes of both particles; d_1 and d_2 are elementary volumes of particles between which distance is equal r; and β is the London constant:

$$\beta = \frac{3\pi}{2}\, \hbar v_0 \alpha_0^2\,. \qquad (5.33)$$

The integration of equation (5.32) appears as:

$$\mathcal{V}_m = -\frac{\mathcal{A}}{6}\Big(\frac{2a_1a_2}{h^2+2ha_1+2ha_2} + \frac{2a_1a_2}{h^2+2ha_1+2ha_2+2a_1a_2} +$$

$$+\ln\frac{h^2+2ha_1+2ha_2}{h^2+2ha_1+2ha_2+2a_1a_2}), \quad (5.34)$$

where $\mathcal{A}=\beta\pi^2 q_r^2$ is the Van der Waals–Gamaker's Constant; and h is the shortest distance between particles' surfaces.

For spherical particles of identical radiuses $(a_1=a_2)$, the equation (5.34) looks like this:

$$\mathcal{V}_m=-\frac{\mathcal{A}}{6}\left(\frac{2a^2}{h^2+4ah}+\frac{2a^2}{h^2+4ah+2a^2}+\ln\frac{h^2+4ah}{h^2+4ah+2a^2}\right). \quad (5.35)$$

If the radius of particles considerably exceeds the distance between them $a \gg h$, it is possible there is a further simplification of formula (5.35).:

$$\mathcal{V}_m=-\frac{\mathcal{A}a}{12h}\ . \quad (5.36)$$

5.8. PLANE-PARALLEL PLATES

The equation for the molecular interaction referred to as the unit of area of two infinite plane–parallel plates by thickness δ, was offered by [189]:

$$\mathcal{V}_m=-\frac{\mathcal{A}}{48\pi}\left[\frac{1}{(\frac{h}{2})^2}+\frac{1}{(\frac{h}{2}+\delta)^2}+\frac{2}{(\frac{a}{2}+\frac{\delta}{2})^2}\right]. \quad (5.37)$$

Let us consider thick plates when $\delta \gg h$:

$$\mathcal{V}_m=-\frac{\mathcal{A}}{12\pi h^2}. \quad (5.38)$$

The force of a molecular attraction is:

$$\mathcal{P}_m=\frac{d\mathcal{V}_m}{dh}=\frac{\mathcal{A}}{6\pi h^3}\ .$$

If the distance between plates is significantly greater than their thickness ($\delta \ll h$), then we get:

$$\mathcal{V}_m = -\frac{\mathcal{A}\delta^2}{2\pi h^4}. \qquad (5.39)$$

It should be noted that the equations for plane-parallel plates and for spherical particles relate to interaction in a vacuum and are applicable only for small distances at which the influence of electromagnetic delay can be neglected.

5.9. PHYSICOCHEMICAL DYNAMICS OF BUBBLE FORMATION

As noted earlier, in the formation of dispersion systems, processes associated with the occurrence of interphase interaction take a special place. The magnitude of the interaction among the individual elements of dispersion systems is determined by the intensity of the fields of external forces and internal forces, including the fields of the chemical potential and their thermodynamic characteristics. Because the results of this interaction are manifested on phase interfaces, it is the molecular–surface forces that determine the dynamics of the emergence, development, and rupture of vapor–gas bubbles, which are an integral part of the process under consideration in most cases.

From the standpoint of formal logic, it is fair to assume, as a result of interphase interaction during the formation of dispersion systems, zones arise in the elementary volumes of the liquid phase in which the relative pressure $\mathcal{P}/\mathcal{P}_S \leq 1$. In this case, because of the diffusion of the molecules of the dissolved gas, vapor–gas bubbles form in these volumes of the liquid phase, which is accompanied by the formation of capillary menisci. Under the condition in which the partial pressure of the liquid vapor at the meniscus at temperature is $T\,(\mathcal{P}_M > \mathcal{P}_0)$, and under the action of pressure gradients, the motion of the dispersion medium layer begins, accompanied by a change in the size of the thickness of the dispersion layer. It should be noted that because of the acceleration of diffusion of the dissolved gas, an increase in the size of the bubbles occurs. At the same time, the process of liquid evaporation into the internal volumes of the bubbles is accelerated, that is leading to their further increase.

Note: $\mathcal{P}_M$ is the partial pressure of the liquid vapor at the meniscus at temperature T, and $\mathcal{P}_S$ is the partial pressure of the liquid vapor at the mouth of the capillary at temperature T.

Thus, during the evaporation of a liquid from a single capillary into a bubble, the mass of the substance is transferred by the mutual diffusion of liquid and gas vapors. At a constant pressure of the vapor–gas mixture $\mathcal{P}_{Bar}$, the vapor diffuses from the meniscus surface into the bubble under the influence of the relative vapor concentration gradient $\nabla \rho_{Vap}$, and the gas (air) diffuses to the surface of the liquid phase under the influence of the relative gas (air) concentration gradient $\nabla \rho_{Air}$. Under these conditions, the vapor stream consists of diffusion, convective flows, and the vapor flow density, or otherwise, the rate of evaporation from the menisci is determined by the Stefan equation [190]:

$$\mathcal{J}^{t}_{\text{диф}} = \frac{\mathcal{D}\mathcal{M}}{\mathcal{R}\mathcal{T}} \frac{1}{1-\rho_{\text{отн}}} \frac{d\mathcal{P}}{dx}, \tag{5.40}$$

where $\mathcal{M}$ is the molecular weight of liquid ($\mathcal{M}$ of water = 18); and $\mathcal{D}$ is the coefficient of mutual diffusion of vapor in air, [m/s²]:

$$\mathcal{D} = \mathcal{D}_0 \left(\frac{\mathcal{T}_i}{273.15}\right)^{1.8} \left(\frac{\mathcal{P}}{Bar}\right), \tag{5.41}$$

where $\mathcal{D}_0$ is the coefficient of mutual diffusion of steam flow through air ($\mathcal{D}_0 = 0.216$ m/s² at 273.15 ⁰K and $\mathcal{P}_{Bar} = 760$ Torr); $\mathcal{P}_{Bar}$ is the barometric pressure, [N/m²]; $\mathcal{T}$ is the ambient temperature, [⁰K]; $\mathcal{P}$ is the partial pressure of vapors, [Pascal = N/m²]; ρ_{rel} is the relative partial vapor pressure; $\mathcal{R} = 8{,}314.67$ is the gas constant, [J/Kmole 1⁰K]; x is the coordinate in the direction of vapors flow through liquid, [m]; and $\frac{1}{1-\rho_{rel}}$ is the factor characterizing the contribution of a convective flow.

The main reason for the deviation from the diffusion theory of the experimental results obtained by various researchers in studying the processes of mass transfer from capillaries to an atmosphere saturated with the vapor of the studied liquid is most likely the additional liquid flow in the adsorption film on the walls of the capillary [191–197]. The solution to this problem was obtained in the linear approximation under the assumption that in any section of the capillary the liquid layer is in thermodynamic equilibrium with the vapor from this liquid. The total flow from a cylindrical capillary of radius r is determined from the equation:

$$Q = \frac{\pi r^2 \mathcal{D}\,(\mathcal{P}_Б - \mathcal{P})}{\mathcal{R}\,\mathcal{T}\ell} + \frac{2\pi r}{3\mathcal{U}_m \mu \ell}\int_{\Pi_M}^{\Pi_0} \theta^3\, d\Pi, \quad (5.42)$$

where μ is the viscosity of the liquid forming the dispersion environment, [N s/m²]; $\mathcal{U}_m$ is the molar volume, [m/kg²]; Π is the proppant pressure (Π_M at a meniscus, Π_0 at the mouth of a capillary slit) films of liquid, [H/m²]; ℓ is the distance from the mouth of a capillary to the meniscus, [m]; $\theta = \sqrt[3]{A/\Pi}$ is the layer thickness on the walls of a capillary, [m]; and A = = 4.9×10^{-19} [J] is the constant of an isotherm of the wedging pressure.

The solutions for equation (5.42) depend on the nature of forces influencing the wedging pressure in a liquid layer as provided in works [193, 198]. From (5.42), it follows that the linear speed of a total flow in a capillary $\mathcal{U}_S$ is equal to:

$$\mathcal{U}_S = \frac{Q\,\mathcal{U}_m \ell}{\pi r^2} = \mathcal{U}_{Dif} + \mathcal{U}_{Film}. \quad (5.43)$$

At the same time, according to the diffusive theory the linear speed of the total flow in a capillary $\mathcal{U}_{Dif}$ is equal to:

$$\mathcal{U}_{Dif} = \frac{\mathcal{DMP}_{Bar}}{\mathcal{RT}\ell} \ln \frac{\mathcal{P}_{Bar} - \mathcal{P}}{\mathcal{P}_{Bar} - \mathcal{P}_S} \quad , \tag{5.44}$$

and the speed of a liquid flow $\mathcal{U}_L$, is:

$$\mathcal{U}_L = \frac{2}{3\mu r} \int_{\Pi_M}^{\Pi_0} \theta^3 \mathrm{d}\Pi, \tag{5.45}$$

where $\Pi_M = \frac{\sigma}{r}$ and $\Pi_0 = \frac{\mathcal{RT}}{\mathcal{U}_m} \ln \frac{\mathcal{P}_S}{\mathcal{P}}$ (5.46)

If the wedging pressure is defined by forces of intermolecular interaction, then the dependence of the wedging pressure on the thickness of a layer is expressed by a formula [198]:

$$\Pi_{\mathrm{I}} = \frac{\mathrm{A}_{\mathrm{I}}}{\theta_{\mathrm{I}}^{3}}, \tag{5.47}$$

and the solution for equation (5.43) looks like:

$$\mathcal{U}_L = \frac{3}{2} \frac{\mathrm{A}_{\mathrm{I}}}{\mu r} \ln \frac{\Pi_0}{\Pi_M} \quad . \tag{5.48}$$

If the wedging pressure is caused by the effect of repulsion of atmospheric ions, the dependence of the wedging pressure on the thickness of the liquid layer has the form [199]:

$$\Pi_{\mathrm{II}} = \frac{\mathrm{A}_{\mathrm{II}}}{\theta_{\mathrm{II}}^{2}}, \tag{5.49}$$

and the equation (5.43) seek a decision in the form of [199]:

$$\mathcal{U}_L = \frac{3}{4}\frac{\sqrt{A_{II}^{\ 2}}}{\mu r}\left(\Pi_0^{-1/2} - \Pi_M^{-1/2}\right). \tag{5.50}$$

When the wedging pressure is caused by the combined action of ion–electrostatic and molecular forces, the solution for equation (5.43) has this appearance:

$$\mathcal{U}_L = \frac{3}{2\mu r}\left[2A_{II}(\theta_I - \theta_{II}) + 3A_I \ln\frac{\theta_I}{\theta_{II}}\right]. \tag{5.51}$$

The quantitative component of the film's flow and diffusive stream for a case when the proppant pressure $\Pi = \frac{-A}{6\pi\theta^3}$ was under various conditions of a mass transfer, were calculated in work [197].

Such excited conditions of a dispersion system can be considered from the perspective of a single bubble development. For this purpose, it is necessary to carry out an analysis of the forces operating on the bubble, which arose during the formation of dispersion systems.

5.10. RESEARCH ON THE FORMATION OF DISPERSION SYSTEMS IN THE MODEL OF A VAPOR-GAS BUBBLE

The most common model of dispersion systems is a system composed of spherical particles that are elements of a dispersed phase. If we imagine that a spherical particle acts as a gas bubble, then such a model can be used to study cavitation processes, the process of bubble formation during boiling, and also to study the formation of dispersion systems by the method of resonance turbulence. Obviously, in the places where spherical particles come into contact when fluid (as a dispersion medium) enters or moves off, its accumulations coalesce in the form of biconcave lenses. In relation to the task posed, it is logically justifiable to replace ordinary spherical elements with flat plates [1, 199], that is, with spheres whose radius tends to infinity. The Laplace pressure that develops in such a lens when ($cos\,\theta = 1$) is equal to:

$$\mathcal{P}_\ell = 2\sigma\mathcal{H}, \qquad (5.52)$$

where $\mathcal{H} = \frac{1}{2}(\frac{1}{r_1} + \frac{1}{r_2})$ is the average curvature of a surface of a lens; and r_1 and r_2 are radiuses of convex and concave surfaces.

Let us consider a model cell formed by two plates (Fig. 5–2). A drop of liquid is sandwiched between two plane-parallel plates, and wetting them forms a three–dimensional figure, in which the side surface is the surface of rotation of a circle around a vertical axis passing through the center of the vertical projection of the drop. Such a figure is called a catenoid (Fig. 5–3). It is known that the catenoid is a surface having a minimum area among all surfaces of rotation of the arcs of lines connecting two given points of the plane.

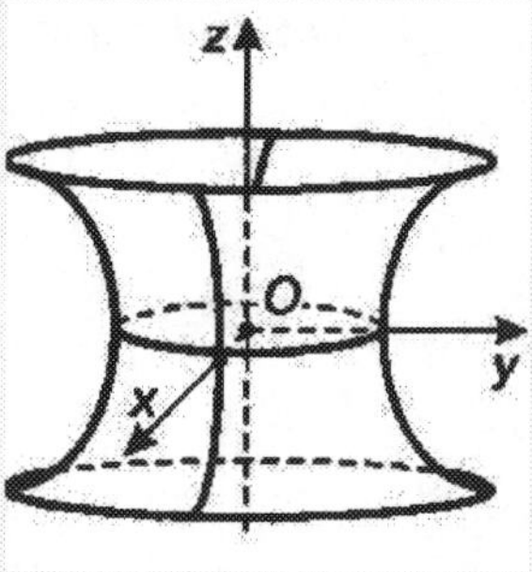

Figure 5-3. Schematic Image of a Catenoid [1]

The internal volume of a catenoid $\mathcal{V}_{Cat}$, which is limited to the side surface of rotation of the sphere and the parallel planes is determined by the formula [169]:

$$\mathcal{V}_{Cat} = \pi \int_0^x y^2\, dx = \frac{\pi a^2}{2}(x + a\, sh\frac{x}{a}\, ch\frac{x}{a}), \qquad (5.53)$$

where x is the distance between parallel planes.

The area of a side surface of a catenoid $\mathcal{S}_{Cat}$ can be calculated by a formula [35]:

$$\mathcal{S}_{Cat} = 2\pi \int_0^{\hbar} y\sqrt{1 + y^2}\, dx = \pi a \left(x + a\, sh\frac{x}{a}\, ch\frac{x}{a}\right), \quad (5.54)$$

where sh is the hyperbolic sine; and ch is the hyperbolic cosine.

It is easy to see that the ratio between the volume $\mathcal{V}_{Cat}$ and the area of a side surface of a catenoid $\mathcal{S}_{Cat}$, is equal to:

$$\mathcal{V}_{Cat} = \frac{a}{2}\mathcal{S}_{Cat}\,.$$

Thus, using one's imagination, one can imagine a drop of liquid as some elementary volume of a dispersion medium, and the surface of rotation of a catenoid can be represented by two imaginary (spherical in shape) elements of the dispersed phase—a gas bubble or a particle of solid matter.

Let us designate the diameter of the horizontal projection of the droplet $\mathcal{D}_D$, and the distance between the plates h (Fig. 5–2). Let us also denote the curves along which the plane passing through the axis of rotation OY intersects with the droplet surface ABC and EFG as the diameter of the smallest horizontal section of the clamped droplet. If the distance between the plates is substantially small ($h \ll D$), then the analytical solution for determining the curvature of the free surface of the dispersion medium is the following [170]:

$$\left(u - \frac{\mathcal{D}_D}{2}\right)^2 + z^2 = \frac{\hbar}{2}\left(u - \frac{\mathcal{D}_D}{2}\right). \quad (5.55)$$

It follows from expression (5.55) that ABC and EFG are circle arches. If the distance between plates is relatively large, then $\hbar$ and $\mathcal{D}_D$ are quantities of the same order. Then the curvature of a surface is defined by this equation [200]:

$$z = \frac{\mathcal{D}_D}{2} \ell g \frac{2u - \sqrt{u^2 - \frac{\mathcal{D}_D}{2}}}{\mathcal{D}}, \tag{5.56}$$

The radiuses of curvature of a free surface of the liquid with sufficient degree of accuracy could be considered equal $\frac{h}{2}$ and $-\frac{\mathcal{D}_D}{2}$. At the same time internal pressure is developing in the dispersive environment that is different from the atmospheric pressure on $2\sigma\,(\frac{1}{h} - \frac{1}{\mathcal{D}_K})$. If plates form a plane–parallel capillary slit, the capillary pressure is equal to:

$$\mathcal{P}_\ell = 2\sigma\,(\frac{1}{h} - \frac{1}{\mathcal{D}_D}). \tag{5.57}$$

Thus, as objects of theoretical analysis is the spherical element of the dispersed phase and its model: the artificial capillary cell formed by two parallel plates—are equivalent [1]. Moreover, the phenomena occurring in a dispersion medium (representing the liquid layer) sandwiched among two parallel plates and imaginary spherical elements of a dispersed phase (impregnated gas bubbles or particle of solid matter or drops of liquid that is immiscible and insoluble with a dispersive medium) are similar, because the relative physical the quantities assigned to similar points of the systems under consideration are the same, and the functional relationships between the individual physical quantities that characterize the process they are identical [1].

The idea of the creation a model of a capillary slit, that I proposed and implemented in the design of the original device [1, 202–210].

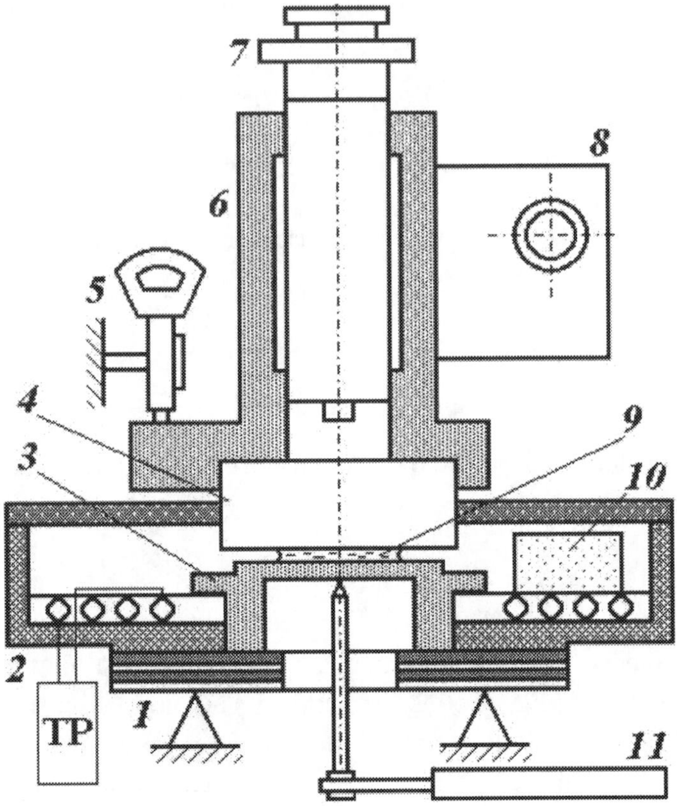

Figure 5-4. The Diagram of the Device for a Research Mechanism for Formation of Dispersion Systems [1]

The device (Fig. 5–4) was installed on a vibration–resistant granite slab, 1, with a thickness of 1.5×10^{-2} meters. It consisted of a sealed chamber, 2, with a heat regulator TP, a measuring microscope, glass plates, 3, and, 4, the mating surfaces that formed a dihedral angle of 10^0 24'. The plate, 4, was attached to the tube of the microscope, 6. The tube was moved in the direction perpendicular to the surface of the plates using the mechanism, 7, to set the required gap between the plates. The width of the gap was measured with a micrometer, 8, with a scale division of 1x 10^{-7} meters. The plate, 3, was rigidly fixed around the perimeter of a thin round membrane and was installed in chamber, 2. The degree of accuracy of a given temperature maintained in the chamber was 0.5 °C. The relative humidity in the chamber was established and maintained with saturated salt solutions placed in the cell, 10.

The pressure arising in the capillary cell caused deformation of the membrane, 3. The membrane, with a thickness of $170 \pm 1x10^{-6}$ m and $15 \pm 1x10^{-3}$ m in diameter, was made of pure quartz glass. The modulus of the elasticity of this glass was 6.65×10^{10} N/m^2 and Poisson's ratio 0.22. The nondeformable plate 4 with a thickness of 40×10^{-3} m was also made of the pure quartz glass. The non-flatness of the surface of the plate in contact with the membrane did not exceed 7×10^{-8} m.

The deflection of the membrane was measured by an electronic displacement sensor, 10, [1, 202-210]. The main element of the sensor was an electronic triode 6MX3S. The triode current changed with the mechanical movement of the measuring probe, rigidly connected to the control grid of the triode located between the anode and cathode. The other end of the probe touched the bottom surface of the membrane. The triode current was measured using a bridge circuit. Preliminary balancing of the bridge was carried out using a micro–ampermeter M 266M. For accurate balancing, a decade-long resistance store R-33 with an adjustment of 0.1 Ohm was connected to one shoulder of the bridge. The deflection of the membrane is counted by the M 195/1 null-galvanometer with a division value of 9.2×10^{-9} A/division. The power sources of the measuring circuit and the incandescent circuits of an electronic triode "mechanotron" were galvanic cells with a constant voltage of 12 volts.

When considering the standard static characteristics of movements of the electronic triode "mechanotron" of the MX3C type, it was found that the sensitivity of the triode is not the same over the entire range of measured movements. The maximum sensitivity was range from $40x10^{-6}$ m to $80x10^{-6}$ m. Therefore, the sensor was set so that the reference point was at a range around $60x10^{-6}$ m, and provided that the measured deflection of the membrane did not exceed $10x10^{-6}$ m, it was possible to achieve the maximum sensitivity of the sensor to the deflection of the membrane and to take measurements on a near-linear section of the standard static characteristic.

During preliminary calibration of the device, the sensitivity of the sensor to movements on the current was over 100 mkA per $1x10^{-6}$ m. The membrane's deformation was measured in a point of the membrane coinciding with the center, with a deviation of $\pm$ 0,066 x 10^{-3} m.

The Laplace pressure, developing in the compressed drop of the liquid placed in the center of the membrane, was defined while taking into account that the capillary force causing a membrane deflection was evenly distributed on a circular surface whose diameter was less than the diameter of the membrane and whose center did not coincide with the center of the membrane. The quantity of the pressure was calculated using formulas [211] generally used to determine the pressure on the elastic surface of round plates with rigidly fixed edges which are under the influence of asymmetrical circular loadings. These formulas were simplified [166] in relation to the considered task.

When the center of a membrane is blocked by a drop spot, the capillary pressure is equal to [1]:

$$\mathcal{P}_\ell = \frac{32\frac{E\delta^3}{3\,(1-\mu^2)\mathcal{D}_K{}^2}\,\mathscr{f}(0,0)}{\left(2c^2+\frac{\mathcal{D}_K{}^2}{4}\right)\ell n\frac{\mathcal{D}_m^2}{4c^2}+\frac{\mathcal{D}_m^2}{2}+\frac{2c^2}{\mathcal{D}_K{}^2}+2c^2}, \qquad (5.58)$$

When the center of a membrane is NOT blocked by a drop spot, the capillary pressure is equal to the following [1]:

$$\mathcal{P}_\ell = \frac{32\frac{E\delta^3}{3\,(1-\mu^2)\mathcal{D}_K{}^2}\,\mathscr{f}(0,0)}{\left(2c^2+\frac{\mathcal{D}_K{}^2}{4}\right)\ell n\frac{\mathcal{D}_m^2}{4c^2}+\frac{\mathcal{D}_m^2}{2}+\frac{2c^2}{\mathcal{D}_K{}^2}-\frac{5}{8}\mathcal{D}_K{}^2}, \qquad (5.59)$$

where E is the modulus of longitudinal elasticity of the membrane material, [N/m^2]; μ is the Poisson's coefficient of the membrane material, [m/m]; δ is the membrane thickness, [m]; $\mathcal{D}_m$ is the membrane diameter, [m]; c is the eccentricity of the center of a drop of liquid near the center of the membrane, [m]; $\mathcal{D}_K$ is the diameter of a horizontal projection of a drop, [m]; and $f_{(0,0)}$ is the deflection of the center of the membrane, [m]. The diameter of a horizontal projection of a drop $\mathcal{D}_K$ and the eccentricity of the center of a drop near the center of a membrane c were measured by optically transparent nondeformable plate, 4, installed in a microscope tube, 6, for an optical reading and measuring microscope with the ability of dividing the eyepiece scale with an accuracy of $\pm$ 0.066x10^{-3} m.

The subject device makes it possible to study processes for the formation of dispersion systems; as well as of sorption and adsorption; to measure the interaction of the capillary and superficial forces and forces of elastic resistance to compression arising between the elements of a dispersed phase divided by layers of the dispersion medium; to investigate directly in a capillary step layer; and to define the coefficient of the superficial tension of various liquids, all fusions of metals and alloys [167] in isometric conditions.

5.11. RESEARCH ON THE CAPILLARY-SURFACE PHENOMENA

As it was repeatedly noted in the previous sections, the mode of torsion-oriented turbulization is characterized by the emergence, development, and a rupture of bubbles of gas. The size of the bubbles significantly depends on dynamics of a condition of the steam-gas (or vapor-gas) mix in a bubble in which intensively there is a mass transfer of steam to the dispersive environment that is mixed up with the gas volume of the dispersed phase [1].

For ease of research, most experiments were carried out using water, glycerin, acetone, gasoline, and ethyl alcohol. In the experiments degassed distilled water of double distillation (pH 6.5) was used. The first distillation was carried out using laboratory apparatus, and the second distillation was done using quartz chemical glassware. The oxidation of organics in a boiling distillate was carried out with potassium permanganate salts $KMnO_4$.

The relative humidity of air φ in the hermetic chamber was maintained via saturated solutions of silica gel and salts: $Na_2SO_4 \cdot 10H_2O$, KBr, $(NH_4)_2SO_4$, and $CaCl_2 \cdot 6H_2O$ were used. Thus, the vapor–gas mixture inside the bubble was simulated. The relative humidity was estimated from dry and wet thermometers with a division value of 0.1 ^0C installed in a thermostat/hygrostat chamber.

The thermal and humidity conditions established inside the chamber were characterized by a certain evaporation rate from the surface of the dispersion medium into the gas bubble $\mathcal{J}_0$. The evaporation rate was estimated from the change in the volume of the liquid $\varrho_0 \Delta V$, referred to the evaporation surface S during the time Δt. A quartz cuvette with a depth of $5 \pm 0.01 x 10^{-3}$ m and a diameter of $19 \pm 0.01 x 10^{-3}$ m was used to determine the intensity of evaporation from the free surface of the liquid. A cuvette with the test liquid was placed in the chamber. After establishing the required stationary thermal and humidity conditions in the chamber, the cuvette was weighed every 30 minutes on a microanalytical balance with a division price of 0.1 mg and with a reading accuracy of 0.05 mg. Previously published results [1, 202-210] provides data on studies of the evaporation rate from the free surface of the liquid $\mathcal{J}_0$, depending on the relative humidity φ and air temperature T.

Before starting the experiments, the surfaces of the plates forming the model were treated with an organic solvent (96% ethanol) and dried. Then, they were treated with an acid solution (pH: 3.5) and washed with a double distillate (pH: 6.5), followed by an alkaline solution (pH: 9.0) they were then washed with the same double distillate for 10 minutes.

In addition, before each test the thermostat was turned on and the required temperature mode was set. Then the surfaces of the plates were wiped several times with the surgical cotton wool that was moistened in ethyl alcohol. After drying, a drop of the studied liquid was applied to the surface of the membrane.

To draw a drop of liquid, the following steps were executed. The mobile plate, 4, (Fig. 5–4) was placed in the upper position. The surface of a membrane was carefully washed out with organic solvent (96% ethanol). Using a 1–ml syringe with a hypodermic needle, the required volume of the tested liquid was placed on the middle of the membrane. Then, moving down the plate, 4, and crushing a drop, the distance between plates was established. As it was noted, the distance between plates was measured using a "mikrokator", 5.

In all experiments the initial diameter of a horizontal projection of the squashed drop of liquid varied from 5 to 6.5 mm. The drop was placed so that the center of the membrane was definitely blocked by this drop therefore the size of Laplace pressure was determined by a formula (4.58). After filling the gap to establish the required humidity level, a cell with certain saturated salt solutions was installed in the chamber. All subsequent measurements were carried out at regular intervals. As calculations and preliminary experiments [1, 202-210] showed, the deflection of the membrane, depending on its size and the physico–mechanical properties of the material, did not exceed the units of a micrometer. Therefore, a change in the curvature of the membrane could be neglected.

The relative error $\xi = \frac{\Delta \mathcal{P}_\ell}{\mathcal{P}_\ell}$ of the detected capillary pressure $\mathcal{P}_\ell$ was defined by addition of private errors of indirect measurements [212, 213]:

$$\xi = \sqrt{\Upsilon^2 + \Psi^2},$$

where the following was true:

$$\Upsilon = \left(\frac{\Delta E}{E}\right)^2 + \left(\frac{3\Delta\delta}{\delta}\right)^2 + \left(\frac{2\Delta\mathcal{D}_K}{\mathcal{D}_K}\right)^2 + \left(\frac{2(1-\mu^2)\Delta\mu}{\mu}\right)^2 + \left(\frac{\Delta f_{(0,0)}}{f_{(0,0)}}\right)^2.$$

$$\Psi = \left[\frac{Q\ell n\frac{\mathcal{D}_m^2}{4c^2} + \left(2c^2 + \frac{\mathcal{D}_K{}^2}{4}\right)\frac{2(c\mathcal{D}_m + \mathcal{D}_m\Delta c)}{c\mathcal{D}_m} + \mathcal{D}_m\Delta\mathcal{D}_m + 4c\Delta c}{\left(2c^2 + \frac{\mathcal{D}_K{}^2}{4}\right)\ell n\frac{\mathcal{D}_m^2}{4c^2} + \frac{\mathcal{D}_m^2}{2} + \frac{2c^2}{\mathcal{D}_K{}^2} + 2c^2}\right]^2.$$

$$Q = \left(4c\Delta c + \frac{\mathcal{D}_K\Delta\mathcal{D}_K}{2}\right).$$

By the substituting extreme quantities in a formula of a relative error ξ the, there are:

$$\frac{\Delta E}{E} = 1 \times 10^{-3};\ \frac{\Delta\mu}{\mu} = 1 \times 10^{-3};\ \mu = 22 \times 10^{-2};\ \mathcal{D}_K = 6{,}5 \times 10^{-3};$$

$$\Delta\mathcal{D}_K = 6{,}5 \times 10^{-6};\ c = 3 \times 10^{-3};\ \Delta c = 3 \times 10^{-6};\ \mathcal{D}_m = 15 \times 10^{-3};$$

$$\Delta\mathcal{D}_m = 0{,}01 \times 10^{-3};\ \delta = 170 \times 10^{-6};\ \Delta\delta = 1 \times 10^{-6};$$

$$f_{(0,0)} = 10 \times 10^{-6};\ \Delta f_{(0,0)} = 0{,}1 \times 10^{-6}.$$

The calculation shows that a relative error did not exceed 3,7% [1].

For determination of the minimum necessary experiment's repetitions, special experiments were conducted with conditions in the chamber at a temperature of 20 ^{0}C and a relative humidity of 93.0% [1].

After establishment of stationary conditions in the thermal-hygrostat, 16, measurements of controlled tests were taken consistently. The results of the measurements and processing of the data obtained are presented in Table 5.1, [1].

During statistical processing of measurement results of the capillary pressure $\mathcal{P}_\ell$, the pressure was defined as:

1. An arithmetic average value of the measured size:

$$\overline{\mathcal{P}_\ell} = \sum_1^n \frac{1}{n}\,(\mathcal{P}_\ell)_i, \text{ at: } \overline{\mathcal{P}_\ell} = 664{,}00 \text{ N/m}^2;$$

where n is the number of measurements.

2. The deviation from average quantity: $(\Delta\mathcal{P}_\ell)_i = \overline{\mathcal{P}_\ell} - (\mathcal{P}_\ell)_i$.
3. The square of the deviations from the average quantity: $(\Delta\mathcal{P}_\ell)_i^2$.
4. The average square error Z_n of each separate measurement is:

$$Z_n = \sqrt{\frac{1}{n-1}\sum_1^n(\Delta\mathcal{P}_\ell)_i^2}, \quad (Z_n = 1{,}245)$$

Table 5–1 [1]

##	$\mathcal{D}_K$	c	$f_{(0,0)}$	$\mathcal{P}_\ell$	$\Delta\mathcal{P}_\ell$	$(\Delta\mathcal{P}_\ell)^2$
1	5.93	2.26	0.91	663.93	0.07	0.005
2	5.89	2.29	0.9	662.22	1.78	3.168
3	5.93	2.26	0.9	663.91	0.08	0.006
4	5.89	2.26	0.91	663.94	0.56	0.314
5	5.93	2.23	0.91	666.01	2.01	4.04
6	5.89	2.26	0.9	663.95	0.07	0.049
7	5.93	2.23	0.91	666.06	2.01	4.04
8	5.93	2.23	0.91	663.93	0.07	0.049
9	5.93	2.26	0.91	663.97	0.08	0.064
10	5.89	2.29	0.9	662.22	1.78	3.168
11	5.96	2.29	0.92	664.23	0.23	0.053
12	5.93	2.26	0.91	663.93	0.07	0.049
13	5.93	2.26	0.91	664.23	0.23	0.053
14	5.93	2.23	0.92	666.01	2.02	4.08
15	5.96	2.26	0.91	663.93	0.08	0.064
16	5.89	2.29	0.9	662.22	1.78	3.168

5. The average square error of an arithmetic average for all n measurements:

$$Z = \frac{Z_n}{\sqrt{n}}, \quad (Z = 0{,}31125)$$

According to the theory of mistakes [213], the quantity of $\mathcal{P}_\ell$ with reliability is in a confidential interval, that is:

$$\overline{\mathcal{P}_\ell} - \Delta \leq \mathcal{P}_\ell \leq \overline{\mathcal{P}_\ell} + \Delta .$$

The size of a confidential interval is: $\Delta = Z \cdot t_{\propto,n,}$, where $t_{\propto,n,}$ is the Student coefficient [213]. At confidential probability $\propto = 0.7$, the size of a confidential interval is $\Delta = 1.1Z$, quite acceptable for those experiments. From the ratio $\xi = \frac{\Delta}{Z_n}$ and in accordance to the table presented by [212, 213], the minimum necessary number of repetitions of each experiment for receiving a random error ξ with reliability $\propto = 0{,}7$ is equal to six (6). All results of further measurements required in average of 6 repetitions of each test.

For Fig. 5–5 the dependences of capillary pressure on the gap width was received by tests and in the following formula:

$$\mathcal{P}_\ell = 2\sigma \left(\frac{1}{h} - \frac{1}{\mathcal{D}_K}\right) + \rho_{\mathcal{D}_K} q h ,$$

It follows from these results that at $h \leq 100 \times 10^{-6}$ m, the Laplace pressure is defined by calculations and by physical tests that coincide with an accuracy within the limits of error. However, at $h \geq 100 \times 10^{-6}$ m the divergence of experimental results with theoretical expectations was observed.

To explain these discrepancies in the course of research [1], photographs were taken of the profiles of a double distillate water drop clamped in a capillary slit. The image scale was 120:1. In the photographs taken [1], for the slit width $h = 500 \times 10^{-6}$ m, the "subsidence" of the droplet was clearly visible, while in the photographs taken for the slit width equal to 100×10^{-6} m, the "subsidence" of the drop was not so obvious. Thus, with an increase in the width of the slit, the role of the gravitational component increases significantly. The change of curvature of the free surface of the liquid reflects the difference between the pressure acting on the side of the concave surface and that operating on the side of the convex surface. That is Laplace pressure. In this case, the diameter of the wet spot on the membrane surface increases, while on the opposite side of the slit, the diameter of the spot decreases. Because the pressure $\mathcal{P}_\ell$ determined by the formula (4.58), depends on the square of the diameter of the liquid spot, even small changes in the acting forces lead to significant differences in theoretical and experimental results at $\hbar \geq 100 \times 10^{-6}$ m.

5.12. ANALYSIS OF FORCES ACTING ON THE SURFACE OF GAS BUBBLES DURING FORMATION OF DISPERSION SYSTEMS

As discussed in the previous sections, a necessary condition for the formation and very existence of a gas–liquid dispersion system is the appearance and cumulative development (compression and collapse) of gas bubbles, leading to the development of internal pressure and temperature fields. It is quite obvious that a condition for the emergence of a dispersed system is a change in the state of the vibrational force field,

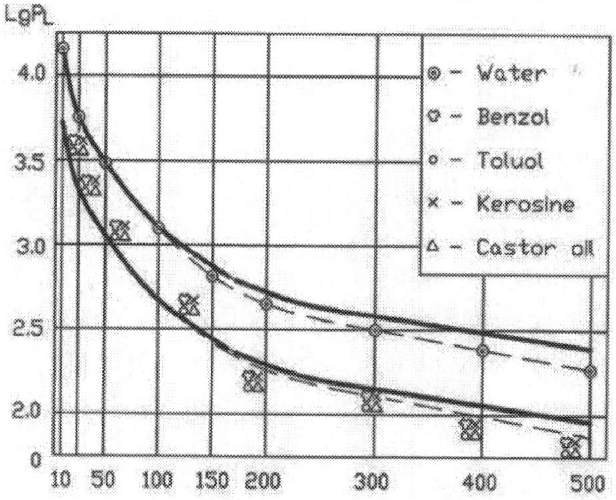

Figure 5-5. Dependence of capillary pressure on the width of the slit gap [1, 208-210]

which, on the one hand, causes mechanical resonance, and, on the other hand, provokes the appearance of a primary shock wave. Under the action of a force field, the components of a dispersed system can begin to do work.

This means that dispersed systems have a certain amount of energy. Therefore, to determine the state of a dispersion system, it is necessary to determine the functional relationships among the various energy fields acting on the system and inside the system.

It is known that force fields are classified as scalar or vector. An example of a scalar field, in this case, is the closed reactor's space in which the components of the forming dispersion system are located—the dispersed phase and the dispersion medium. An example of a vector field is the gravitational and vibrational components of external disturbing forces.

To consider the dynamic processes occurring in dispersion systems at the phase boundary—if we understand a dispersion system to be a set of material points that continuously fill a certain space, between which there are internal forces: intermolecular interaction and external forces as well as surface tension (molecular surface forces). Obviously, the accepted initial conditions do not contradict the generally accepted ones but open up the possibility of creating a mathematical model to elucidate the mechanism of interaction among the individual elementary volumes (material points) of a given dispersed system, the medium under study, and the vibrating device.

Let us return to the definition of a condition under which a dispersion system can be considered as a certain set of material points, the mechanical bonds of which can be reduced only to geometric, or otherwise, to holonomic bonds [1], that is, to those that come down only to restrictions on the possible spatial positions of material points of this system. The equilibrium state for any point included in the adopted system and subordinate to k holonomic stationary bonds is [1]:

$$f_j(x_1, y_1, z_1, x_2, y_2, z_3, \ldots x_n, y_n, z_n, t) = 0, \quad (j = 1, 2, 3, \ldots, k), \qquad (5.60)$$

where: x_i, y_i, z_i are coordinates; t is the time; and k is the number of the imposed bonds, which for any timepoints are defined by this condition [1]:

$$\sum_i^n \overrightarrow{\mathfrak{F}}_i \delta \mathfrak{r}_i + \sum_i^n \overrightarrow{\mathfrak{R}}_i \delta \mathfrak{r}_i = 0\,, \qquad (5.61)$$

where i is the point number; $\overrightarrow{\mathfrak{F}}_{\mathrm{i}}$ is the vector resultant of all active forces closer to point number i; $\overrightarrow{\mathfrak{R}}_{\mathrm{i}}$ is the vector resultant from all internal forces closer to point number i; and $\delta\mathfrak{r} = \delta x_{\mathrm{i}} + \delta y_{\mathrm{i}} + \delta z_{\mathrm{i}}$ is the vector virtual relocation of the point number i.

The condition (5.61) can be written down as:

$$\sum_{\mathrm{i}}^{\mathrm{n}}(Fx_{\mathrm{i}}\,\delta x_{\mathrm{i}} + Fy_{\mathrm{i}}\delta y_{\mathrm{i}} + Fz_{\mathrm{i}}\delta z_{\mathrm{i}}) +$$

$$+ \sum_{\mathrm{i}}^{\mathrm{n}}(Rx_{\mathrm{i}}\,\delta x_{\mathrm{i}} + Ry_{\mathrm{i}}\delta y_{\mathrm{i}} + Rz_{\mathrm{i}}\delta z_{\mathrm{i}}) = 0, \qquad (5.62)$$

where Fx_i, Fy_i, Fz_I and Rx_i, Ry_i, Rz_i are projections of active and internal forces to axes of coordinates.

It should be noted that variations of coordinates δx δy, δz are a result of definition [1], by which virtual relocation of points of the dispersion system are subordinated to kind of k-bonds (5.60), are a set of infinitesimal vectors:

$$\delta\vec{r} = \delta\mathfrak{x}\cdot i + \delta\mathfrak{y}\cdot j + \delta\mathfrak{z}\cdot k,$$

whose projections satisfy the system of these equations:

$$\sum_{i}^{\mathrm{n}}\left[\frac{\partial f(j)}{\partial x_{\mathrm{i}}}\delta x_{i} + \frac{\partial f(j)}{\partial y_{\mathrm{i}}}\delta y_{i} + \frac{\partial f(j)}{\partial z_{\mathrm{i}}}\delta z_{i}\right] = 0, \qquad (5.63)$$

where $j = 1, 2, \ldots k$ are also subordinated to k-equations (5.63).

By analogy, as it was done in [1], let us designate the condition (5.62) for the internal points of the disperse system (*index*: ✳), for points of the free surface, or otherwise, the liquid–gas interface (*index*: ★) and points of the contact layer of the dispersion medium with the surface of the gas bubble or with particles of solid matter (*index*: ◊).

All the active forces of the system under consideration are predetermined; therefore, let denote all three sums of these forces with one symbol and sum the results. The result of this summation is the following [1]:

$$\sum_{i}^{n}(Fx_i\delta x_i + Fy_i\delta y_i + Fz_i\delta z_i) +$$

$$+\sum_{i}^{n-m-k}(\mathcal{R}^{*}x_i\delta x_i + \mathcal{R}^{*}y_i\delta y_i + \mathcal{R}^{*}z_i\delta z_i)+$$

$$+\sum_{i}^{k}(\mathcal{R}^{\star}x_i\delta x_i + \mathcal{R}^{\star}y_i\delta y_i + \mathcal{R}^{\star}z_i\delta z_i) +$$

$$+\sum_{i}^{m}(\mathcal{R}^{\diamond}x_i\delta x_i + \mathcal{R}^{\diamond}y_i\delta y_i + \mathcal{R}^{\diamond}z_i\delta z_i) = 0, \qquad (5.64)$$

where $n > k$ and $n > m$.

Thus, internal forces $\overrightarrow{\mathfrak{R}}_i$ of the considered dispersion system have potential and, therefore, have a certain power function $U = U(x_i, y_i, z_i)$.

The sum of elementary works of forces $\overrightarrow{\mathfrak{R}}_i$ on any movement of the system will be a full differential of the function U depending upon n points of coordinates of the system. In this case:

$$dU = \sum_{i}^{n}(Rx_i\,\delta x_i + Ry_i\delta y_i + Rz_i\delta z_i),$$

where Rx_i, Ry_i, Rz_i are the projections of forces $\overrightarrow{\mathfrak{R}}_i$ on coordinate axes.

Thus:

$$Rx_i = \frac{\partial U}{\partial x_i};\ Ry_i = \frac{\partial U}{\partial y_i};\ Rz_i = \frac{\partial U}{\partial z_i}.$$

Let us enter a concept of potential energy of the system $E_p = E_p(x_i, y_i, z_i)$, which is defined as the amount of work, that forces of the potential field have to do in order to turn a system from position (x_i, y_i, z_i) into position (x_{i0}, y_{i0}, z_{i0}), chosen randomly. Therefore:

$$E_p\,(x_i, y_i, z_i) = \sum_i^n \int_{(x_i,y_i,z_i)}^{(x_{i0},y_{i0},z_{i0})} (Rx_i + Ry_i\delta y_i + Rz_i\delta z_i)$$

Changing an order of summation and integration there is:

$$E_p\,(x_i, y_i, z_i) = \int_{(x_i,y_i,z_i)}^{(x_{i0},y_{i0},z_{i0})} dU.$$

After integration:

$$E_p\,(x_i, y_i, z_i) = U(x_{i0}, y_{i0}, z_{i0}) - U(x_i, y_i, z_i),$$

where the potential energy E_p, accurate to the additive constant, is equal to the force function U taken with the opposite sign:

$$E_p\,(x_i, y_i, z_i) = -\,U(x_i, y_i, z_i).$$

Writing down the principle of virtual displacements using the potential energy Ep, there is:

$$\sum_i^n (Rx_i\,\delta x_i + Ry_i\delta y_i + Rz_i\delta z_i) =$$
$$= \sum_i^n \left(\frac{\partial U}{\partial x_i}\delta x_i + \frac{\partial U}{\partial y_i}\delta y_i + \frac{\partial U}{\partial z_i}\delta z_i\right) = -\,\delta U = 0\,.$$

Thus, we get this system of the equations:

$$\sum_i^{n-m-k} (\mathcal{R}^* x_i\delta x_i + \mathcal{R}^* y_i\delta y_i + \mathcal{R}^* z_i\delta z_i) = -\,\delta U^*\,;$$

$$\sum_i^k\,(\mathcal{R}^\star x_i\delta x_i + \mathcal{R}^\star y_i\delta y_i + \mathcal{R}^\star z_i\delta z_i) = -\,\delta U^\star; \quad (5.65)$$

$$\sum_{i}^{m} (\mathcal{R}^{\diamond}x_i\delta x_i + \mathcal{R}^{\diamond}y_i\delta y_i + \mathcal{R}^{\diamond}z_i\delta z_i) = -\,\delta U^{\diamond}.$$

The potential U^{*} is the function of mass forces and depends on the density of this dispersion system ρ. Potentials $U^{\star}, U^{\diamond}$and $U^{\diamond}$ are functions of the density of the system $\rho$and blanket thickness of the surface film ϑ on the free surface, or a dispersion layer of the contact with the particle of solid matter, or with the gas bubble. Therefore:

$$U^{*}= U^{*}(\rho^{*}),\;\; U^{\star}=U^{\star}(\rho^{\star},\vartheta^{\star}),\;\; U^{\diamond}= U^{\diamond}\,(\rho^{\diamond},\delta^{\diamond}).$$

Let us denote as N^{*} the ratio of the potential amount U^{*} to the unit of volume dv^{*}. Let us denote also by $N^{\star}$ and $N^{\diamond}$ the specific values of the potentials $U^{\star}$ and $U^{\diamond}$ referred to the unit of the free surface $ds^{\star}$ or to the unit of the surface of the vapor–gas bubble or the solid particle of the dispersed phase $ds^{\diamond}$.

Because of the continuity of this dispersion medium and the continuity of the contact of the dispersion medium with elements of the dispersed phase, there is:

$$U^{*} = U^{*}\,dv^{*},\; U^{\star} = \int U^{\star} ds^{\star} \text{ и } U^{\diamond} = \int U^{\diamond} ds^{\diamond}. \qquad (5.66)$$

Replacing the action of the active forces upon the system in question from a free surface and by not violating the condition of equilibrium, it is possible to assume the fairness of the following equality:

$$\sum_{i}^{n} \vec{\mathfrak{F}}_i\,\delta\vec{r}_i = \int(\mathcal{R}^{*}x_i\delta x_i + \mathcal{R}^{\star}y_i\delta y_i + \mathcal{R}^{\diamond}z_i\delta z_i)\,dv^{*} +$$

$$+\int(\mathcal{R}^{\star}x_i\delta x_i + \mathcal{R}^{\star}y_i\delta y_i + \mathcal{R}^{\star}z_i\delta z_i)\,ds^{\star}. \qquad (5.67)$$

Writing down (5.64) with consideration of (5.65), (5.66), and (5.67), there is:

$$\int(\mathcal{R}^* x_i \delta x_i + \mathcal{R}^* y_i \delta y_i + \mathcal{R}^* z_i \delta z_i)\ d\mathcal{v}^* +$$

$$+\int(\mathcal{R}^\star x_i \delta x_i + \mathcal{R}^\star y_i \delta y_i + \mathcal{R}^\star z_i \delta z_i)\ ds^\star - \delta\int U^*(\rho^*)\ d\mathcal{v}^* -$$

$$-\ \delta\int U^\star(\rho^\star, \vartheta^\star) ds^\star\ - \delta\int U^\circ(\rho^\circ, \delta^\circ)\ ds^\circ = 0\ . \qquad (5.68)$$

Equation (5.68) represents the condition of equilibrium of the considered dispersion medium with the surface of a drop of liquid, which is insoluble and immiscible in the dispersion environment, or a gas bubble or a particle of the solid matter. Wherein, the action of the first and the third integrals extends to all points of volume of system $\mathcal{v}^*$and the action of the second integral extends to all points of a free surface $s^\star$.

The projections $\mathcal{R}_x^*, \mathcal{R}_y^*$ and $\mathcal{R}_z^*$ are the results of forces depending on the density of the considered components of the systems, and projections $\mathcal{R}_x^\star, \mathcal{R}_y^\star$ and $\mathcal{R}_z^\star$ are the resultant of the system of surface forces. The fourth and fifth integrals extend the action to the surface points of a liquid that is insoluble and immiscible in the dispersive medium, or a gas bubble, or a solid particle.

Defining the variations of the integrals in the equation (4.68) shows that:

$$\delta\int U^*(\rho^*)\ d\mathcal{v}^* = \int \frac{\partial U^*}{\partial \rho^*}\ \delta\rho^*\ d\mathcal{v}^*\ + U^* \delta\, d\mathcal{v}^*; \qquad (5.69)$$

$$\delta\int U^\star\, (\rho^\star, \vartheta^\star) ds^\star = \int(\frac{\partial U^\star}{\partial \rho^\star}\ \delta\rho^\star + \frac{\partial U^\star}{\partial \vartheta^\star}\ \delta\vartheta^\star) ds^\star + \int U^\star \delta ds^\star \quad (5.70)$$

$$\delta\int U^\circ(\rho^\circ, \vartheta^\circ) ds^\circ = \int(\frac{\partial U^\circ}{\partial \rho^\circ}\ \delta\rho^\circ + \frac{\partial U^\circ}{\partial \vartheta^\circ}\ \delta\vartheta^\circ) ds^\circ\ + \int U^\circ \delta\, ds^\circ. \quad (5.71)$$

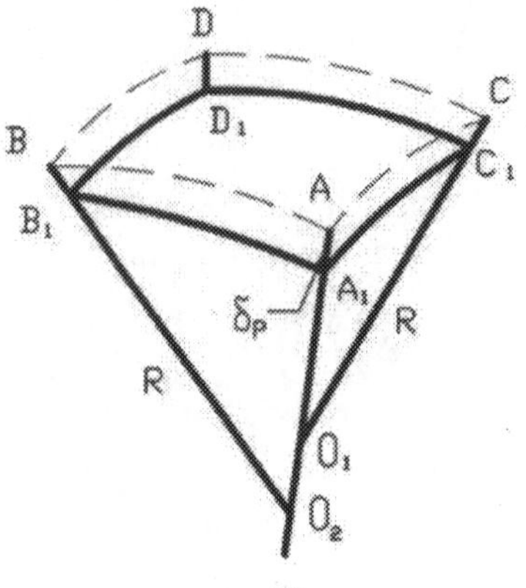

Figure 5–6

The variation of the free surface element $\delta ds^{\star}$, depending on the magnitude of the virtual displacement of the points of the free surface, is determined by the Bertrand method [172].

Let us assume (Fig. 4–6) that $ABCD = ds_1^{\circ}$ is the element of a free surface of displacement prior to displacement and $A_1B_1C_1D_1 = ds_2^{\circ}$ is the same element of a free surface after completion of displacement. Based on the definition of virtual displacement: $\delta ds^{\circ} = ds_1^{\circ} - ds_2^{\circ}$.

If $AB$and $AC$are the elements of two orthogonal lines of curvature, drawn on the surface through the basis A of the normal $\overrightarrow{\mathfrak{P}}$, which is directed inside the system, then:

$$ds_1^{\circ} = AB \cdot AC \quad \text{and} \quad ds_2^{\circ} = A_1 B_1 \cdot A_1 C_1.$$

It should be noted that the normal $\overrightarrow{\mathfrak{P}}$ is the vector. However, it is quite obvious (Fig. 5–6) that:

$$\delta ds^{\circ} = (\frac{1}{R_1} + \frac{1}{R_2})\ ds^{\circ} d\overrightarrow{\mathfrak{P}},$$

where $AA_1 = \mathrm{d}\overrightarrow{\mathfrak{P}}$ is the normal displacement of the point A in the direction $\overrightarrow{\mathfrak{P}}$.

The expression $(\frac{1}{R_1} + \frac{1}{R_2})$ should be taken as an absolute value because it is possible that the direction of displacement may not coincide with the direction of the normal to the surface. Thus:

$$\delta\, ds^{\diamond} = \pm\, (\frac{1}{R_1} + \frac{1}{R_2})\; ds^{\diamond} \mathrm{d}\overrightarrow{\mathfrak{P}}. \qquad (5.72)$$

From a condition of the continuity of the dispersion system, which is considered in the form of the accepted system of material points and continuity of contacts of the material points located on a surface point of the liquid that is insoluble and immiscible in the dispersion medium, or a gas bubble, or a solid particle, we get:

$$\delta\, ds^{\diamond} = 0. \qquad (5.73)$$

defining variations $\delta\rho^{*}$, $\delta\rho^{\star}$and $\delta\rho^{\diamond}$. From the condition of continuity: δ $(\rho d\upsilon) = 0$. Therefore:

$$\delta d\upsilon^{*} = \nabla d\upsilon^{*} \text{ and } \delta\rho^{*} = -\, \delta\nabla\rho^{*}, \quad (4.74)$$

where $$\nabla = \frac{\partial}{\partial x}\,\delta x + \frac{\partial}{\partial y}\,\delta y + \frac{\partial}{\partial z}\,\delta z.$$

For the surface layer is fair the equality $\delta\, (\rho^{*}, \mathrm{d}\overrightarrow{\mathfrak{P}}, ds^{\,*}) = 0$ is valid, and so (5.72), by virtue of the commutative property:

$$\delta\rho^{\star} ds^{\star} = \pm\, \rho^{\star} (\frac{1}{R} + \frac{1}{R})\; ds^{\star}\, \delta\overrightarrow{\mathfrak{P}}. \qquad (5.75)$$

For a layer of a dispersive medium that is in direct contact with the surface of a liquid drop insoluble in a dispersion medium, or with the surface of a gas bubble or a solid particle, by virtue of (5.73):

$$\delta\rho^{\ltimes} ds^{\ltimes} = 0. \qquad (5.76)$$

Expressing $\delta\,\overrightarrow{\mathfrak{P}}$ in functions of $\delta x,\ \delta y,\ \delta z$ and considering that $\overrightarrow{\mathfrak{P}}$ is the vector, its virtual displacement is equal:

$$\delta\,\overrightarrow{\mathfrak{P}} = \cos\,(px)\delta x + \cos\,(py)\delta y + \cos\,(pz)\delta z. \qquad (5.77)$$

Finally, $\delta\vartheta^{\star}$and $\delta\vartheta^{\circ}$ from (5.63), are equal:

$$\delta\vartheta^{\star} = \frac{\partial w}{\partial x}\,\delta x^{\star} + \frac{\partial w}{\partial y}\,\delta y^{\star} + \frac{\partial w}{\partial z}\,\delta z^{\star}; \qquad (5.78)$$

$$\delta\vartheta^{\circ} = \frac{\partial w}{\partial x}\,\delta x^{\circ} + \frac{\partial w}{\partial y}\,\delta y^{\circ} + \frac{\partial w}{\partial z}\,\delta z^{\circ}. \qquad (5.79)$$

Equations (4.69), (4.70) and (4.71) with consideration of equations from (4.72) to (4.79) will look this:

$$\delta\int U^{*}(\rho)d\tau = \int(U^{*}(\rho) - \rho\frac{\delta U^{*}}{\partial \rho})\nabla d\tau; \qquad (5.80)$$

$$\delta\int U^{\star}\,(\rho^{\star},\vartheta^{\star})ds^{\star} = \int\Big\{\pm(\frac{1}{R_1} + \frac{1}{R_2})\ \mathrm{x}$$

$$\mathrm{x}\left[U^{\star}(\rho^{\star},\vartheta^{\star}) - \rho\frac{\partial U^{\star}\,(\rho^{\star},\vartheta^{\star})}{\partial \rho^{\star}}\right]\mathrm{x}$$

$$\mathrm{x}\left[\cos\,(px)\delta x + \cos\,(py)\,\delta y + \cos(pz)\,\delta z\right\}$$

$$\text{x}\left[\frac{\partial U^{\star}(\rho^{\star},\vartheta^{\star})}{\partial \rho^{\star}}\nabla\vartheta^{\star}\right]ds^{\star}; \tag{5.81}$$

$$\delta\int U^{\circ}(\rho^{\circ},\vartheta^{\circ})\,ds^{\circ}=\int\frac{\partial U^{\circ}}{\partial\vartheta^{\circ}}\nabla\vartheta^{\circ}\,ds^{\circ}. \tag{5.82}$$

Substituting values from equations (5.80), (5.81) and (5.82) into (5.68) and using the Green's method of integrated transformations [35], there is:

$$\int_{(v)}(\nabla\psi\nabla\varphi)dv=-\int_{(S)}\varphi\nabla^{2}\psi dv-\int_{(S)}\varphi\frac{\partial\psi}{\partial\rho}\,ds,$$

where φ is the scalar function; and $\overrightarrow{\mathfrak{P}}(\nabla\varphi)=\frac{\partial\psi}{\partial p}$ is the vector function.

Thus:

$$(\mathcal{R}_x^{*}\,\delta x+\mathcal{R}_y^{*}\delta y+\mathcal{R}_z^{*}\delta z)d\tau+(\mathcal{R}_x^{\star}\delta x+\mathcal{R}_y^{\star}\delta y+\mathcal{R}_z^{\star}\delta z)\,ds^{\star}+$$

$$+\mathcal{L}_{(\rho)}\left[\cos(px)\delta x+\cos(py)\,\delta y+\cos(pz)\,\delta z\right]ds^{\star}+$$

$$+\mathcal{L}_{(\rho)}\left[\cos(px)\delta x+\cos(py)\,\delta y+\cos(pz)\,\delta z\right]ds^{\circ}+$$

$$+\int\left[\frac{\partial\mathcal{L}_{(\rho)}}{\partial x}\delta x+\frac{\partial\mathcal{L}_{(\rho)}}{\partial y}\delta y+\frac{\partial\mathcal{L}_{(\rho)}}{\partial z}\delta z\right]dv+$$

$$+\int\left\{\pm\left(\frac{1}{R_1}+\frac{1}{R_2}\right)\sigma^{\star}(\rho^{\star},\vartheta^{\star})\,\text{x}\right.$$

$$\left.\text{x}\left[\cos(px)\delta x+\cos(py)\delta y+\cos(pz)\delta z\right]\right\}ds^{\star}-$$

$$-\int\frac{\partial U^{\star}}{\partial\vartheta^{\star}}\nabla\vartheta^{\star}ds^{*}-\int\frac{\partial U^{\circ}}{\partial\vartheta^{\circ}}\nabla\vartheta^{\circ}ds^{\circ}=0, \tag{5.83}$$

where:

$$\mathcal{L}_{(\rho)} = U^*{}_{(\rho)} - \rho \frac{\partial U^{\diamond}_{(\rho)}}{\partial p},$$

$$\sigma^{\star}{}_{(\rho^{\star}, \vartheta^{\star})} = U^{*}{}_{(\rho^{\star}, \vartheta^{\star})} - \rho^{\star} \frac{\partial U^{\star}(\rho^{\star},\vartheta^{\star})}{\partial \rho^{\star}}.$$

The physical means of the function $\mathcal{L}_{(\rho)}$ is the internal pressure, which develops in the subject dispersion system and is a function of mass forces that are acting in all points and on all elementary volumes of this system.

Thus, the internal pressure is the total action of molecular and surface forces referred to the unit of volume dv, and $\sigma_{(\rho^{\star}\vartheta^{\star})}$ represents the free energy of unit of the surface.

Variations of coordinates $\delta x, \delta y, \delta z$, by the definition given in [172], are subordinated to k equations (5.63). By multiplying these equations upon the uncertain Lagrange's multiplier: $\lambda_1, \lambda_2 ..., \lambda_n$, and then taking the sum of the received expressions, it is:

$$\sum_j^k \lambda_j \sum_i^n \left(\frac{\partial f_j}{\partial x_i} \delta x_i + \frac{\partial f_j}{\partial y_i} \delta y_i + \frac{\partial f_j}{\partial z_i} \delta z_i \right) = 0. \quad (5.84)$$

Taking the sum of the (5.83) and (5.84) and choosing λ_j, that the coefficients at k variations would become zero. Ruther than being independent from them, the coefficients $(3n - k)$ variations will become equal to zero, too. Therefore, for internal points of the system:

$$\mathcal{R}^{\diamond}_{x} = \frac{\partial L_{(\rho)}}{\partial x}; \ \mathcal{R}^{\diamond}_{y} = \frac{\partial L_{(\rho)}}{\partial y}; \ \mathcal{R}^{\diamond}_{z} = \frac{\partial L_{(\rho)}}{\partial z}. \quad (5.85)$$

Thus, it is obvious that for the material points of a free surface to be satisfied, the following system of equations has to be satisfied:

$$\mathcal{L}_{(\rho)} \cos(px) \pm \left(\frac{1}{R} + \frac{1}{R}\right) \sigma^{\star}{}_{(\rho^{\star}, \omega^{*})} \cos(px) - \frac{\partial U^{\star}}{\partial \vartheta^{\star}} \frac{\partial \vartheta^{\star}}{\partial x} \mathcal{R}^{\star}_{x} = 0;$$
$$\mathcal{L}_{(\rho)} \cos(py) \pm \left(\frac{1}{R} + \frac{1}{R}\right) \sigma^{\star}{}_{(\rho^{\star}, \omega^{*})} \cos(py) - \frac{\partial U^{\star}}{\partial \vartheta^{\star}} \frac{\partial \vartheta^{\star}}{\partial y} \mathcal{R}^{\star}_{y} = 0;$$
$$\mathcal{L}_{(\rho)} \cos(pz) \pm \left(\frac{1}{R} + \frac{1}{R}\right) \sigma^{\star}{}_{(\rho^{\star}, \omega^{*})} \cos(pz) - \frac{\partial U^{\star}}{\partial \vartheta^{\star}} \frac{\partial \vartheta^{\star}}{\partial z} \mathcal{R}^{\star}_{z} = 0. \quad (5.86)$$

For points of the contact layer of the subject dispersion system with surface points of the liquid that is insoluble and immiscible in the dispersion medium, or a gas bubble, or a solid particle, the condition of equilibrium, corresponds to the following system of equations:

$$\mathcal{L}_{(\rho)} \cos(px) - \frac{\partial U^{\circ}}{\partial \vartheta^{\circ}} \frac{\partial \vartheta^{\circ}}{\partial x} \mathcal{R}^{\circ}_{x} = 0;$$
$$\mathcal{L}_{(\rho)} \cos(py) - \frac{\partial U^{\circ}}{\partial \vartheta^{\circ}} \frac{\partial \vartheta^{\circ}}{\partial y} \mathcal{R}^{\circ}_{y} = 0; \quad (5.87)$$
$$\mathcal{L}_{(\rho)} \cos(pz) - \frac{\partial U^{\circ}}{\partial \vartheta^{\circ}} \frac{\partial \vartheta^{\circ}}{\partial z} \mathcal{R}^{\circ}_{z} = 0.$$

As thicknesses of the layers are measured upon normal to their surfaces, it is always possible to define vectors $\overrightarrow{\mathfrak{M}}\,(\vartheta^{\star})$and $\overrightarrow{\mathfrak{P}}\,(\vartheta^{\star})$ that the following conditions will be satisfied [1]:

$$\frac{\partial U^{\star}}{\partial \vartheta^{\star}} \frac{\partial \vartheta^{\star}}{\partial x} \overrightarrow{\mathfrak{M}}\,(\vartheta^{\star}) \cos(px) \text{ ... and so on,} \quad (5.88)$$

and

$$\frac{\partial U^{\circ}}{\partial \vartheta^{\circ}} \frac{\partial \vartheta^{\circ}}{\partial x} \overrightarrow{\mathfrak{P}}\,(\vartheta^{\circ}) \cos(px) \text{ ... and so on.} \quad (5.89)$$

Thus, the system (4.86) converts to the following system of equations:

$$\mathcal{R}^{\star}_{x} = [\mathcal{L}_{(\rho)} \pm \left(\frac{1}{R_1} + \frac{1}{R_2}\right) \sigma^{*}{}_{(\rho^{\star}, \vartheta^{\star})} - \overrightarrow{\mathfrak{M}}\,(\vartheta^{\star}) \cos(px);$$

$$\mathcal{R}_y^\star = [\boldsymbol{\mathcal{L}}_{(\rho)} \pm (\frac{1}{R_1} + \frac{1}{R_2})\, \sigma^*{}_{(\rho^\star,\,\vartheta^\star)} - \overrightarrow{\mathfrak{M}}_{(\vartheta^\star)} \cos{(py)}; \quad (5.90)$$

$$\mathcal{R}_z^\star = [\boldsymbol{\mathcal{L}}_{(\rho)} \pm (\frac{1}{R_1} + \frac{1}{R_2})\, \sigma^*{}_{(\rho^\star,\,\vartheta^\star)} - \overrightarrow{\mathfrak{M}}_{(\vartheta^\star)} \cos{(pz)}.$$

It is easy to see that the following condition has to correspond to a free surface or the surface of the phase separation:

$$\mathcal{C}_{(x,y,z)} = \boldsymbol{\mathcal{L}}_{(p)} + \overrightarrow{\mathfrak{M}}_{(\vartheta^\star)} \pm \sigma^\star{}_{(\rho^\star,\,\vartheta^\star)} (\frac{1}{R_1} + \frac{1}{R_2}),$$

where:

$$\mathcal{C}_{(x,y,z)} = \sqrt{(\mathcal{R}_x^\star)^2 + (\mathcal{R}_y^\star)^2 + (\mathcal{R}_z^\star)^2}\,.$$

Thus, in a layer in which action of surface forces is shown the internal pressure depends on forces of surface tension $\mathcal{C}_{(x,y,z)}$, which are dependent on the form of the surface of the liquid $\sigma^\star{}_{(\rho^*,\,\vartheta^\star)} (\frac{1}{R_1} + \frac{1}{R_2})$ and potential forces of various nature $\overrightarrow{\mathfrak{M}}_{(\vartheta^\star)}$, are determined by layer thickness ϑ.

On the surface of a drop of liquid that is insoluble and immiscible with the dispersion medium, the surface of a vapor–gas bubble, or a particle of the solid matter, the condition of equilibrium is taking into consideration (5.89) could be written down as:

$$\boldsymbol{\mathcal{L}}_{(p)} = \overrightarrow{\mathfrak{P}}_{(\vartheta^\circ)}, \qquad (5.91)$$

That is, the internal pressure that is acting on a surface of a drop of liquid, insoluble and immiscible with the dispersion medium, a surface of a vapor–gas bubble or particle of the solid matter, is equal to the internal pressure of the system.

Going back to the equation (5.67), it should be noted, that the internal energy characterizing the potential of internal forces $\boldsymbol{U}$ of the dispersion systems, that in a mode of the torsion-oriented turbulization, is connected to external revolting forces $\boldsymbol{Q}$ and to the work of surface forces $\boldsymbol{W}$ [215]:

$$\delta U = \delta Q + \delta W.$$

The work of surface forces $\boldsymbol{W}$ is equal to the sum of elementary works of displacement of the surface tension and works of the deformations [215]:

$$\delta W_{\text{surface forces}} = \delta W_{\text{displacement}} + \delta W_{\text{deformation}}$$

The work of deformations $W_{(def)}$ for the isotropic system, in which is observed the similarity of all mechanical, physical, and chemical and other properties in all directions, is equal to [215]:

$$W_{(def)} = \mu'\delta\left[e^2_{xx} + e^2_{yy} + e^2_{zz} + \frac{1}{2}\left(e^2_{xy} + e^2_{yz} + e^2_{zx}\right)\right] +$$
$$+ \frac{1}{2}\lambda'\,\delta(\text{div}\,\mathfrak{U})^2,$$
$$Diss\,f_{(\mathfrak{u})} = \left[e^2_{xx} + e^2_{yy} + e^2_{zz} + ½\left(e^2_{xy} + e^2_{yz} + e^2_{zx}\right)\right],$$

where $\overrightarrow{\mathfrak{U}}$ is the elastic displacement of particles; μ' and λ' are the elastic modules of isotropic substances; $\text{div}\,\mathfrak{U} = \frac{\partial U}{\partial x} + \frac{\partial U}{\partial y} + \frac{\partial U}{\partial z}$ is the relative volume of the expansion, and $Diss\,f_{(\mathfrak{u})}$ is the dissipative function of Rayleigh.

The specific elementary work of the surplus surface forces upon displacements, is equal to:

$$\delta W_{\text{пов}} = \frac{\partial R_x}{\partial x} + \frac{\partial R_y}{\partial y} + \frac{\partial R_z}{\partial z},$$

where R_x, R_y, R_z are projection of surface forces onto coordinate axes.

Amount δQ is the excess of heat brought to the system ($\delta Q = \mathrm{div}\vec{\mathbf{q}}\delta t$).

For the isotropic systems the heat flow is expressed using Fourier's formula [187]:

$$\vec{\mathbf{q}} = -\,\Lambda\,\mathrm{grad}\,\mathbf{T}.$$

The final expression for internal energy will look:

$$\mathrm{U} = \left[\frac{\partial R_x}{\partial x} + \frac{\partial R_y}{\partial y} + \frac{\partial R_z}{\partial z}\right]\delta\vec{\mathfrak{u}} + \mu'\delta\left[\mathrm{Diss}\ \mathrm{f}_{(\mathrm{u})}\right] + $$
$$+\frac{1}{2}\lambda'\delta(\mathrm{div}\vec{\mathfrak{u}})^2 + \mathrm{div}(\Lambda\,\mathrm{grad}\,\mathbf{T}). \qquad (5.92)$$

5.13. SUMMARY OF THE CHAPTER 5.

Because of the difference in internal pressures (tensions or stresses), which develops during the formation of dispersion systems in the mode of toreion-oriented turbulization between the elementary volumes of a dispersion system, it is possible to evaluate the nature of the fields of internal pressure between different zones of mass transfer and heat transfer inside the reactor.

Thus, vapor droplets and solid particles inside a dispersed system and droplets of liquid insoluble in a dispersive medium, are under the influence of internal pressure, which is the main characteristic of dispersion systems in a state of torsion-oriented turbulization.

Therefore, the magnitude of the internal tension is the main characteristic of the formed dispersion system.

CHAPTER 6

EFFICIENCY OF THE REALIZATION OF RESONANCE CAVITATION AND TORSION-ORIENTED TURBULIZATION PHENOMENA

It has been considered earlier, dispersion systems possess several special characteristics including the excess of a free energy, super-large surface separation between phases, elevated chemical activity, and others. Given the developed interface between phases, such systems are unstable. The main characteristic of dispersion system is the size of the specific surface, which is determined by the size of the surface related to the allocated volume of the dispersed phase carried to unit of the same volume. Also, the most important characteristic of the dispersion medium is its continuity.

The main research methods for mechanical phenomena are developed non-additive, or otherwise, non-extensive thermodynamics. The concept of non-additivity (or otherwise, non-extensiveness) assumes that some thermodynamic, mechanical, and physical properties of system do not depend on the change of volume in this system.

Additivity or non-additivity is defined by the relation between an integral object and its components. The concept of additivity can be expressed by the following definition: the whole is equal to the sum of its parts. And, respectively, the non-additivity can be presented as the whole is not equal to the sum of its parts. Furthermore, if the whole is less than the sum of its parts, then it defines sub-additivity. Conversely, if the whole is larger than the sum of its parts, this defines the concept of super additivity.

To further develop these representations, it is possible to assume that any additive material system has additive properties. For example, the mass of the physical system is equal to the sum of the masses of the parts of this system. Because many properties of those complicated systems are not additive, they do not have similar properties to other parts of the system.

The non-additivity of the system assumes the difference between properties of this system and sums of properties of elements of the same system if they do not interact definitely.

In orthodox thermodynamics the major geometrical parameter is the volume. As a rule, the volume and the related thermodynamic functions are extensive and independent of a geometrical form of the system. Therefore, the dispersion systems, as a rule, differ in non-extensiveness of the entropy, thermodynamic functions, and other physical characteristics. Considering the complicated heterogeneous systems such as solid–liquid, solid–liquid–liquid, liquid–gas and other similar systems, that are under the influence of the external revolting field of forces, it is possible to assume that any thermodynamic system possesses non-extensive properties.

The sign of the completion formation of dispersion systems under vibration in the mode of toreion-oriented turbulization is the rupture of a continuum of the dispersion medium.

Also, as it was noted earlier that the considered phenomenon of torsion-oriented turbulization arises under conditions in which the components of the future dispersion systems are placed in the reactor. The necessary requirement for the reactor is the rigidity. The reactor assumes the formation of dispersion systems under the influence of the external revolting force to change the volume of the formed system. Such change can take place as the result of deformation of reactor's elements: in other words, in the conditions of non-extensive behavior of the forming dispersion system. The phenomena of mechanical resonance and fluid (hydraulic) hammer impact, arising at certain parameters of vibration, lead to resonance cavitation and torsion-oriented turbulization, that is the condition of the formation of dispersion systems.

If the components, that fill the reactor are liquid metals, then, at the corresponding temperature parameters and under external vibration influence of the revolting force, they formed alloys with special characteristics such as a crystal lattice and special physical and mechanical characteristics [2-5].

As already repeatedly noted, the physical and chemical processes happening at the molecular level, including heat exchange and a mass transfer, are on the surface of separation and through an interface between phases. For this reason, the main problem of modern chemical, thin technologies and nanotechnologies is the increase of the interface. The main objective of the research of efficiency of chemical processes by traditional methods of chemical technology is to define the certain parameters as function of time, under controlled thermodynamic conditions.

6.1. SPEED OF FORMATION OF DISPERSION SYSTEMS

For research on the speed of the formation of the dispersion systems in the modes such as resonance cavitation and torsion-oriented turbulization, it is necessary to add to the usual conditions parameters of vibration where the phenomenon of resonance cavitation occurs. Thus, the target of a such research is to find the corresponding equation that will allow for modeling the subject technological process [216]. Usually, such equations could be determined by an experimental method.

For the purpose of finding the type of the kinetic equation, the first of all, it is necessary to test the stoichiometric equation of the reaction. The stoichiometric equation is the chemical formula describing to the ideal combined structure of a chemical compound from atoms, that meets the requirement of valency (that is, the ability of the atom to form chemical bonds with other atoms or groups of atoms).

Let us consider a rather trivial situation when the speed of chemical reaction in modes of resonance cavitation and torsion-oriented turbulization is the function of time and parameters of vibration. Let us consider a virtual process:

$$aA + \text{в}B \rightarrow cC + \ldots,$$

describing the formation of dispersion system in conditions of constant volume of the reactor V and at a constant temperature T. The kinetic equation of such a process has the following appearance:

$$\frac{dv}{dt} = k\,(n_{a0} - x)^{a}\,(n_{a0} - \frac{bx}{a})^{b}, \qquad (6.1)$$

where a, b and k are permanent amounts of substances, that have to be defined for each process on the basis of the experimental data.

In the equation (6.1) the internal space of the chemical reactor V is permanent and the total area of the phase's interface is included, composed from the some constant of chemical process k. In some cases, dispersion systems are formed parallel with collateral chemical reactions, because of which multicomponent and multiphase dispersion systems are formed with blurry phases and a weakly expressed dispersion medium.

It is necessary to understand, that at the point of emergence of the phenomena of vibrational cavitation and resonance turbulization the total size of the phase interface is a function of parameters of vibration, a surface tension, and the geometrical dimensions of the internal chamber of the chemical reactor. It is quite obvious that, in the maintenance of the mode of torsion-oriented turbulization when the formed dispersion system is in a turbulent state, the size of the phase interface changes constantly. But nevertheless, during the relatively long the turbulent condition of the dispersion system, there is an average size of the phase interface S, which could be calculated using formula (3.114):

In addition, it should be noted that the key parameter that characterizes the efficiency of the formation of a dispersion system is not the volume of the internal chamber of the chemical reactor, but the total area of the phase interface S, being a function of the size of the chemical reactor.

In the equation (6.1) constants a, b and k could be found experimentally. The algorithm of determining the sizes of a, b and k could be based on the simplest case, when $a = b$. The initial quantities of the processed components of the planned dispersion system are equal. It is easy to see that in this case the kinetic equation (6.1) can be written down as:

$$\frac{dv}{dt} = k\,(n_{a0} - x)^n . \qquad (6.2)$$

In the kinetic equation (6.2), the quantities of the some constant of the chemical processes k and n can be found by integrated equation, differentiation, or half-decay.

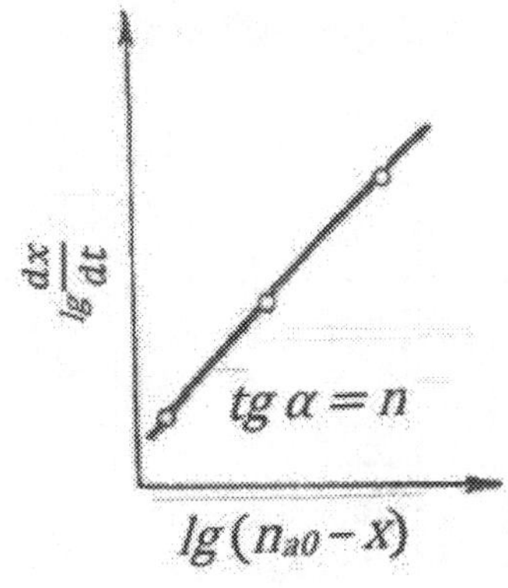

Figure 6-1

1. **The Method of the Differentiation**

The derivative $\frac{dx}{dt}$ can be determined graphically on the basis of skilled data, as follows:

$$\lg\frac{dx}{dt} = n\lg(n_{a0} - x) + \lg k,$$

and parameters of the chemical process k and n could be determined by the plot (Fig. 6-1) constructed based on the logarithmic function determined by two points:

$$n = \frac{\lg(\frac{dx}{dt})_2 - \lg(\frac{dx}{dt})_1}{\lg(n_{a0} - x_2) - \lg(n_{a0} - x_1)}; \qquad (6.3)$$

and

$$k = \frac{(\frac{dx}{dt})_1}{(n_{a0} - x_1)^n}. \qquad (6.4)$$

If the line on the plot (Fig. 6-1) the line is not straight, then the considered process formation of dispersion systems is complicated. The dispersion systems are formed parallel with collateral chemical reactions, as a result of which multicomponent and multiphase dispersion systems are formed with blurry phases and a weakly expressed dispersion medium.

2. The Method of the Integrated Equation

Except for the case when $n = 1$, the integral of the equation (6.2) is:

$$(\frac{1}{n_{a0} - x})^{n-1} - (\frac{1}{n_{a0}})^{n-1} = kt(n-1). \qquad (6.5)$$

For creation of the plot in $(\frac{1}{n_{a0} - x})^{n-1}$ coordinates, it is necessary to accept some amounts for n and time t. If the plot (Fig. 6-2) represents a

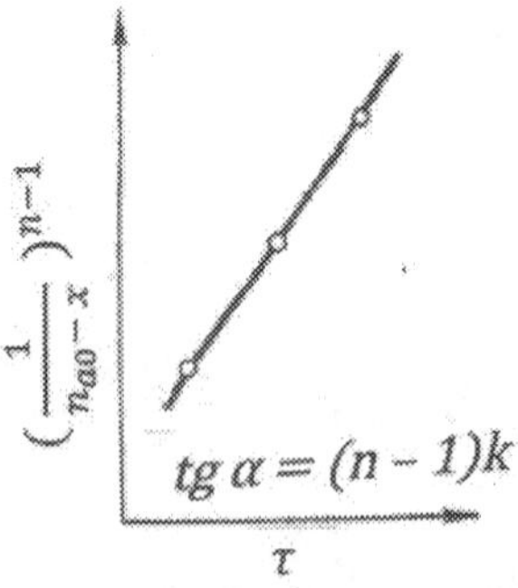

Figure 6-2

straight line, then a choice of value n is made correctly. At the same time, the amount k is determined by the line of inclination of the tangent of angle $tan \propto = k(n-1)$ on the plot (Fig. 6-2). It is necessary to pay attention that, at $n = 1$ the plot is constructed in $\lg\ (n_{a0} - x)$ coordinate and t .

The change of the amount k in a rather wide range for all checked values of n, indicates that the considered process of formation of dispersion systems is complicated. The subject dispersion systems are formed parallel with collateral chemical reactions.

3. The Method of the Half-Decay

For about 50% of all transformations, at $x = \frac{n}{2}$, the integrated equations of kinetics are converted into simple forms:

$$\frac{dx}{dt} = k(n_{a0} - x); \quad \frac{t}{2} = \frac{\lg 2}{2}; \tag{6.6a}$$

$$\frac{dx}{dt} = k(n_{a0} - x)^2; \quad \frac{t}{2} = \frac{1}{k n_{a0}}; \tag{6.6b}$$

$$\frac{dx}{dt} = k(n_{a0} - x)^n \quad \frac{t}{2} = \frac{2^{n-1} - 1}{k(n-1) n_{a0}^{n-1}}, \tag{6.6c}$$

and $n \neq 1$

Let us to present the equality (6.6c) in the following form:

$$\lg \frac{t}{2} = \lg \frac{2^{n-1} - 1}{k(n-1)} - (n-1) \lg n_{a0}\,. \tag{6.7}$$

Then the graph (Fig. 6-3) for $\lg \frac{t}{2}$, is concerning $\lg n_{a0}$ must be a straight line of inclination of the tangent of angle $tan \propto = 1 - n$. In this case, the amount of the parameter k can be defined from equality:

$$k = \frac{2^{n-1} - 1}{(\frac{t}{2})^{n-1} n_{a0}^{n-1}}. \tag{6.8}$$

This method could be recommended, when the process of formation of dispersion systems is considered under the variable conditions of the frequency and acceleration of vibration, temperature and other parameters causing change to k.

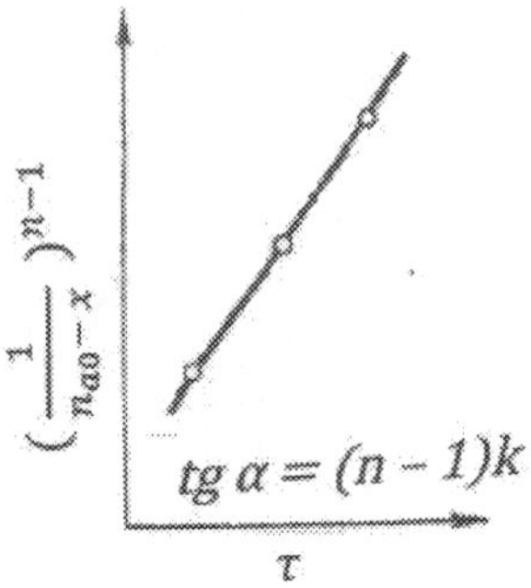

Figure 5-3

6.2. GENERAL EQUATION OF THE FORMATION OF DISPERSION SYSTEMS IN A HOMOGENEOUS ENVIRONMENT

Let us consider some virtual irreversible processes in the formation of a dispersion system:

$$aA + bB + cC \rightarrow dD + eE + fF, \qquad (6.9)$$

where a, b, and c are stoichiometric (pre-calculated) moles of the components of the planned dispersion system and the interacting substances A, B, and C, that correspond to the ideal integer composition of a chemical compound of atoms that satisfy the valency requirement (i.e., the ability of an atom to form chemical bonds with other atoms or groups of atoms).

Let N_A represent the number of moles A, available in time point t. Then $\frac{dN_A}{dt}$ represents the number of moles A, reacting per unit of time. If t increases, the amount N_A decreases. Therefore, the derivative $\frac{dN_A}{dt}$ is negative. Thus, the derivative $\frac{dN_A}{dt}$ is proportional to the number of moles of a substance A, i.e. is proportional to N_A.

Equation (6.9) could be presented as:

$$A + (a-1)\,A + bB + cC \rightarrow dD + eE + fF. \qquad (6.10)$$

Therefore, the differential equation determining the speed of dispersion of substance A at a constant temperature will look like this:

$$\frac{dN_A}{dt} = -\,k\,N_A\,C_A^{a-1}\,B_B^{b}\,C_C^{c}, \qquad (6.11)$$

where C is the concentration expressed in moles per unit of volume.

Equation (6.11) represents the general equation of the speed of formation of dispersion systems in homogeneous environment.

If the initial quantities of components of the planned dispersion system are known, then by means of the equations for material equilibrium and stoichiometric ratios, obviously, it is possible to express all concentrations as function of N_A. Then, the variables N_A and t, with their differentials can be regrouped in a way that will make equation (6.11) possible to integrate.

In case of adiabatic reaction, the temperature of the interacting substances will change. The parameter of the chemical reaction k, that is the function of temperature, will become a variable. Knowing the thermal capacity of substances, it is possible to express the temperature of the reaction as the function of N_A and, therefore, to receive the parameter k as the function of N_A. Under these conditions, the analytical receptions of the solution for equation (5.11) are rather difficult, and so it is more convenient to write down this equation as:

$$\int_0^t dt = -\int_{N_{A0}}^{N_A} \frac{dN_A}{k\,NAC_A^{a-1}B_B^{b}C_C^{c}}, \qquad (6.12)$$

and to apply a method of graphic integration.

For a special case, when the process of the formation of a dispersion system proceeds in the rigid reactor under at the constant volume $\mathcal{V}$, the following formulas would be used:

$$C_A = \frac{N_A}{\mathcal{V}} \text{ and } N_A = \mathcal{V} dC_A ,$$

Then, the equation (6.11) takes this form:

$$\frac{dC_A}{dt} = - k\, C_A^a\, B_B^b\, C_C^c\,. \tag{6.13}$$

Equation (6.13) defines the speed of the reaction under ideal conditions. However, it cannot be applicable in the mode of resonance cavitation, characterized by the formation, development, and collapse of vapor–gas bubbles, that occurring under the constant pressure, unless, at the same time, there is no change in the total number of moles, which leads to constant volume ($\mathcal{V}=$ const.) or the increment of volume $\frac{d\mathcal{V}}{dt}$ it is at its negligible smallest size.

Having defined the stoichiometric ratios between mix components, the content of the dispersion system, and products of collateral chemical reaction from the equation (6.10), it is possible to convert equation (6.10), that is, to make it applicable to any kind of the interaction of molecules. For example, it is possible to track the formation of a substance D by substitution, in equation (6.10), of the following expression:

$$- dN_A = \frac{a}{d}\, dN_D\,.$$

After this conversion, the equation (6.10) will look like this:

$$\frac{dN_D}{dt} = -k\left(\frac{d}{a}\right) C_A^{a-1}\, B_B^{b}\, C_C^{c}. \qquad (6.14)$$

When using equations like (6.10) and (6.14), some difficulties may arise. First, the general process represented by equation (6.10) could be reversible. Substance A could be consumed during the formation of dispersion systems and the implementation of direct collateral chemical reactions. Additionally, it could be formed because of reversed chemical reactions. To track quantitative changes of any substance over time, equation (6.10) must be written down for all processes, including direct and reversed collateral chemical reactions.

Additional complications could arise when the stoichiometric formula does not exactly correspond to the mechanisms of the main process and collateral chemical reactions. For example, during the formation of a dispersion system, the collateral intermediate chemical compounds, which can form the other products over the time, could be received. In this case, the equation of the speed is constructed for the process of the formation of dispersion systems, and the amounts entered it would be defined from the general stoichiometric equation.

Finally, we have the possible processing of some collateral reactions as an addition to the main process, some transformations of substances, and intermediate products. If the amount of the substance, entering into the interaction of these collateral reactions is large, then construction up the equation is made for the speed of the conversion of any of reagents on the basis of the data obtained experimentally.

6.3. ASSESSMENT OF THE AVERAGE SPEED OF THE FORMATION OF DISPERSION SYSTEMS

The formula for the definition of time t necessary for the processing of any chemical reaction, [162, 216], is:

$$t = \frac{1}{k} \ln \frac{a}{a-x}, \tag{6.15}$$

where a is the amount of the substance involved in the beginning of the reaction; and k is the coefficient, that is constant for each reaction and possibly defined experimentally.

From here:

$$x = a\,(1 - e^{-kt}). \tag{6.16}$$

Let us determine the dependence of the speed of formation of dispersion systems (in the modes of resonance cavitation and torsion-oriented turbulization) on the amount of x. For this purpose, let us indicate the speed of the process with w and then differentiate function (6.16) with respect to time t:

$$w = \frac{\partial x}{\partial t} = ake^{-kt}. \tag{6.17}$$

Excluding e^{-kt} from the formula (6.17), formula (6.16), looks like this:

$$w = k\,(a - 1). \tag{6.18}$$

Equation (6.17) expresses the speed of process w of the formation of a dispersion systems in the modes of resonance cavitation and torsion-oriented turbulization based on the process duration t and the equation (6.18) on the basis of the amount of the dispersed substance.

Now, let us determine the average speed of process for both cases. Using a formula for average value of function, this is the formula:

$$w_t = \frac{1}{t_1 - t_0} \int_{t_0}^{t_1} ake^{-kt}\,dt =$$

$$= \frac{a(ke^{-kt_0} - ke^{-kt_1})}{t_1 - t_0} = \frac{w_0 - w_1}{\ln w_0 - \ln w_1}, \tag{6.19}$$

and

$$w_x = \frac{1}{x_1 - x_0} \int_{x_0}^{x_1} k(a - x)\, dx =$$

$$= \frac{k\,(x_1 - x_0)(2a - x_1 - x_0)}{2(x_1 - x_0)} = \frac{w_0 - w_1}{2}. \qquad (6.20)$$

As is apparent from formulas (6.19) and (6.20), the average value of the changing speed depends on the choice of an argument. The reasoning behind this is as follows: the average value of function y is the extreme value of an arithmetic average from the values of function y, taken through equal intervals of an argument x.

Let us conduct the following: if between $a = x_0$ and $b = x_n$ to insert $x_1, x_2, \dots, x_{n-1}$, than:

$$x_1 - x_0 = x_2 - x_1 = \dots = x_n - x_{n-1} = \frac{b - a}{n}.$$

So, that the average arithmetic values are:

$$y_0 = \varphi\,(x_0)\,,\, y_1 = \varphi\,(x_1), \dots\, y_{n-1} = \varphi\,(x_{n-1})\,,$$

and equally:

$$\frac{\varphi\,(x_0) + \varphi\,(x_1) + \dots + \varphi\,(x_{n-1})}{n} =$$

$$= \frac{\varphi\,(x_0)\,(x_1 - x_0) + \varphi\,(x_1)\,(x_2 - x_1) + \dots + \varphi\,(x_{n-1})\,(x_n - x_{n-1})}{n \cdot \frac{b - a}{n}} =$$

$$= \frac{\sum \varphi\,(x_i)\,(x_{i+1} - x_i)}{b - a}.$$

Now, if instead of an argument x to enter the other argument, for example, t, than at regular intervals of changes of time, the function y will not accept those values anymore. Furthermore, it may transpire (for example, in the interval where y accepts rather greater values) that it will be extended. Thus, the average value of the function will be a relatively larger, than in the first case.

From a mathematical point of view, the suitable replacement for an independent variable is any average value of function y in an interval between a and b.

6.4. PROCESS OF FORMATION OF DISPERSION SYSTEMS AND COLLATERAL CHEMICAL REACTIONS AT THE PERMANENT INTERNAL VOLUME OF THE REACTOR

Let us consider the process of the formation of dispersion systems running parallel to the collateral reversible chemical reactions happening at some average size S of an interface between phases, which as a first approximation, can be a constant ($n = \text{const.}$). That formula is as follows:

$$S = \lim \sum_1^n S_1 + S_2 + \dots S_n \qquad (6.21)$$

Let us consider two reversible reactions proceeding according to the scheme:

$$A \rightleftarrows B \qquad (a)$$
$$B \rightleftarrows C \qquad (b)$$

Let us suppose that at the beginning of the reaction there is a single mole of initial substance. Let us designate x, y, z as the number of moles, respectively: A, B, and C, which were present or were formed by the time t. Also, suppose, k_1 and k_2 - are constants of speed of direct reaction (a), and k_3 and k_4 – are constants of speed of the return reaction (b). In that case, based on equation (6.13), the speed of transformation A is equal to:

$$\frac{dx}{dt} = -k_1 x + k_2 y, \qquad (6.22)$$

and the speed of transformation B, is equal to:

$$\frac{dy}{dt} = -(k_2 + k_3)y + k_1 x + k_4 z \qquad (6.23)$$

According to the condition set above: $x + y + z = 1$.

After differentiation, the equation (6.22) on t, looks like this:

$$\frac{d^2x}{dt^2} = -k_1 \frac{dx}{dt} + k_2 \frac{dy}{dt}. \qquad (6.24)$$

Substituting instead of $\frac{dy}{dt}$ its expression from the formula (5.23), the new formula is:

$$\frac{d^2x}{dt^2} + P_1(t) \frac{dx}{dt} + P_2(t)\, x - Q(t) = 0, \qquad (6.25)$$

where:

$$P_1(t) = k_1 + k_2 + k_3 + k_4;$$

$$P_2(t) = k_1 k_3 + k_2 k_4 + k_1 k_4;$$

$$Q(t) = k_2 k_4.$$

Replacing z with it with value $(1 - x - y)$, then substituting y from the equation (6.22) and finally regrouping it, we get:

$$\frac{d^2x}{dt^2} + P_1(t) \frac{dx}{dt} + P_2(t)\, x - Q(t) = 0.$$

The equation (6.25) is the linear equation of the second order with constant coefficients. By replacing coefficients $P_1(t)$, $P_2(t)$ and $Q(t)$ in the equation (6.25), we get:

$$\frac{d^2x}{dt^2}+\frac{dx}{dt}\mathcal{P}_1(t)+x\mathcal{P}_2(t)=Q.(t) \qquad (6.26)$$

When $Q(t)=0$, the subject equation is called uniform, and when $Q(t) \neq 0$, the equation is called nonuniform.

Let us construct the equations for both cases being considered:

1. Uniform equation when $Q(t)=0$

$$\frac{d^2x}{dt^2}+\frac{dx}{dt}\mathcal{P}_1(t)+x\mathcal{P}_2(t)=0. \qquad (6.27)$$

a) If $x_1(t)$ and $x_2(t)$ are any two private integrals of the uniform equation (6.26), then the function is the following:

$$x=C_1x_1(t)+C_2x_2(t)$$

where C_1 and C_2 are any arbitrary constants.

b) If $x_1(t)$ and $x_2(t)$ are linearly independent integrals, i.e., $\frac{x_1}{x_2} \neq$ const., then in the function $x = C_1x_1(t) + C_2x_2(t)$ there is a general integral of the equation (6.26).

Thus, to find the common solution for the equation (6.26), it is sufficient to find two of its linearly independent private solutions.

2. Non-uniform equation when $Q(t) \neq 0$

If the common integral of this uniform equation is known, then by applying a method of variations of arbitrary constants, it is possible to find private and consequently the common integral of the nonuniform equation. This method is applicable to any equation, irrespectively of what kind of appearance. For some private types of the right side of the equation, for the finding of private integrals, the so-called method of uncertain coefficients is applicable.

Consideration of methods of arbitrary variable constants and the method of uncertain coefficients is far beyond the scope of this work.

6.5. CONSIDERATION OF THE CONTINUOUS FORMATION OF DISPERSION SYSTEMS

The differential equation (6.11), which determines the speed of dispersion of substance A

$$\frac{dN_A}{dt} = -k\, N_A C_A^{a-1}\, B_B^{b}\, C_C^{c} \qquad (6.11)$$

could be applied to the formation of dispersion systems by the resonance cavitation in the continuous mode, with continuous loading into the reactor of components of the mixture along with simultaneous unloading of the final product. This mode proceeds in isothermal conditions under the constant pressure and the constant changing of the volume. This leads to additional conditions because the time at the location inside the reactor is under continuous influence by the external revolting force. It means that the time of formation is the function of speed of the movement of components and the sizes of the reactor's chamber.

Since the vast majority of processes underpinning physical and chemical technologies are carried out continuously, it was proposed (See Chapter 2, Fig. 2-18.) the technological scheme for the formation of dispersion systems in the continuous mode [2–7].

Let us designate as N_{A0} the number of moles of the components of a mix of a future dispersion system continuously loading into the reactor for the duration of one hour. In addition, let us designate as t the time at which components are passing through the reactor. After some period from the beginning of process N_A moles that remain as non-dispersed components.

Applying the equation (6.11) to the simplest case, when the dispersion system consists of two components—one of which is the gas forming a dispersed phase, and the other is the liquid forming the dispersion phase—we get:

$$\frac{dN_A}{dt} = -\,k\,N_A\,C_A\ . \qquad (6.28)$$

To find a solution for this equation, it is necessary to exclude one of the variables of the equation (6.28). However, it is more appropriate to express variables C_A and t through the variable of the volume of a reactor's zone V_R.

Let us assume that, at any moment after the beginning of the process V, the total amount of non-dispersed components and the corresponding final product is N_A. Using the equation for the condition of the ideal gas and the stoichiometric equation for the considered process, we get:

$$V = \frac{RT}{P} = \left[N_{A0} + (N_{A0} - N_A)\right].$$

If designating (Chapter 1. Fig. 2-18) x as the distance from the middle of the entrance of feeding hoses 7, 10, or 11, to any section of the reactor, the volume of this part of the reactor throughout the length x will be equal to Sx, where S is the cross section of the reactor. Therefore, $dV_R = Sdx$.

Let us accept a condition that the speed of gas is constant in any section of the reactor. Then the linear speed U of the volumes of gas, that is passing the distance dx for a period of time dt, will be equal:

$$U = \frac{dx}{dt} = \frac{dV_R}{Sdt},$$

from which:

$$dt = \frac{S}{V}dx = \frac{dV_R}{V}\ . \qquad (6.29)$$

The value V represents the volume of the dispersion system formed after loading N_{A0} moles of the mixture per unit of time into the reactor, and it can be considered as the volume of the vapo-gas mixture passing per unit of time through the reactor's section X. Equation (6.29) establishes the relationship between the contact time t during the formation of the dispersion system inside the reactor and reactor volume $\mathcal{V}_{\mathcal{R}}$.

It is necessary to express a variable component C_A through N_A. It is known that:

$$C_A = \frac{N_A}{\mathcal{V}} = \frac{\mathcal{P} N_A}{\mathcal{R}\mathcal{T}\,(2N_{A0} - N_A)}. \qquad (6.30)$$

A substitution of the equations (6.29) and (6.30) for (6.28), gives:

$$\frac{dN_A}{d\mathcal{V}_{\mathcal{R}}} = -\,k\,\frac{N_A^2}{\mathcal{V}^2} = -\,k\,\left(\frac{\mathcal{P}}{\mathcal{R}\mathcal{T}}\right)^2 \left(\frac{N_A}{2N_{A0} - N_A}\right)^2.$$

A separation of variables leads to the equation:

$$\left(\frac{4N_{A0}^2}{N_A^2} - \frac{4N_{A0}}{N_A} + 1\right) dN_A = -k\left(\frac{\mathcal{P}}{\mathcal{R}\mathcal{T}}\right)^2 d\mathcal{V}_{\mathcal{R}}. \qquad (6.31)$$

In this problem, it is required to determine the molar fraction of the formed dispersion system for a given reactor volume $\mathcal{V}_{\mathcal{R}}$, i.e., $\frac{N_A}{N_{A0}}$.

Let us designate: $\frac{N_A}{N_{A0}} = \psi$, then the equation (6.31) takes this form of:

$$N_{A0}\left(\frac{4}{\psi^2} - \frac{4}{\psi} + 1\right) d\psi = -\,k\left(\frac{\mathcal{P}}{\mathcal{R}\mathcal{T}}\right)^2 d\mathcal{V}_{\mathcal{R}}.$$

Now, let us integrate the left part of this equation into ψ, ranging from 1 to ψ, and the right part on $\mathcal{V}_{\mathcal{R}}$, ranging from 0 to $\mathcal{V}_{\mathcal{R}}$. Neglecting a minor change of pressure $\mathcal{P}$, caused by friction inside the reactor, the equation will be:

$$4 - \frac{4}{\psi} - 4\ln\psi + (\psi - 1) = -\frac{k}{N_{A0}}\left(\frac{\mathcal{P}}{\mathcal{R}\mathcal{T}}\right)^2 \mathcal{V}_{\mathcal{R}}. \qquad (6.32)$$

Formula (6.32) allows us to calculate ψ for this speed of formation of the dispersion system and for the set speed of the loading of components of mixed-in moles in the unit of time for the reactor with a volume $\mathcal{V}_{\mathcal{R}}$.

The other questions demand further study.

6.6. GAS ABSORBTION BY THE LIQUID IN TORSION-ORIENTED TURBULIZATION MODE

Absorption takes an important place in modern chemical technology. The basis of this processes is the ability of gases to interact with liquids to form solutions. For example, the artificial saturation of liquid oxygen is called an aeration. The artificial saturation of carbon dioxide is called a saturation and so on. The mechanism of the absorption is as follows: a boundary layer is formed on gas–liquid interface, consisting of two layers adjacent to each other—one of which consists of gas molecules, the other consists of liquid molecules. It should be noted that gas–liquid layer resists the passage of gas from the dispersed phase to the dispersion medium.

It is quite obvious that gas absorption process by liquid in the mode of torsion-oriented turbulization is caused by an essential increase of the phase interface and intensive agitation, allowing new opportunities for acceleration and optimization of the considered process. The use of torsion-oriented turbulization for absorption lets us to consider the dissolution of carbon dioxide CO_2 in water H_2O, for example.

The solubility of gas in liquid is characterized by the coefficient of absorption $\propto$. This defines what volume of gas can be dissolved in a unit of liquid volume. That is, the coefficient of absorption $\propto$ is the amount of the volume of gas that could be absorbed by one volume of liquid under partial pressure of gas 101.3 kN/m^2 (that is equal 760 mm of Hg.) and the temperature of 0 ^{0}C. Thus:

$$\propto = \frac{\mathcal{v}_{\mathcal{g}}}{\mathcal{V}_{\ell}},$$

where $\mathcal{v}_{\mathcal{g}}$ is the volume of gas, [m^3]; and $\mathcal{V}_{\ell}$ is the volume of solvent, [m^3].

The solubility of gas in water can be characterized, by the amount of gas (in grams) that could be dissolved in 100 grams of water under the general pressure of gas and vapors of water of 101.3 kN/m^2.

The interacting of the carbon dioxide CO_2 with water H_2O, forms a coal acid that is dissociated on ions of a carbonate and bicarbonate:

$$H_2O + CO_2 \rightleftarrows H_2\,CO_3 \rightleftarrows H^+ + HCO_3 \rightleftarrows 2\,H^+ + CO_3^{2-}.$$

The private coefficients of the speed of absorption for a gas dispersion phase and solvent (the dispersive environment) are set by the criteria equations [217]:

$$K_G = f_1 \frac{D_G}{d} \boldsymbol{Re}_G^k \boldsymbol{Pr}_G^l \left(\frac{d}{h}\right)^m;$$

$$K_L = f_2 \frac{D_L}{d} \boldsymbol{Re}_L^n \boldsymbol{Pr}_L^p \left(\frac{d}{h}\right)^q;$$

For the considered process, the equation for the general coefficient of speed of absorption K [Kg/m ^{2} x hour x mm of Hg] makes an appearance [217]:

$$K = \frac{1}{f_1 \frac{D_G}{d} \boldsymbol{Re}_G^k\, \boldsymbol{Pr}_G^l \left(\frac{d}{h}\right)^m \cdot \frac{3600M}{22.4 \cdot 760} + f_2 \frac{D_L}{d} \boldsymbol{Re}_L^n\, \boldsymbol{Pr}_L^p \left(\frac{d}{h}\right)^q \cdot \frac{3600H}{760}}.$$

or

$$K = \frac{1}{0.211 \cdot f_1 \frac{D_G}{d} \boldsymbol{Re}_G^k\, \boldsymbol{Pr}_G^l \left(\frac{d}{h}\right)^m \cdot M + 4.73 \cdot f_2 \frac{D_L}{d} \boldsymbol{Re}_L^n\, \boldsymbol{Pr}_L^p \left(\frac{d}{h}\right)^q \cdot H},$$

where:

- f_1 and f_2 are amounts, that have to be determined.
- $k, l, m, n, p,$ and q are exponents of criteria of similarity.
- M is the molecular mass of the dissolved gas.
- H is the Henry's constant, [kg/m^2 x atmospheric pressure].
- $\boldsymbol{Re}_G$ is the Reynolds number for gas $\left(\boldsymbol{Re}_G = \frac{d w_G}{\upsilon_G}\right)$.

- Re_L is the Reynolds number for liquid $\left(Re_L = \frac{dw_L}{\upsilon_L}\right)$.
- Pr_G is the Prandtl's number for gas $\left(Pr_G = \frac{\upsilon_G}{D_G}\right)$.
- Pr_L is the Prandtl's number for liquid $\left(Pr_L = \frac{\upsilon_L}{D_L}\right)$.
- D_G is the coefficient of diffusion for gas, [m²/s].
- D_L is the coefficient of diffusion for liquid, [m²/s].
- d is the internal diameter of the reactor, [m].
- h is the reactor's height, [m].
- υ_G is the kinematic viscosity of gas (disperse phase), [m²/s].
- υ_L is the kinematic viscosity of liquid (dispersive phase), [m²/s].

In compliance with Henry's Law, the dependence of the solubility of the gas in a specific liquid at a constant temperature is directly proportional to the pressure of this gas above the solution. It must be understood, that this law is suitable only for **ideal** solutions and with relatively low pressure. The Henry's Law can be expressed as:

$$C = H\mathcal{P}$$

where $\mathcal{P}$ is the partial pressure of gas over the solution; C is the molar concentration of gas in the solution; and N is the Henry's constant, that is depending on the physical and mechanical properties of gas, solution and temperature.

1. Determination of the Coefficient k

It is necessary to experimentally determine the general coefficients of the speed of absorption k at the variable amount of the Re_G:

$$\text{For } Re_{G1}: \quad K_1 = \frac{1}{\frac{A}{Re_{G1}^{k}} + \frac{1}{K_L}}.$$

For Re_{G2}: $$K1 = \frac{1}{\frac{A}{Re_{G2}^{k}} + \frac{1}{K_L}}.$$

For Re_{G3}: $$K1 = \frac{1}{\frac{A}{Re_{G3}^{k}} + \frac{1}{K_L}}.$$

where:

$$A = \frac{1}{0.211 \cdot f_1 \frac{D_G}{d} Re_G^k Pr_G^l (\frac{d}{h})^m \cdot M}.$$

Thus, there are three equations with three unknowns: A, k and $\frac{1}{K_L}$. At the joint solution of these equations, k could be defined by the equation:

$$(\alpha^k - 1) = B(1 - \beta^k).$$

where:

$$\alpha = \frac{Re_{G2}}{Re_{G1}}, \ \beta = \frac{Re_{G3}}{Re_{G1}} \text{ and } B = \frac{\frac{1}{K_1} - \frac{1}{K_2}}{\frac{1}{K_2} - \frac{1}{K_3}}.$$

The amounts A and $\frac{1}{K_L}$ are:

$$A = \frac{\frac{1}{K_1} - \frac{1}{K_2}}{\frac{2}{Re_{G1}^k} - \frac{1}{Re_{G2}^k}} \quad \text{and} \quad \frac{1}{K_L} = \frac{1}{K_1} - \frac{A}{Re_{G1}^k}.$$

2. Determination of the Coefficient m

Let us define the general coefficient of speed of absorption K at the variable values $\frac{d}{h}$. Because the amount of A depends upon $\frac{d}{h}$, it is necessary for each of the values of $\frac{d}{h}$ to find A from the three values of K.

Let us assume that $(\frac{d}{h})_1$ and $(\frac{d}{h})_2$ correspond to A_1 and A. Then:

$$A_1 = \frac{1}{0.211 \cdot f_1 \frac{D_G}{d} Re_G^k Pr_G^l (\frac{d}{h})_1^m \cdot M}.$$

$$A_2 = \frac{1}{0.211 \cdot f_2 \frac{D_G}{d} Re_G^k \, Pr_G^l \, (\frac{d}{h})_2^m \cdot M}.$$

To construct the ratio $\frac{A_1}{A_2}$, let us take the logarithm and definition from the equation received at the same time m:

$$m = \frac{\lg\frac{A_1}{A_2}}{\lg\frac{h_1}{h_2}}.$$

3. Determination of the Coefficient l

In this case K is defined at variable amounts Pr, which can be received by testing the other gases. However, it is not only Pr that is changing. M and D_G are changing also. The amount of A depends upon Pr_G, therefore it is necessary for various gases to determine A from three values of K. Let us assume that for the gas, for which Pr_1, D_{G1}, and M_1 are known, the amount A_1 has been found. For the other gas for which Pr_2, D_{G2}, and M_2 are known, the amount A_1 is also found. Thus:

$$A_1 = \frac{1}{0.211 \cdot f_1 \frac{D_{G1}}{d} \, Pr_{G1}^l \, (\frac{d}{h})^m \cdot M_1}.$$

$$A_2 = \frac{1}{0.211 \cdot f_2 \frac{D_{G2}}{d} \, Pr_{G2}^l \, (\frac{d}{h})^m \cdot M_2}.$$

from where:

$$l = \frac{\lg \frac{A_1}{A_2} \frac{M_1}{M_2} \frac{D_{G1}}{D_{G2}}}{\lg\frac{Pr_{G2}}{Pr_{G1}}}.$$

4. Determination of the Coefficient f_1

If coefficients l and m are known, then the value of the f_1 function is easy to define from the equation:

$$f_1 = \frac{1}{0.211 \cdot A\, D_G\, \boldsymbol{Pr}_G^l\, (\frac{d}{h})^m \cdot M}.$$

where A is the average value of this amount as coefficients k, l and m are calculated upon several values of A.

5. Determination of the Coefficient n

The amount K is at the variable amounts of $\boldsymbol{Re}_G$, meaning that K is under a condition in which the frequency of the vibration impact are approaches the frequency of natural fluctuations of components of the processed dispersion system. As a result, the quantity of vapor-gas bubbles increases, and we have the following resulting equations:

$$\text{For } \boldsymbol{Re}_{G1}:\ K_1 = \frac{1}{\frac{1}{K_G} + \frac{E}{\boldsymbol{Re}_{G1}^n}}.$$

$$\text{For } \boldsymbol{Re}_{G2}:\ K_1 = \frac{1}{\frac{1}{K_G} + \frac{E}{\boldsymbol{Re}_{G2}^n}}.$$

$$\text{For } \boldsymbol{Re}_{G3}:\ K_1 = \frac{1}{\frac{1}{K_G} + \frac{E}{\boldsymbol{Re}_{G3}^n}}.$$

where:

$$E = \frac{1}{4.73 \cdot f_2\, \frac{D_L}{d}\, \boldsymbol{Pr}_L\, (\frac{d}{h})^q \cdot H}.$$

The exponent n, when solving these equations, is determined from the relation:

$$(\alpha^n - 1) = z\,(1 - \beta^n)$$

where:

$$\alpha = \frac{\boldsymbol{Re}_{G2}}{\boldsymbol{Re}_{G1}}; \qquad \beta = \frac{\boldsymbol{Re}_{G2}}{\boldsymbol{Re}_{G3}}; \qquad z = \frac{\frac{1}{K_1} - \frac{1}{K_2}}{\frac{1}{K_2} - \frac{1}{K_3}}.$$

Amounts:

$$E = \frac{\frac{1}{K_1} - \frac{1}{K_2}}{\frac{2}{Re_{G1}^{n}} - \frac{1}{Re_{G2}^{n}}} \quad \text{and} \quad \frac{1}{K_G} = \frac{1}{K_1} - \frac{A}{Re_{G1}^{n}} .$$

6. Definition of the Exponent p

In this case, the variable amount is Pr_L . At the same time with Pr_L, which changes when the other gas is in use, amounts D_L and Henry's constant H are changing as well. So:

$$P = \frac{\lg \frac{E_1}{E_2} \frac{H_1}{H_2} \frac{D_{G1}}{D_{G2}}}{\lg \frac{Pr_{G2}}{Pr_{G1}}} .$$

7. Definition of the Function f_2

In the presence of the known exponents p and q, this function is defined as:

$$q = \frac{1}{4.73 \cdot D_L \; Pr_G^{p} \; (\frac{d}{h})^{q} \cdot H \, E} .$$

Applying a method [216], developed during study of the processes of dissolution of NH_3, SO_2, and HCl in a mixture with air in water, after mathematical processing, confirmed by experimental data, the following values were also obtained for the coefficients of the absorption rate, which can be used in the calculations in relation to this process:

$$K_G = 0.044 \frac{D_G}{d} Re_G^{0.752} \, Pr_G^{0.620} \left(\frac{d}{h}\right)^{0.066} . \qquad [\text{м/s}]$$

$$K_L = 471 \frac{D_L}{d} Re_L^{0.324} \, Pr_L^{0.165} \left(\frac{d}{h}\right)^{0.503} . \qquad [\text{м/s}]$$

CHAPTER 7

DIRECT METHOD OF MEASUREMENT OF THE INTERNAL PRESSURE DURING THE FORMATION OF DISPERSION SYSTEMS

As established in the above, the internal pressure, to be more specific, fields of the internal tensions, is the main characteristic of formed dispersion systems.

7.1. ANALYSIS OF FORCES ACTING ON THE SURFACE OF A SENSITIVE ELEMENT OF THE DEVICE FOR THE MEASUREMENT OF THE INTERNAL PRESSURE

As was discussed in the previous chapters, the resonance cavitation and the torsion-oriented turbulization are phenomena resulting from combined and simultaneous influence of the revolting forces of a shock wave, coincidence of frequency of harmonic oscillations of the external forces (indignant influence) forces, called resonance, and frequency of internal (natural) fluctuations of the dispersion system. A necessary condition of the formation and the future existence of the dispersion system is the emergence and cumulative development (compression and collapse) of bubbles, which leads to development of fields of internal pressure. As shown in Chapter 3, the one of the major characteristics of the considered processes is development of differences of internal pressure between adjacent elementary volumes of the dispersion system, that is the development of the fields of internal tension.

Simplest, at first sight, is the direct method of measurement of internal pressure when the sensitive element of the measuring device is placed inside of the system in question. In this case there is some mechanical connection: "dispersion system—a sensitive element". It is quite obvious, that the sensitive element placed inside dispersion system is a foreign object that, being placed into the considered system, changes the character of the fields of force acting in this system. Thus, the registered signal is reflection of this indignant state. Naturally, there is a question of the nature of forces are operating on the measuring device.

To carrying out the analysis of the physical nature of forces, let us consider the effect of the three–phase dispersion system—solid particles–liquid–gas—on the condition of equality of pressure in the dispersion medium (liquid) and a dispersed (gas and solid particles) phase, wherein, in rather small bubbles (the size of < 2 mm), the heat exchange conditions are significantly difficult. Under such conditions, the gas in the bubbles cannot cool to the temperature of the liquid phase, which serves as the basis for applying the adiabatic model [215]. Another limitation in the system under consideration is the neglect of small–scale bubble pulsations, which is acceptable for gas–liquid systems with a low gas content [172]. Under such initial conditions, this dispersion system can be considered as holonomic [214], that is, those that impose restrictions only on the possible positions of the material points of the given system.

The equilibrium state for any point in the adopted system and subordinate to holonomic stationary bonds, as was noted [1] as:

$$f_j(x_1, y_1, z_1, x_2, y_2, z_3, \dots x_n, y_n, z_n, t) = 0, \quad (j = 1, 2, 3, \dots, k), \quad (7.1)$$

where x_i, y_i, z_i, are coordinates; t is the time; and k is the number of the imposed bonds, which for any time point are defined by the condition [168]:

$$\sum_i^n \vec{\mathfrak{F}}_i \delta \mathfrak{r}_i + \sum_i^n \vec{\mathfrak{R}}_i \delta \mathfrak{r}_i = 0 \quad (7.2)$$

where i is the point number; $\vec{\mathfrak{F}}_i$ is the vector resultant from all active forces closer to point number i; $\vec{\mathfrak{R}}_i$ is the vector resultant from all internal forces closer to point number i; and $\delta\mathfrak{r} = \delta x_i + \delta y_i + \delta z_i$ is the vector virtual relocation of the point number i.

The condition (7.2) can be written down as:

$$\sum_{i}^{n}(Fx_i\,\delta x_i + Fy_i\delta y_i + Fz_i\delta z_i) +$$
$$+\sum_{i}^{n}(Rx_i\,\delta x_i + Ry_i\delta y_i + Rz_i\delta z_i) = 0, \quad (7.3)$$

where Fx_i, Fy_i, Fz_i and Rx_i, Ry_i, Rz_i are projections of indignant (active) and internal forces to axes of coordinates.

It should be noted that variations of coordinates δx δy, δz caused by the definition [1], by which virtual relocation of points of the dispersion system are subordinated to k bonds, is version of equation (7.1) called a set of infinitesimal vectors:

$$\delta\vec{r} = \delta\mathfrak{x}\cdot i + \delta\mathfrak{y}\cdot j + \delta\mathfrak{z}\cdot k, \quad (7.3a)$$

with which the following projections satisfy the system of equations:

$$\sum_{i}^{n}\left[\frac{\partial f(j)}{\partial x_i}\delta x_i + \frac{\partial f(j)}{\partial y_i}\delta y_i + \frac{\partial f(j)}{\partial z_i}\delta z_i\right] = 0, \quad (7.4)$$

where $j = 1, 2, \ldots k$ are also subordinated to k.

Using the analogy as in [1], it is possible to write a condition (7.4) for internal points of dispersion medium D, for points of a free surface, or otherwise, interfaces of phases P and for points of a contact layer of the studied dispersion system with the surface of the measuring device M.

All active forces of the considered system are set. Therefore, let designate all three sums of these forces in one symbol and record the received results. As a result of such summation will be:

$$\sum_{i}^{n}\left(Fx_i\delta x_i + Fy_i\delta y_i + Fz_i\delta z_i\right) +$$
$$+\sum_{i}^{n-m-k}\left(R_D x_i\delta x_i + R_D y_i\delta y_i + R_D z_i\delta z_i\right) +$$
$$+\sum_{i}^{k}\left(R_P x_i\delta x_i + R_P y_i\delta y_i + R_P z_i\delta z_i\right) +$$

$$+\sum_{i}^{m}\left(R_M x_i\delta x_i + R_M y_i\delta y_i + R_M z_i\delta z_i\right) = 0 \quad (7.5)$$

where n > k and n > m.

Because internal forces $\overrightarrow{\mathfrak{R}}_i$ of the dispersion system in question have potential and, therefore, have a power function $U = U(x_i, y_i, z_i)$, the sum of elementary works of forces $\overrightarrow{\mathfrak{R}}_i$ on any movement of system will be a full differential of the function U depending on n of coordinates of points of the system. In this case:

$$dU = \sum_{i}^{n}\left(Rx_i\delta x_i + Ry_i\delta y_i + Rz_i\delta z_i\right), \quad (7.5a)$$

where Rx_i, Ry_i, Rz_i are projections of forces $\overrightarrow{\mathfrak{R}}_i$ to coordinate axes. From this it is visible that:

$$R = x_i\frac{\partial U}{\partial x_i};\ Ry_i = \frac{\partial U}{\partial y_i};\ R = z_i\frac{\partial U}{\partial z_i}. \quad (7.5b)$$

Let us enter a concept of potential energy of the system:

$$E_p = E_p\ (x_i, y_i, z_i).$$

This energy is defined by work that forces of the potential field must perform to convert the system from position (x_i, y_i, z_i) to position (x_{i0}, y_{i0}, z_{i0}), chosen randomly. Therefore,

$$V(x_i, y_i, z_i) = \sum_{i}^{n}\int_{(x_i,y_i,z_i)}^{(x_{i0},y_{i0},z_{i0})}\left(Rx_i + Ry_i\delta y_i + Rz_i\delta z_i\right). (7.5c)$$

Changing the order of summation and integration there is:

$$V(x_i, y_i, z_i) = \int_{(x_i,y_i,z_i)}^{(x_{i0},y_{i0},z_{i0})} dU. \quad (7.5d)$$

After the integration:

$$V(x_i, y_i, z_i) = U(x_{i0}, y_{i0}, z_{i0}) - U(x_i, y_i, z_i), \qquad (7.5e)$$

where the potential energy V, accurate to the additive constant, is equal to the force function U, taken with the opposite sign:

$$V(x_i, y_i, z_i) = -U(x_i, y_i, z_i). \qquad (7.5f)$$

Expressing the principle of virtual displacements by means of the potential energy V, we get:

$$\sum_i^n (Rx_i\, \delta x_i + Ry_i \delta y_i + Rz_i \delta z_i) =$$

$$= \sum_i^n \left(\frac{\partial U}{\partial x_i} \delta x_i + \frac{\partial U}{\partial y_i} \delta y_i + \frac{\partial U}{\partial z_i} \delta z_i \right) = - \delta U = 0 \quad (7.5g)$$

Thus:

$$\sum_i^m (R_D x_i \delta x_i + R_D y_i \delta y_i + R_D z_i \delta z_i) = - \delta U_D$$

$$\sum_i^k (R_P x_i \delta x_i + R_P y_i \delta y_i + R_P z_i \delta z_i) = -\delta U_P \qquad (7.6)$$

$$\sum_i^{n-m-k} (R_M x_i \delta x_i + R_M y_i \delta y_i + R_M z_i \delta z_i) = - \delta U_M$$

If to accept that the deformation ability of a sensitive element of the measuring device can to some extent can be considered as a semblance of density (ρ_M), then the physical sense of the system of the equations (7.6) in this case is as follows:

- Potential U_D is the function of mass forces and depends on the density of this dispersion system (ρ);
- Potentials U_P and U_M are functions of the density of system ρ, the deformation ability of a sensitive element ρ_M, and the thickness of a layer of the dispersion medium λ on a free surface as well as the

thickness of a layer of contact with a surface of a sensitive element of the measuring device.

Therefore:

$$U_D = U_D\,(\rho_D),\ U_P = U_P\,(\rho_P, \lambda_P),\ U_M = U_M\,(\rho_M, \lambda_M). \quad (7.6a)$$

Let us designate through N_D the potential size relation U_D to a unit of volume of the dispersion system $d\tau_D$. Also, let us similarly designate through N_P and N_M specific values of potentials U_P and U_M, carried to a unit of a free surface or, otherwise, to the limit of the section of phases ds_P and to the unit of the surface of the measuring device ds_M.

Because of the continuity of the considered disperse system and continuity of contact with a sensitive element of the measuring device, there is:

$$U_D = \int U_D d\tau_D \quad U_P = \int U_P ds_P \text{ and } U_M = \int U_M\, ds_M, \quad (7.7)$$

Replacing the action of active forces with the subject dispersion system from a free surface, and not violating the equilibrium condition, it is possible to assume that the justice of the equality is:

$$\sum_i^n \overrightarrow{\mathfrak{F}_i\, \delta \mathfrak{r}_i} = \int (R_D x_i \delta x_i + R_D y_i \delta y_i + R_D z_i \delta z_i)\, d\tau_D + $$
$$+ \int (R_p x_i \delta x_i + R_p y_i \delta y_i + R_p z_i \delta z_i)\, ds_P\,, \quad (7.8)$$

where $\delta \mathfrak{r} = \delta x_i + \delta y_i + \delta z_i$ is the vector virtual relocation of the point number *i*.

By writing down (6.5) and taking into account (7.6), (7.7), and (7.8), there is:

$$\int (R_D x_i \delta x_i + R_D y_i \delta y_i + R_D z_i \delta z_i)\, d\tau_D +$$

$$+ \int (R_P x_i \delta x_i + R_P y_i \delta y_i + R_P z_i \delta z_i)\, ds_P -$$
$$- \delta \int U_D\,(\rho_D) d\tau_D \; - \delta \int U_P\,(\rho_P, \lambda_P) ds_P -$$
$$- \delta \int U_M\,(\rho_M, \lambda_M)\, ds_M = 0. \qquad (7.9)$$

Equation (7.9) represents a condition of equilibrium of the considered dispersion system with the sensitive element of the measuring device placed inside it. Projections $(R_D)_x, (R_D)_y$, and $(R_D)_z$ are equally effective forces depending on the density of the dispersion system, and projections $(R_P)_x$, $(R_P)_y$and $(R_P)_z$ make an equally effective system of surface forces operating on an interface between phases. The action of the first and third integrals extends to all points of the volume of the system, and the action of the second integral extends to all points of the free surface, in other words, the interface. The third and fourth integrals extend their action to all points of the volume of the dispersion system and the interface, while the fifth integral extends its action to all points of the surface of the measuring device.

Let us define variations of the integrals entering the equation (7.9):

$$\delta \int U_D\,(\rho_D) d\tau_D = \int \frac{U_D}{\partial \rho}\, \delta\rho\, d\tau + U_D\, \delta d\tau; \qquad (7.10)$$

$$\delta \int U_P\,(\rho_P, \lambda_P) ds_P =$$
$$= \int \Big(\frac{\partial U_P}{\partial \rho_P}\, \delta\rho_P + \frac{\partial U_P}{\partial \omega_P}\, \delta\lambda_P\Big) ds_P + \int U_P \delta ds_P\,; \qquad (7.11)$$

$$\delta \int U_M\,(\rho_M, \lambda_M) ds_M =$$
$$= \int \Big(\frac{\partial U_M}{\partial \rho_M}\, \delta\rho_{ИУ} + \frac{\partial U_{ИУ}}{\partial \lambda_M}\, \delta\lambda_M\Big) ds_M + \int U_M\, \delta ds_M \quad (7.12)$$

For the variation of an element of a free surface δds_P, which depends on the virtual movements of points of a free surface, let us to use Bertrán's method [172].

Let us assume that $ABCD = ds_{P-1}$is an element of a free surface of movement (Fig. 7.1) and $A_1B_1C_1D_1 = ds_{P-2}$is the same element of a free surface after movement. Then, based on the definition of virtual movement, we get:

$$\delta ds_P = ds_{P-1} - ds_{P-2} \,. \qquad (7.12a)$$

AB and AC are elements of two orthogonal lines of curvature, which drawn on the surface through the basis A of the normal $\overrightarrow{\mathfrak{P}}$ directed into the system, there is:

$$ds_{P-1} = AB \cdot AC \text{ and } ds_{P-2} = A_1 B_1 \cdot A_1 C_1. \qquad (7.12b)$$

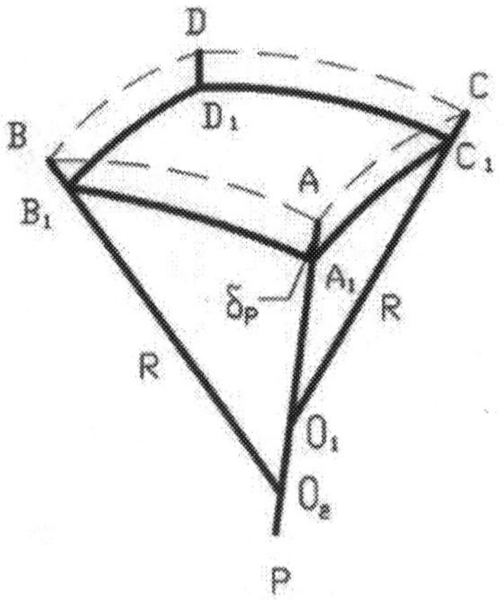

Figure 7-1. Scheme of the Calculation

Let us note that the normal $\overrightarrow{\mathfrak{P}}$ is the vector's amount, and it is quite obvious (Fig. 7.1) that:

$$A_1B_1 = \left(1+\frac{\delta\rho}{R_1}\right)AB \text{ and } A_1C_1 = \left(1+\frac{\delta\rho}{R_2}\right) AC. \quad (7.12c)$$

Therefore,

$$\delta \mathrm{d}s_P = \left(\frac{1}{\mathrm{R}_1} + \frac{1}{\mathrm{R}_2}\right) \mathrm{d}s_P \mathrm{d}\overrightarrow{\mathfrak{P}}, \quad (7.12d)$$

where $AA_1 = \mathrm{d}\overrightarrow{\mathfrak{P}}$ is the normal movement of a point A in the direction $\overrightarrow{\mathfrak{P}}$.

The expression in parentheses should be taken as an absolute value, that the direction of movement cannot coincide with the direction of a normal to a surface. Therefore:

$$\delta \mathrm{d}s_P = \pm \left(\frac{1}{\mathrm{R}_1} + \frac{1}{\mathrm{R}_2}\right) \mathrm{d}s_P \mathrm{d}\overrightarrow{\mathfrak{P}}, \quad (7.13)$$

From a condition of continuity of the dispersion medium, that is considered in the form of an accepted system of material points and continuity of the contacts between these points located on a surface of the sensitive element with said surface, we get:

$$\delta \mathrm{d}s_M = 0. \quad (7.14)$$

Let is define the variations $\delta\rho_D$, $\delta\rho_P$ and $\delta\rho_M$ now.

From the condition of continuity $\delta(\rho \mathrm{d}\tau) = 0$. From this it follows that:

$$\delta \mathrm{d}\tau = \nabla \mathrm{d}\tau \text{ and } \delta\rho = -\delta\nabla\rho, \quad (7.15)$$

$$\nabla = \frac{\partial}{\partial x}\delta x + \frac{\partial}{\partial y}\delta y + \frac{\partial}{\partial z}\delta z. \quad (7.15a)$$

For the surface film, there is a similar equality:

$$\delta\left(\rho_P \mathrm{d}\overrightarrow{\mathfrak{P}}\, \mathrm{d}s_P\right) = 0,$$

that from (6.13), as a result of commutative property:

$$\delta\ \rho_P \mathrm{d}s_P = \pm\ \rho_P(\frac{1}{\mathrm{R}} + \frac{1}{R})\mathrm{d}s_P \delta \overrightarrow{\mathfrak{P}}. \qquad (7.16)$$

For the layer of the dispersion system, that is in directly contact with the surface of the sensitive element, due to (7.14):

$$\delta\rho_M \mathrm{d}s_M = 0 \qquad (7.17)$$

Writing down $\delta\overrightarrow{\mathfrak{P}}$ in functions of $\delta x,\ \delta y,\ \delta z$ and considering that $\overrightarrow{\mathfrak{P}}$s is the vector, we get:

$$\delta\ \overrightarrow{\mathfrak{P}} = cos\ (p\,x)\,\delta x + cos\ (p\,y)\ \delta y + cos\ (p\,z)\ \delta z. \quad (7.18)$$

Finally, $\delta\lambda_P$ and $\delta\lambda_M$, because of (7.4), are equal to:

$$\delta\lambda_P = \frac{\partial w}{\partial x}\ \delta x\ _P + \frac{\partial w}{\partial y}\ \delta y_P + \frac{\partial w}{\partial z}\delta z_P; \qquad (7.19)$$

$$\delta\lambda_M = \frac{\partial w}{\partial x}\ \delta x\ _M + \frac{\partial w}{\partial y}\ \delta y_M + \frac{\partial w}{\partial z}\delta z_M. \qquad (7.20)$$

Let us to write down the equations (7.10), (7.11) and (7.12) while taking into account the above equations from (7.13) to (7.20):

$$\delta \int U_D\ (\rho)\,d\tau = \int (U_D(\rho) - \rho\frac{\delta U_D}{\partial \rho})\nabla\, d\tau; \qquad (7.21)$$

$$\delta \int U_P\ (\rho_P, \lambda_P) ds_P = \int \{\pm(\frac{1}{\mathrm{R}_1} + \frac{1}{\mathrm{R}_2})\ [U_P\ (\rho_P, \lambda_P) -$$

$$- \rho\frac{\partial U_P\ (\rho_P, \lambda_P)}{\partial \rho_P}](cos\,(px)\,\delta x + cos\ (py)\ \delta y + cos(pz)\ \delta z)\}\ \mathrm{x}$$

$$\mathrm{x}\ [\frac{U_P\ (\rho_P, \lambda_P)}{\partial \rho_P}\ \nabla\ (\rho_P, \lambda_P)\ ]\ ds_P; \qquad (7.22)$$

$$\delta \int U_M(\rho_M, \lambda_M) ds_M = \int \frac{\partial U_M}{\partial \lambda_M} \delta\lambda_M \nabla \lambda_M ds_M. \quad (7.23)$$

By substituting (7.21), (7.22) and (7.23) in (7.9) and using Green's method of integrated transformations [35], we get:

$$\int_{(v)} \nabla \psi \nabla \varphi) d\tau = -\int_{(s)} \varphi \nabla^2 \psi d\tau - \int_{(s)} \varphi \frac{\partial \psi}{\partial \rho} ds,$$

where φ is the scalar function; $\overrightarrow{\mathfrak{P}} (\nabla\varphi) = \frac{\partial \psi}{\partial p}$, there is:

$$(R_D\delta x + R_D\delta y + R_D\delta z)\, d\tau + (R_P\delta x + R_P\delta y + R_P\delta z)\, ds_P +$$
$$+ L_{(\rho)}\left[\cos(p) + \cos x\, \delta x\, (py)\, \delta y + \cos(pz)\, z\delta\right] ds_P +$$
$$+ L_{(\rho)}\left[\cos(px)\delta x + \cos(py)\, \delta y + \cos(pz)\, \delta z\right] ds_M +$$

$$+ \int \left[\frac{\partial L_{(\rho)}}{\partial x} \delta x + \frac{\partial L_{(\rho)}}{\partial y} \delta y + \frac{\partial L_{(\rho)}}{\partial z} \delta z\right] d\tau +$$
$$+ \int\left\{\pm\left(\frac{1}{R^1} + \frac{1}{R^2}\right)\sigma_P(\rho_P, \lambda_P)\ \mathrm{x}\right.$$
$$\mathrm{x}\left.\left[\cos(px)\delta x + \cos(py)\, \delta y + \cos(pz)\, \delta z\right]\right\} ds_P -$$
$$- \int \frac{U_P}{\partial \lambda_P} \nabla\lambda_P ds_P - \int \frac{\partial U_M}{\partial \lambda_M} \nabla\lambda_M\, ds_M = 0, \quad (7.24)$$

where $L_{(\rho)} = U_D(\rho) - \rho \frac{\partial m}{\partial \rho}$;

and $\sigma_P(\rho_P, \lambda_P) = U_P(\rho_P, \lambda_P) - \rho_P \frac{U_P(\rho_P, \lambda_P)}{\partial \rho_P}$.

The physical sense of the function $L_{(\rho)}$ is the internal pressure that develops in the subject dispersion system and is the function of the mass forces that are acting at all points and upon all elementary volumes in this system. Thus, the internal pressure is the combined action of molecular–

surface forces related to unit of volume $d\sigma$. The $\sigma(\rho_P, \lambda_P)$ represents free energy of the unit of the phase interface. Variations of coordinates δx, δy, δz , by the definition provided by [1], are subordinated k equations (7.4).

Multiplying (7.4) using uncertain multipliers of Lagrange $m_1, m_2, \ldots, m_n$, and then adding the received expressions, there is:

$$\sum_j^k m_j \sum_i^n \left(\frac{\partial f_j}{\partial x_i}\, \delta x_i + \frac{\partial f_j}{\partial y_i}\, \delta y_i + \frac{\partial f_j}{\partial z_i}\, \delta z_i\right) = 0. \quad (7.25)$$

Adding ratios (7.24) and (6.25) and choosing m_j in a way that would ensure coefficients at variations k, would converted into zero, they would then be converted into zero and coefficients at the others' $(3n - k)$ variations, as a result of their independence. Therefore, for internal points of system, there are:

$$R_{(D)x} = \frac{\partial L_{(\rho)}}{\partial x};\ R_{(D)y} = \frac{\partial L_{(\rho)}}{\partial y}\ ;\ R_{(D)z} = \frac{\partial L_{(\rho)}}{\partial z}. \quad (7.26)$$

Thus, it is obvious, that, for material points of a free surface, the following system of equations must be satisfied:

$$\begin{aligned}
&L_{(\rho)} \cos(px) \pm \left(\frac{1}{R} + \frac{1}{R}\right) \sigma_P(\rho_P, \lambda_P) \cos(px) - \\
&- \frac{U_P}{\partial \lambda_P} \frac{\partial \lambda_P}{\partial x} R_{(P)x} = 0; \\
&L_{(\rho)} \cos(y) p \pm \left(\frac{1}{R} + \frac{1}{R}\right) \sigma_P(\rho_P, \lambda_P) \cos(py) - \\
&- \frac{U_P}{\partial \lambda_P} \frac{\partial \lambda_P}{\partial y} R_{(P)y} = 0; \qquad (7.27) \\
&L_{(\rho)} \cos(z) p \pm \left(\frac{1}{R} + \frac{1}{R}\right) \sigma_P(\rho_P, \lambda_P) \cos(pz) - \\
&- \frac{U_P}{\partial \lambda_P} \frac{\partial \lambda_P}{\partial z} R_{(P)z} = 0;
\end{aligned}$$

For points of a contact layer of the considered system and a sensitive element of the measuring device, the condition of the balance must answer the following system of equations:

$$\begin{aligned} &\mathrm{L}_{(\rho)} \cos(px) - \frac{U_M}{\partial\lambda_M}\frac{\partial\lambda_M}{\partial x} R_{(M)x} = 0 \\ &\mathrm{L}_{(\rho)} \cos(py) - \frac{U_M}{\partial\lambda_M}\frac{\partial\lambda_M}{\partial y} R_{(M)y} = 0 \\ &\mathrm{L}_{(\rho)} \cos(pz) - \frac{U_M}{\partial\lambda_M}\frac{\partial\lambda_M}{\partial z} R_{(M)z} = 0 \end{aligned} \qquad (7.28)$$

As the thickness of layers is measured as normal to their surfaces, it is always possible to define vectors $\overrightarrow{\mathfrak{M}}_{(\lambda_P)}$ and $\overrightarrow{\mathfrak{P}}_{(\lambda_M)}$ so that the following conditions are satisfied:

$$\frac{U_P}{\partial\lambda_P}\frac{\partial\lambda_P}{\partial x} = \overrightarrow{\mathfrak{M}}_{(\lambda_P)} \cos(px)\text{... and so on} \qquad (7.29)$$

$$\frac{U_M}{\partial\lambda_M}\frac{\partial\lambda_M}{\partial x} = \overrightarrow{\mathfrak{P}}_{(\lambda_M)} \cos(px)\text{... and so on} \qquad (7.30)$$

In this case the system of the equations (7.27) converts to the system of the equations (7.31):

$$\begin{aligned} &R_{(P)x} = \left[\mathrm{L}_{(\rho)} \pm \left(\frac{1}{R_1} + \frac{1}{R_2}\right) \sigma_P\left(\rho_p, \lambda_P\right) - \overrightarrow{\mathfrak{M}}_{(\lambda_P)} \cos(px);\right. \\ &R_{(P)y} = \left[\mathrm{L}_{(\rho)} \pm \left(\frac{1}{R_1} + \frac{1}{R_2}\right) \sigma_P\left(\rho_p, \lambda_P\right) - \overrightarrow{\mathfrak{M}}_{(\lambda_P)} \cos(py);\right. \quad (7.31) \\ &R_{(P)z} = \left[\mathrm{L}_{(\rho)} \pm \left(\frac{1}{R_1} + \frac{1}{R_2}\right) \sigma_P\left(\rho_p, \lambda_P\right) - \overrightarrow{\mathfrak{M}}_{(\lambda_P)} \cos(pz).\right. \end{aligned}$$

It is easy to see that some free surface, that is to an interface of liquid-gas phases, must correspond to this condition:

$$\mathrm{C}_{(x,\,y,\,z)} = \mathrm{L}_{(p)} + \overrightarrow{\mathfrak{M}}_{(\lambda_P)} \pm \sigma_P\left(\rho_p, \lambda_P\right) - \left(\frac{1}{R_1} + \frac{1}{R_2}\right),$$

where:

$$\mathbf{C}_{(x,\,y,\,z)} = \sqrt{(R_{(P)x})^2 + (R_{(P)y})^2 + (R_{(P)z})^2}.$$

Thus, we can conclude that on the layer on which the action of surface forces is manifested, the internal pressure depends on the surface tension forces $\mathbf{C}_{(x,\,y,\,z)}$, which in turn depend on the surface shape of the liquid $\sigma_P(\frac{1}{R_1} + \frac{1}{R_2})$ and on the potential of forces of various nature $\overrightarrow{\mathfrak{M}}_{(\lambda_P)}$, determined by the layer thickness λ.

The condition of balance on the surface of a sensitive element, considering (7.30) is equal to:

$$\mathrm{L}_{(p)} = \overrightarrow{\mathfrak{P}}_{(\lambda_M)}. \tag{7.32}$$

Therefore, the pressure perceived by a sensitive element of the measuring device is equal to the internal pressure of the dispersion system at this very point of measurement.

Returning back to equation (7.9), it should be noted that the internal energy characterizing the potential of the internal forces of the dispersion system in the state of torsion-oriented turbulization is associated with the action of external indignant forces and the work of surface forces [217]:

$$\delta \mathrm{U} = \mathrm{Q}\,\delta + \delta \mathrm{W}.$$

The work of surface forces is equal to the sum of elementary works of movements of the surplus tension of surface forces and works of deformations [214]:

$$\delta \mathrm{W}_{\text{surface forces}} = \delta \mathrm{W}_{\text{movement}} + \delta \mathrm{W}_{\text{deformation}}.$$

The work of deformations for isotropic system is equal to [216]:

$$\delta W_{def} = \mu\delta\left[e^2_{xx} + e^2_{yy} + e^2_{zz} + \right.$$
$$\left. + \frac{1}{2}(e^2_{xy} + e^2_{yz} + e^2_{zx})\right] + \frac{1}{2}\Psi\,\delta(\text{div}\,\vec{\mathfrak{U}})^2$$

and

$$\text{Diss } f_{(\mathfrak{U})} = \left[e^2_{xx} + e^2_{yy} + e^2_{zz} + ½\,(e^2_{xy} + e^2_{yz} + e^2_{zx})\right],$$

where Diss $f_{(\mathfrak{U})}$ is the dissipative function of Rayleigh; $\vec{\mathfrak{U}}$ is the elastic shift of particles; μ and Ψ are elastic modules of isotropic substance; and $\text{div}\,\vec{\mathfrak{U}} = \frac{\partial U}{\partial x} + \frac{\partial U}{\partial y} + \frac{\partial U}{\partial z}$ is the relative volume expansion.

The specific elementary work of the surplus of surface forces upon movements, is equal:

$$\delta W_{surface} = \frac{\partial R_x}{\partial x} + \frac{\partial R_y}{\partial y} + \frac{\partial R_z}{\partial z},$$

where Rx, Ry, Rz are projections of surface forces onto coordinate axes.

The amount δQ is an excess of heat brought to the system:

$$\delta Q = \text{div}\,\vec{q}\,\delta t$$

For isotropic systems the stream of heat is expressed with Fourier's formula [218]:

$$\vec{q} = -\Lambda\,\text{grad}\,T.$$

Therefore, the expression for internal energy is:

$$U = \left[\frac{\partial R_x}{\partial x} + \frac{\partial R_y}{\partial y} + \frac{\partial R_z}{\partial z}\right]\delta\vec{\mathfrak{U}} + \mu'\delta\left[\text{Diss} f_{(\vec{\mathfrak{U}})}\right] +$$

$$+ \frac{1}{2}\lambda'\delta(\text{div}\vec{\mathfrak{U}})^2 + \text{div}\,(\Lambda\,\text{grad}\,T). \qquad (7.33)$$

Thus, the sensitive element of the measuring device, placed inside the dispersion system under study, perceives the internal pressure, which is the main characteristic of dispersion systems that form in the modes of resonance cavitation and torsion-oriented turbulization. From the difference in internal pressures between the adjacent volumes of the dispersed phase, it is possible to evaluate the internal state of the fields of internal tension between the adjacent volumes as well as to research the processes of mass transfer and heat exchange inside the reactor. When the direct-type sensitive elements are placed in a measured medium, they measure the energy of the medium. They perceive the pressure acting in the medium on the surface of the sensitive element.

For correct measurements, the surface of the sensitive element placed in the medium to measure the internal pressure must be in contact with all points of the dispersion medium over its entire surface. This means that various pressures are acting on this surface. Their action is independent of the shape of the surface and is directed perpendicular to any point on this surface. Therefore, the direction of pressure forces can be determined by the direction of action of the internal pressure forces of the dispersion system on the surface of the sensitive element. Depending on this, it must take a positive or negative sign for the surface of the sensitive element, but not with respect to the selected coordinate system.

Since the internal pressure forces are acting in a sufficiently large volume of the dispersion system, by comparison with the volume on the sensitive element, there is a certain value within the limit of the surface of this element. The location of the sensitive element relative to the direction of the pressure forces in the dispersion system and the surface of the sensitive element of any shape apply equally to scalar and vector fields of internal pressure forces. This principle holds true for both static and dynamic fields of internal pressure.

7.2. DIRECT METHOD OF MEASUREMENT OF INTERNAL PRESSURE

As it was discovered in the previous chapters, the process of formation of dispersion systems is followed by development of fields of tension among adjacent volumes of the system. The cause of such tension is the joint and simultaneous action of a mechanical resonance, the continuous occurrence of fluid hammers impacts, and interaction of molecular-surface forces as well as forces of the resistance to compression. As the result of non-uniform changes, which result from non-uniform development and collapse of the gas bubbles in adjacent volumes, fields of internal tension develop among adjacent volumes of the system.

Thus, it would be fair to assume that, during formation of dispersion systems, fields of internal tensions are occurring inside those systems as follows:

- The first kind: When the sizes of volumes in which this tension works, they have a macroscopic character, that covers the entire internal space of the reactor or a part of it.
- The second kind: When the sizes of elementary volumes have a microscopic character that covers volume proportional to one or more united in the unit, several gas bubbles, drops of liquid or solid particles.
- The third kind: When the sizes of volumes have an ultramicroscopic character that covers the volume of one or several macromolecules, which are in a layer of the dispersion medium, surrounding the element volume of the dispersion phase.

The first kind of tension is a direct consequence of the indignant influence of an external field of vibratory forces that are forces of a mechanical nature. Internal tensions of the second and third kinds occur from interaction of intermolecular and capillary-surface forces.

The measurement of internal pressure in the formed dispersion systems by a direct method—the introduction into the system of a sensitive element—raises a question about the nature of forces operating on the measuring device. It is quite obvious that when the measuring device is placed inside the dispersion system, it changes the character of the field of force, and the registered signal is a reflection of this indignant state.

In the previous section, the mathematical analysis of forces operating during the process of measuring of the internal pressure with a direct method was carried out. The analysis showed that the sensitive element perceives internal pressure to be average on its surface.

It is also necessary to consider the influence of the discrepancy of physical, mechanical, and physicochemical properties of dispersion systems on characteristics of measuring devices and to develop special requirements guaranteeing the accuracy of measurements. Regarding the establishment of theoretical dependence of the size of a relative error on physical, mechanical, and rheological characteristics of dispersion systems, as well as on the deformation characteristics of measuring devices, by analogy with prior research [219-220], let us proceed from the followings:

1. The internal space of the reactor is infinitely large by comparison with the volume of a sensitive element of the measuring device.
2. The sensitive element of the measuring device perceives pressure that is evenly distributed upon its surface and while the points of the middle surface of the sensitive element move along the normal to its surface.
3. The sliding particles of the dispersed phase on a surface of a sensitive element are relatively small and could be neglected.

If the deformation ability (sensitivity) of the measuring device differs from rheological properties of the dispersion medium (liquid), then, with equal amounts of the integrated pressure operating on a surface of a sensitive element (a capsule) and inside the dispersion environment, the volume of dispersion system will change at an amount different from the amount of the deformation of the capsule of similar volume. Therefore, when maintaining continuity of the dispersion environment in the area adjoining a surface of a sensitive element on the surface of the capsule, there is additional pressure:

$$\mathcal{P}_{RP} = \mathcal{P}_{IP} \pm \mathcal{P}_{A},$$

where $\mathcal{P}_{RP}$ is the registered pressure, [N/m^2]; $\mathcal{P}_{IP}$ is the internal pressure developing in the dispersion system, [N/m^2]; and $\mathcal{P}_{A}$ is the additional pressure depending on deformation ability (sensitivity) of the measuring device, [N/m^2].

On the condition of constant preservation of the contact between the dispersion environment and the surface of a sensitive element (capsule), the equality for each point of time has to remain equal to:

$$(\Delta \mathcal{V}_D)_C = (\Delta \mathcal{V}_C)_{\mathcal{P}_{IP}} \pm (\Delta \mathcal{V}_C)_{\mathcal{P}_A}, \tag{7.34}$$

where $(\Delta \mathcal{V}_D)_C$ is the change of the elementary volume of a dispersion system equal to the volume of a capsule, [m^3]; and $(\Delta \mathcal{V}_C)_{\mathcal{P}_{IP}}$ and $(\Delta \mathcal{V}_C)_{\mathcal{P}_A}$ are the changes of the volume of the capsule under the influence of internal pressure $\mathcal{P}_{IP}$ and the additional $\mathcal{P}_A$ pressure.

The change of the selected elementary volume of a dispersion system depends on the internal pressure $\mathcal{P}_{IP}$, developing because of external power influence, the action of molecular-surface forces, the internal friction forces (dynamic viscosity ξ) of a dispersion system, and the coefficient of compressibility β of the liquid. These four parameters characterize the volume changes of the system. It should be noted that kinematic viscosity μ is the characteristic of the dispersion medium and is independent of changes to the volume of the system.

The size of the allocated elementary volume is significantly smaller than the internal space of the reactor. Thus, a priori, it is possible to assume that change of the allocated volume for any point of time, with a sufficient degree of accuracy, is described by this equation [221]:

$$\mathcal{V}_i = \mathcal{V}_{i\,0}\,(1+\frac{\mathcal{P}^3}{\xi_i^3}\beta_i), \tag{7.35}$$

where $\mathcal{V}_i$ is the size of the allocated volume that corresponds to the registration moment i; and $\mathcal{V}_{i0}$ is the size of the allocated volume that corresponds to the registration moment i_0.

Therefore, it is possible to calculate the change of the volume of a dispersion system as being equal to the volume of a sensitive element of the measuring device, as:

$$(\Delta\mathcal{V}_D)_C = \mathcal{V}_C \frac{\mathcal{P}^3}{\xi_i^3} \beta_i, \qquad (7.36)$$

where $\mathcal{V}_C$ is volume of the sensitive element.

7.3. CALCULATION OF A RELATIVE ERROR OF SPHERICAL CAPSULES AND FLAT MEMBRANES

Let us consider the change of volume of a sensitive element made in the form of the spherical shell connected to the measuring chamber with a tube. The deformation of the tube by comparison with deformation of the capsule can be neglected. For the spherical shell combined with a cylindrical cover (Fig. 7-2) the horizontal deflection $\mathcal{U}_H$ is equal to [226]:

$$\mathcal{U}_H = \frac{1-\mu_C}{2} \frac{\mathcal{P}\mathcal{R}^2}{\mathcal{V}\mathrm{E}_C} \sin\vartheta \qquad (7.37)$$

and vertical $\mathcal{U}_V$ deflection is equal to:

$$\mathcal{U}_V = \frac{1-\mu_C}{2} \frac{\mathcal{P}\mathcal{R}^2}{\mathcal{V}\mathrm{E}_C} (\cos\vartheta_1 - \cos\vartheta). \qquad (7.38)$$

The radial movement of points of a median surface w, or, otherwise, the change of radius of a median surface of a spherical cover is equal to [226]:

$$w = \mathcal{U}_H \sin\vartheta - \mathcal{U}_V \cos\vartheta. \qquad (7.39)$$

Substituting (7.37) and (7.38) with (7.39) and with the consideration, that:

$$\cos\vartheta_1 = \cos(\arcsin\frac{r}{R}),$$

there is:

$$w = \frac{1-\mu_C}{2}\frac{\mathcal{P}\mathcal{R}^2}{\mathcal{V}E_C}\left[1-\cos(\arcsin\frac{r}{R})\right], \tag{7.40}$$

where μ_C is the Poisson ratio that is the measure of the Poisson effect that describes the expansion of the capsule's material in the direction perpendicular to the direction of a compression.

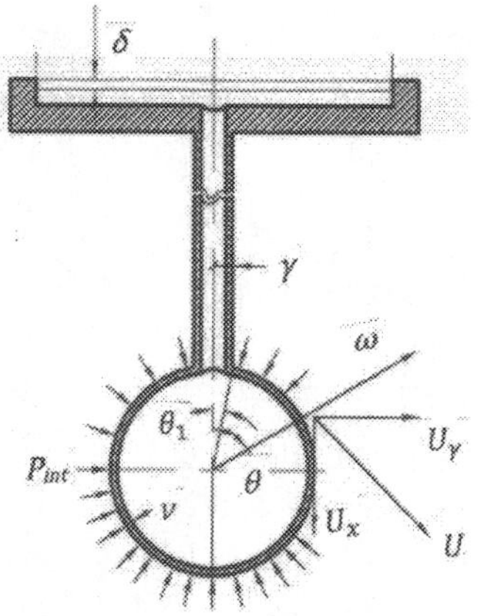

Figure 7-2. Principal Scheme of a Spherical Sensitive Element

The volume of the sphere is equal to: $\frac{4}{3}\pi\mathcal{R}^3$, therefore, change of volume of the spherical capsule is equally:

$$(\Delta\mathcal{V}_C)_{\text{per}} = \frac{4}{3}\pi w^3,$$

or

$$(\Delta\mathcal{V}_K)_R = \frac{4}{3}\pi\frac{\mathcal{P}^3\mathcal{R}^6}{8E_K^3\nu^3}(1-\mu_K)^3\left[1-\cos(\arcsin\frac{r}{R})\right]^3, \tag{7.41}$$

where $\mathcal{P}$ is the internal pressure, [N/m²]; ν is the thickness of the walls of a sensitive element, [m]; $\mathcal{R}$ is the radius of a median surface of the sensitive element (capsule), [m]; E_C is the module of the elasticity, [N/m²]; μ_C is the Poisson coefficient of the capsule's material; r is the radius of the tubing, [m]; and $(\Delta \mathcal{V}_K)_R$ is the registered change of the volume of the spherical capsule, [m³].

The change of the volume of the spherical capsule under the influence of additional pressure is equal to:

$$(\Delta \mathcal{V}_C)_{\mathcal{P}_A} = \frac{4}{3}\pi \frac{\mathcal{P}_A^3 \mathcal{R}^6}{8E_C^3 \nu^3}(1-\mu_C)^3\left[1-\cos(\arcsin\frac{r}{R})\right]^3. \quad (7.42)$$

Substituting (7.36), (7.41) and (7.42) for (7.34), there is:

$$\mathcal{V}_C \frac{\mathcal{P}^3}{\xi_i^3}\beta_i = \frac{4}{3}\pi \frac{\mathcal{P}_A^3 \mathcal{R}^6}{8E_C^3 \nu^3}(1-\mu_C)^3\ (\mathcal{P}^3 \pm \mathcal{P}_A^3)\ \left[1-\cos(\arcsin\frac{r}{R})\right]^3. \quad (7.43)$$

It is easy to see that the relative error $\eta = \pm\frac{\mathcal{P}_A}{\mathcal{P}}$, is equal:

$$\eta = \pm\sqrt[3]{\frac{8\beta_i E_C^3 \nu^3}{\xi_i^3 \mathcal{R}^3 (1-\mu_C)^3\left[1-\cos(\arcsin\frac{r}{R})\right]^3} - 1}. \quad (7.44)$$

Since the internal volume of the measuring device is completely filled with a relatively incompressible fluid, which transfers the perceived pressure onto the membrane (elastic element of the measuring transducer), the deformation capacity of the entire measuring device is determined by the flexibility of the membrane. The equivalent deformation ability of the measuring device E_C can be expressed as:

$$E_C = \frac{f}{2\mathcal{R}}E, \quad (7.45)$$

where f is the deflection of the center of a flat membrane, [m]; and E is the module of elasticity of the material of a membrane, [N/m²].

The Poisson's coefficient of the capsule's material could be replaced with the Poisson's coefficient of the membrane's material, that is: $\mu_C = \mu$. In this case the deflection of the center of the flat round membrane, that is rigidly jammed on a contour, is determined by the formula [1]:

$$f = \frac{\mathcal{P} d_{\text{M}}^3}{256\, D},\qquad (7.46)$$

where $D = \frac{\mathrm{E}\delta^3}{12(1-\mu^2)}$ is the cylindrical rigidity; and d_{M} and δ are the diameter and thickness of the membrane.

By applying the restriction at which the material of a membrane has to be in a zone of elastic deformations, the maximum permissible pressure would be permissible to measure is equal to:

$$\mathcal{P}_{max} = \frac{4}{0.783}[\sigma_{\Pi}]\left(\frac{\delta}{d_{\text{M}}}\right)^2 \qquad (7.47)$$

where σ_{Π} is limit of proportionality of the membrane's material.

Substituting values of equivalent deformation ability of all measuring device (membrane), from (7.45), (7.46) and (7.47), for (7.44), the expression for the definition of a relative error of the direct method of measurements of the internal pressure in dispersion systems for devices with spherical sensitive elements is:

$$\eta = \pm \sqrt[3]{\frac{2.16 \cdot 10^{-6}\,[\sigma_{\Pi}]^3 (1-\mu)^3 d_{\text{M}}^6 \beta_i\, v^3}{\xi_i^3 \delta^3 \mathcal{R}^6 [1-\cos(\arcsin\frac{r}{R})]^3}} - 1. \qquad (7.48)$$

7.4. CALCULATION OF A RELATIVE ERROR OF CYLINDRICAL CAPSULES AND FLAT MEMBRANE

Let us define a relative error for a cylindrical sensitive element, provided that mutual influence of the ends of a cylindrical shell can be neglected.

For the cylindrical cover (Fig. 7-3), perceiving the external pressure that is evenly distributed upon a surface, the deflection of points of the median surface $\mathcal{U}_{\text{X}}$ in the longitudinal direction [1], is equal to:

$$\mathcal{U}_{\text{X}} = \frac{\mu_C \mathcal{P} \mathcal{R}^2}{v \mathrm{E}_C} \frac{L}{\mathcal{R}}, \qquad (7.49)$$

and in the radial direction $\mathcal{U}_R$, is equal to:

$$\mathcal{U}_R = \frac{\mathcal{P}\mathcal{R}^2}{\mathcal{V}\mathrm{E_K}}. \qquad (7.50)$$

Considering that the volume of the cylindrical capsule is equal: $\pi\mathcal{R}^2 L$, so that the change of volume $(\Delta\mathcal{V}_D)_C = \pm\,\pi\Delta\mathcal{R}^2\Delta L$.

Since $\Delta L = \mathcal{U}_{\mathrm{X}}$ and $\Delta\mathcal{R} = \mathcal{U}_R$, we get:

$$(\Delta\mathcal{V}_D)_C = \pm\,\pi(\mathcal{U}_R)^2\mathcal{U}_{\mathrm{X}} \qquad (7.51)$$

Substituting (7.49) and (7.50) for (7.51), we get an expression for calculation of the change of the volume of a cylindrical sensitive element under the influence of the internal pressure developing during the formation of dispersion systems:

$$(\Delta\mathcal{V}_D)_C = \pm\,\pi\,\mu_{\mathrm{K}}\frac{\mathcal{P}^3\mathcal{R}^6}{\nu^3 E_C^3}\cdot\frac{L}{\mathcal{R}}. \qquad (7.52)$$

It is quite obvious that a change in the volume of the cylindrical capsule under the influence of additional pressure is equal to:

$$(\Delta\mathcal{V}_C)_{\mathcal{P}_A} = \pm\,\pi\,\mu_{\mathrm{K}}\frac{{\mathcal{P}_A}^3\mathcal{R}^6}{\nu^3 E_C^3}\cdot\frac{L}{\mathcal{R}}. \qquad (6.53)$$

Substituting (7.36), (7.51) and (7.52) for (7.34) and considering expressions (7.45), (7.46) and (7.47), we get a formula for defining a relative error of the direct method of measurements by devices with cylindrical sensitive elements [228]:

$$\eta = \pm\sqrt[3]{\frac{0.27\cdot 10^{-6}\,[\sigma_{\Pi}]^3(1-\mu^2)^3 d_{\mathrm{M}}^6\beta_i\,\nu^3}{\mu\xi_i^3\delta^3\mathcal{R}^6}} - 1 \qquad (7.54)$$

The received expressions (7.48) and (7.54) are applicable for measuring devices with the elastic element of the converter made as a flat membrane, that is for strain gauge converters.

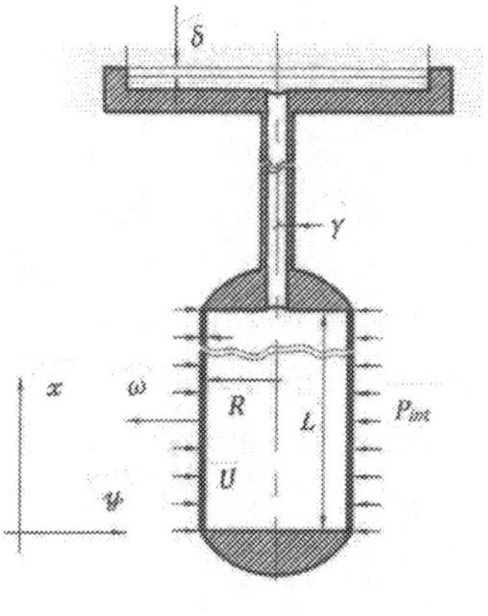

Figure 7-3. Principal Scheme of a Cylindrical Sensitive Element

7.5. CALCULATION OF A RELATIVE ERROR OF CYLINDRICAL CAPSULES AND CORRUGATED MEMBRANE

For measuring devices with a converter made as corrugated membrane the expressions for definition of a relative error are different. The deflection of the center of corrugated membranes f_{Cor} on the straight section can be determined by the formula [228]:

$$f_{Cor} = \frac{1}{16a} \frac{d_{\text{М}}^6}{\mathrm{E}\delta^3} \mathcal{P}_{\text{макс}}, \qquad (7.55)$$

where a is the coefficient that depends on a profile of a corrugation, the relative depth of a goffering and the Poisson's coefficient of the membrane material; $\mathcal{P}_{\text{макс}}$ is the size of the most admissible measured pressure at which the characteristic of a corrugated membrane remains linear; $d_{\text{М}}$ and δ are the diameter and thickness of a corrugated membrane; and E is the module of elasticity of the membrane material.

Substituting (7.55) for (7.45), the value for the equivalent deformation ability of measuring devices in which the elastic element is executed in the form of a corrugated membrane is:

$$\mathrm{E}_C = \frac{1}{32a}\frac{d_{\text{м}}^4}{\mathcal{R}\delta^3}\mathcal{P}_{\text{макс}}\,. \tag{7.56}$$

By writing down (7.48), (7.54), and taking into consideration (7.56), formulas are obtained for the determination of the size of the relative error of a direct method of measurements of internal pressure by means of measuring devices with spherical capsules in which the elastic element of the converter is made of a corrugated membrane:

$$\eta = \pm\sqrt[3]{\frac{24.0\cdot 10^{-5}\,\mathcal{P}_{\text{макс}}{}^3(1-\mu^2)^3 d_{\text{м}}^{12}\beta_i\,\nu^3}{\xi_i^3\delta^9\mathcal{R}^6a^3\,(1-\mu)^6\,[1-\cos(\arcsin\frac{r}{R})]^3}} - 1, \tag{7.57}$$

For the same but with cylindrical capsules, it is:

$$\eta = \pm\sqrt[3]{\frac{3.05\cdot 10^{-5}\,\mathcal{P}_{\text{макс}}{}^3 d_{\text{м}}^{12}\beta_i\,\nu^3}{\xi_i^3\delta^9\mathcal{R}^6a^3\,\mu}} - 1. \tag{7.58}$$

The analysis carried-out by [1] showed that for measuring devices with spherical capsules, the size of a relative error on two orders exceeds the size of a relative error of devices with cylindrical capsules. This results from the fact that in the location where a joint of a spherical cover meets the tubing, additional concentration of tension perceived by the measuring device develops.

The theoretical analysis made it possible to develop a device design to measuring internal pressures that is practically free of the shortcomings of measuring devices that did not provide the minimum value of the relative measurement error caused by the difference in the deformation properties of the measuring device and the dispersion systems under study.

7.6. ANALYSIS OF THE SYSTEMATIC ERROR OF MEASUREMENTS OF THE INTERNAL PRESSURE

When measuring internal pressures in the subject dispersion systems, the measuring device determines the quantitative values of the mechanical state of the working fluid filling the entire internal volume of the measuring device. The perceived change in the mechanical state of the working fluid is transmitted through the cross-section S of the elastic element of the sensor, causing a change in the mechanical state of the elastic element of the measuring transducer, after the output of which a measured electrical signal appears. To limit the deflection, the elastic element of the transducer counteracts it in the form of a membrane reaction. The displacement of each point of the membrane can be written as the sum [1]:

$$U = U_0(\tau) + \tilde{U}'(\tau),$$

where $U_0(\tau) = \frac{1}{L}\int_0^l U\, d\ell$ is the average value of shift in the direction of a sensor capsule axis; L is the length of a sensitive element of the pressure sensor; $d\ell$ is the element of the sensor length; and $d\tilde{U}'(\tau)$ is the amount, characterizing the shift of points of a sensitive element.

As pressure acts during the formation of the dispersion systems, it does not cause essential deformation of liquid, so that $U_0(\tau) \gg \tilde{U}'(\tau)$.

The mechanical condition of an elastic element of the capsule is described by the conservation law of impulses. Let us consider some volume of the working liquid of the measuring device located between the elementary sections of the capsule, which are at distance ℓ and from the beginning of coordinates $d\ell$. In this volume liquid is affected by the following forces:

1. Forces of the inertia: $\rho \frac{\partial^2 U}{\partial \tau^2}\, d\ell$;
2. Forces of the friction: $f \frac{\partial U}{\partial \tau}\, d\ell$;

3. Forces of the elasticity: ES $\frac{\partial^2 U}{\partial S^2} d\ell$;

4. Forces of the reaction of an elastic element of the capsule: $\overrightarrow{\mathfrak{P}}\, d\ell$,

where ρ is the density of the working liquid of the measuring device, [N/m^3]; E is the module of elasticity of material of the membrane, [N/m^2]; f is the coefficient of the friction, [is dimensionless]; and $\overrightarrow{\mathfrak{P}}$ is the vector resultant from all reaction forces of the elastic element of the measuring device (membrane), equal to the pressure acting in the considered measuring device.

The conservation law of impulses for the considered measuring device could be written as follows:[1]:

$$f\,\frac{\partial U}{\partial \tau} + \overrightarrow{\mathfrak{P}} = \mathrm{ES}\,\frac{\partial^2 U}{\partial S^2} - \rho\,\frac{\partial^2 U}{\partial \tau^2}. \qquad (7.59)$$

The condition of equilibrium of the measuring device has the following appearance [230]:

$$-\,\mathrm{ES}\,\frac{\partial U}{\partial l}\bigg|_{l=L} = \overrightarrow{\mathfrak{P}} - \mathrm{ES}\,\frac{\partial U}{\partial l}\bigg|_{l=0} - P_{\text{АТМ}}, \qquad (7.60)$$

where $\overrightarrow{\mathfrak{P}}$ is the vector amount of the internal pressure that developing in dispersion systems; and P_A is the atmospheric pressure.

The solution for the equations (7.59) and (7.60), which meets the entry conditions, was found by the author [203]:

$$U\Big|_{\tau=0} = 0 \quad \text{and} \quad \frac{\partial U}{\partial \tau}\Big|_{\tau=0} = 0$$

where:

$$U_0(\tau) = \left(\frac{\mathfrak{P}-\mathfrak{P}_a}{C} - \frac{\mathfrak{P}-\mathfrak{P}_a}{C}\right)\exp\left(-\frac{f \times L}{2m}\tau\right)\cos\frac{\sqrt{4mc - (f \times L)^2}}{2a}\tau +$$

$$+\frac{f \times L}{\sqrt{4mc - (f \times L)^2}} \sin \frac{\sqrt{4mc - (f \times L)^2}}{2a} \tau . \quad (7.61)$$

The received solution unambiguously defines the nature of the deformation of an elastic element. From the equation (6.61) it follows that, based on the nature of deformation of an elastic element of the measuring device (membrane) $U_0(\tau)$, it is possible to estimate the size of the internal pressure $\overrightarrow{\mathfrak{P}}$ developing in dispersion systems.

It is easy to see, that [1]:

$$\lim_{\tau \to \infty} U_0 = \frac{P - P_A}{C}, \quad (7.62)$$

where C is the rigidity of a membrane of the measuring device.

Therefore, having determined the atmospheric pressure value P_A, the average displacement value in the direction of the axis of the sensor capsule $U_0(\tau)$ and the stiffness of the membrane C, by extrapolating, it is possible to determine the internal pressure in the considered dispersion systems $\overrightarrow{\mathfrak{P}}$, which could also be achieved by the tasting of the measuring device.

To evaluate the results of measuring the internal pressure in dispersion systems, it is necessary to analyze the error of the measuring device, the source of which is the measuring device itself. As a result of the analysis, the following sources of error were identified:

1. The hydraulic measuring device: They are depending on the change of volume of the working liquid of the measuring device, as a result of thermal expansion, compressibility of the working liquid and

compressibility of the remains of free air in the measuring device after the filling its internal volume with the working liquid.

2. The strain gauge converter: The sizes of resistance of the strain gauge, which depends on change of ambient temperature, creep of materials of strain gauge element, changes of sensitivity and humidity of strain gauges.
3. The additional measuring devices, such as the amplifier, power supply, etc.

Let us consider the each of the listed sources of error:

1. It is known that a change in the volume of liquid as a result of thermal expansion is equal to:

$$V_t = V_0 (1 + \beta t).$$

At the change of pressure, as a result of deformation of an elastic element of the sensor, there is a change of volume under a membrane V_m, which is equal to [231]:

$$V_m = \frac{\pi}{12} \omega_0 d^2{}_m, \qquad (7.63)$$

where ω_0 is the change of an arrow of a deflection of the center of the membrane.

The deflection of the center of the membrane ω_0 is equal to [232]:

$$\omega_0 = \frac{3(1-\mu^2)}{256} \frac{Pd^4}{\hat{E}\delta^3}, \qquad (7.64)$$

where $\hat{E}$ is the equivalent deformation of an ability of the measuring device:

$$\hat{E} = \frac{\omega_0}{2\mathcal{R}} E, \qquad (7.64a)$$

where ω_0 is the deflection of the center of a flat membrane, [m]; and E is the module of elasticity of the material of a membrane, [N/m²].

The additional deflection of the membrane as a result of the increment of the volume of the working liquid of the measuring device as a result of thermal expansion, is equal to:

$$\omega_\beta = \frac{12}{\pi} \frac{\beta \nabla t}{d^2} V_0 \qquad (7.65)$$

Substituting values ω_β from (6.65) and Ê from (6.64a) for (7.64), the amount of the additional pressure is obtained depending on the thermal expansion of working liquid:

$$P_A = \frac{30.72\,[\sigma]\,\delta^2\,\beta\,\nabla t}{\pi R d_M{}^4} V_0 \;, \qquad (7.66)$$

where $[\sigma]$ is the limit of the proportionality (the maximum mechanical stress at which Hooke's law is satisfied, that is, the deformation of the body is directly proportional to the applied force) of the membrane material; δ is the thickness of a membrane; β is the coefficient of volume expansion of working liquid; V_0 is the volume of the sensor capsule, R is the radius of the capsule of the sensor; and d_M is the membrane diameter.

Thus, at the change of 1°C from the temperature, at which the hydraulic system of the measuring device is filled, the additional pressure does not exceed 23.3 x10^{-5} N/м^2.

2. The compressibility of liquid can be determined by the following formula [233]:

$$\frac{V_P}{V_0} = 1 - 10^{-4} \,,$$

where V_P is the liquid volume under the pressure P; and V_0 is the liquid volume under the normal pressure.

When the pressure is $P \simeq 0.1$ [MN/м^2], the error is equal to 0.002% and when the pressure P is in the range from 1.0 to 10.0 [MN/м^2], the error is equal to 0.02% to 0.2% respectively.

3. The air remains inside the hydraulic system after it is filled with working liquid, increasing it compressibility. Per recommendations for filling the hydraulic measuring devices [220], the deformation of a membrane as the result of air compression, has to be 10 times less than the deformation caused by the measured pressure. Therefore, the allowed volume of vials of air is:

$$V_{air} \leq 0.1 \frac{V_0}{\hat{E}},$$

where V_{air} is the total volume of vials of air, that remains in the system; V_0 is the volume of the liquid under a normal pressure; and $\hat{E}$ is the equivalent deformation ability of the measuring device.

It is obvious, that his kind of error it is possible to neglect.

4. As it was already noted, the electrical resistance of strain gauges is measured according to the bridge scheme. At this method of measurement, the relative increments of the resistance of the strain gauges, which are switched on in the active compensation shoulders, tied with an increment of counting on a scale of the secondary device, are [234]:

$$(\varphi - \varphi_0) = \frac{1}{G}\left[\left(\frac{\Delta R}{R}\right)_a - \left(\frac{\Delta R}{R}\right)_e\right] \qquad (7.67)$$

where $(\varphi - \varphi_0)$ is the increment of counting of a scale of the secondary device; G is the device constant; and $\left(\frac{\Delta R}{R}\right)_a$ and $\left(\frac{\Delta R}{R}\right)_e$ are the relative resistance of strain gauges.

The relative change of the resistance of strain gauges during the measuring of the deformation of elastic elements, is equal to [234]:

$$\frac{\Delta R}{R} = \varepsilon S, \qquad (7.68)$$

where S is the sensitivity of the strain gage to deformation; and ε is the deformation of the elastic element.

The general formula for measurement of deformation, is equal to [235]:

$$\varepsilon_a = \frac{1}{S(1-m)} \{(\varphi - \varphi_0)S - [(\frac{\Delta R}{R})_a - (\frac{\Delta R}{R})_e]_t - . \qquad (7.69)$$

$$-[(\frac{\Delta R}{R})_a - (\frac{\Delta R}{R})_e]_g - [(\frac{\Delta R}{R})_a - (\frac{\Delta R}{R})_e]_u - [(\frac{\Delta R}{R})_a - (\frac{\Delta R}{R})_e]_b$$

where m is the coefficient, characterizing the ratio of deformations ε_a and ε_e in the places of the sticker of active and compensation strain gauges; $[(\frac{\Delta R}{R})_a - (\frac{\Delta R}{R})_e]_t$ represents the temperature increments of the resistance of strain gauges at the change of temperature from t_{a0} and t_{e0} (at the time of counting φ_0) to t_a and t_e (at the time of counting φ); $[(\frac{\Delta R}{R})_a - (\frac{\Delta R}{R})_e]_g$ represents the relative increments of the resistance of strain gauges caused by creep during the time that passed between counting φ_0 and φ; $[(\frac{\Delta R}{R})_a - (\frac{\Delta R}{R})_e]_u$ represents the relative changes of the resistance of strain gauges from the change in environment humidity during the time that passed between counting φ_0 and φ; $[(\frac{\Delta R}{R})_a - (\frac{\Delta R}{R})_e]_b$ represents the relative changes of resistance of strain gauges at the change of the resistance of isolation b_{a0} and b_{e0} (at the time of counting φ_0) to b_a and b_e (at the time of counting φ)

To determine m (the coefficient that characterizes the ratio of strains ε_a and ε_e in the places of the sticker of the active and compensation strain gauges), the following formulas could be used [235]:

$$\varepsilon_a = \frac{3P}{8\delta^2}\frac{1-\mu^2}{E}\left(R^2 - 3r^2\right) \text{ and } \varepsilon_e = \frac{3P}{8\delta^2}\frac{1-\mu^2}{E}\left(R^2 - r^2\right).$$

The influence of moisture on the resistance of isolation and the strain gage is excluded on the application of a protective covering. The isolation resistance increase remains with increase of the temperature, even at the maximum working temperatures. Therefore, in the equation (7.69) it is possible to exclude:

$$\left[\left(\frac{\Delta R}{R}\right)_a - \left(\frac{\Delta R}{R}\right)_e\right]_b \text{ and } \left[\left(\frac{\Delta R}{R}\right)_a - \left(\frac{\Delta R}{R}\right)_e\right]_u.$$

It should also be noted that the private errors of the readings φ, as well as the error of the device, can be considered to have little effect on the measurement results. In this case, equation (6.69) can be written as follows:

$$\varepsilon_a = \frac{1}{S(1-m)}\left\{\left[\left(\frac{\Delta R}{R}\right)_a - \left(\frac{\Delta R}{R}\right)_e\right]_t - \left[\left(\frac{\Delta R}{R}\right)_a - \left(\frac{\Delta R}{R}\right)_e\right]_g\right\}. \quad (7.70)$$

Entering the designations:

$$D_t^2 = \left[\left(\frac{\Delta R}{R}\right)_a - \left(\frac{\Delta R}{R}\right)_e\right]_t \text{ and } D_g^2 = \left[\left(\frac{\Delta R}{R}\right)_a - \left(\frac{\Delta R}{R}\right)_e\right]_g.$$

Let us write (7.70) as follows:

$$\varepsilon_a = \frac{1}{S(1-m)}\left(D_t^2 - D_g^2\right). \quad (7.71)$$

Based upon consideration of the law of addition of private errors of indirect measurements (7.71), the error of measurement for deformation $\Delta\varepsilon_a$ has the appearance as:

$$\Delta\varepsilon_a = \pm\,(D_s^2 + D_t^2 + D_g^2)^{-2}\ . \qquad (7.72)$$

It is convenient to present a total error of measurement (7.72) in the form of relative amount of $\vartheta = \dfrac{\Delta\varepsilon_a}{\varepsilon_a}$, then:

$$\vartheta = \pm\frac{1}{\varepsilon_a}\,(D_s^2 + D_t^2 + D_g^2)^{-2}\,. \qquad (7.73)$$

The terms D_S, D_t, and D_g, included in the radical expression of formula (7.73) are equal to [234]:

$$\frac{Ds}{\varepsilon_a} = \delta S_t \Delta t,\ \frac{Dt}{\varepsilon_a} = 3\sqrt{2}\,\frac{[\sigma]\Delta t}{S(1-m)\varepsilon_a},\ \frac{Dg}{\varepsilon_a} = \pm\,\Pi_{Max}\,\varepsilon_a. \quad (7.74)$$

Substituting $\Delta\varepsilon_a$ amounts from (7.72) for (7.73), a total relative limit error of the measurement of the strain gauge converter is:

$$\vartheta = \frac{1}{\varepsilon_a}\left[\ (\varepsilon_a\delta S_t\Delta t)^2 + (3\sqrt{2}\,\frac{[\sigma]\Delta t}{S(1-m)})^2 + (\Pi_{max}\,\varepsilon_a{}^2)^2\right]^{-2}. \ (7.75)$$

where δS_t is the average change of sensitivity of the strain gauge referred to change at 1°C; Π_{Max} is the most observed relative creep of this batch of strain gauges; $[\sigma]$ is the standard deviation of the temperature increments of the resistance of a given batch of strain gages; and S is the strain gage sensitivity to the deformation.

From (7.73) it is visible that relative private errors on creep and on sensitivity do not depend on deformation ε_a. The private errors from temperature increments will be the greater the smaller the measurement value is.

Applying the received expression (7.75) to definition of an error ϑ there are:

- The average sensitivity of the strain gauge to deformation S is approximately 2.2; the average change of the sensitivity of the strain gauge to deformation δS_t at temperatures lower than 80 °C is equal to 0.1%.
- The relative standard deviation of the sensitivity of individual strain gauges from the average sensitivity of the entire batch is ≃ 0.5%.
- The dependence $\frac{\Delta R}{R} = f(\varepsilon)$ is linear up until the deformation is no larger than 4.0%.
- The creep of strain gauges at the current of about 30 mA and at the temperature of about of 20 °C does not exceed $\Pi_{max} = 0.1\%$ per 1 hour.
- The temperature increment of the resistance in the field of temperatures from 20 to 30 °C does not exceed 2×10^{-5} units.
- The isolation resistance size $(\frac{\Delta R}{R})_b$ is no less than 5×10^{5} [MΩ] and the relative standard deviation of temperature increments $(\frac{\Delta R}{R})_t$ does not exceed 11.3×10^{-5} units.

Substituting the provided characteristics of the strain gauges into formula (7.75) for determination of relative amount of the total error of a strain gauge ϑ, a conclusion is reached that, at temperatures below 80 °C the relative error does not exceed 2,0%. As the measuring device for the resistance of strain gauges, it is desirable to use the Null Galvanometer with a current scale of $9{,}2 \times 10^{-9}$ Amps per division. The relative error of this device is negligible. Therefore, the total systematic error of measurement of the amount of the internal pressure by devices with strain gages is about 2.0%.

CONCLUSION

For the practical use of the considered phenomena in physicochemical technology, it is necessary to conduct studies of the development of the fields of internal tension(s); the influence of the external revolting forces, the vibration impact on the development of the capillary-surface forces, and the forces of intermolecular interaction that develop in the course of formation of dispersion systems, composite materials and alloys in the modes of resonance cavitation and torsion-oriented turbulization in batch and continuous modes.

Besides, it is necessary to define the influence of various factors on stability, as well as physical, chemical and rheological characteristics of dispersion systems; to conduct technological research for definition of the most expedient fields of their application and to consider the economic efficiency of the considered modes for the solution of specific objectives.

From a position of fundamental science, the developed reactor, built with transparent walls, allows for research and for carrying out measurements of mechanical and physicochemical parameters of the subject applications and, in addition, allows for the observation of the "in live" emergence and development of turbulence as a special case of the general theory of chaos.

REFERENCES

1. Л.Г. Амусин. Исследование механизма развития полей капиллярных давлений при высушивании коллоидных капиллярно-пористых тел с целью управления их структурно-механическими свойствами. Диссертация на соискание ученой степени к.т.н. Калининский Политехнический институт. Калинин. 1976.
   (Dissertation: ***Research of the Mechanism of the Development of Capillary Pressure Fields during Sorption of Colloidal Capillary-Porous Substances in order to control their structural and mechanical properties.*** The Dissertation for the Ph.D. Doctorate. Kalinin Polytechnic University. City of Kalinin. Russia. 1976)
2. L. G. Amusin. Title: System and Method for Processing Dispersed Systems. United States Patent Application Publication. US 2015/0217244 A1. August 6, 2015.
3. L. G. Amusin. Title: System and Method for Processing Dispersed Systems. International Application Published Under The Patent Cooperation Treaty (PCT). International Publication Number WO 2015/119652 A1. August 13, 2015.
4. L. G. Amusin. Title: Method of Processing Molten Metals and Alloys. United States Patent Application Publication. US 2016/0040936 A1. February 11, 2016.
5. Л.Г. Амусин. Теоретические основы физико-химической динамики процесса формирования дисперсных систем в режимах вибрационной кавитации и резонансной турбулентности. Израиль. Июнь, 27 2019.
   http://www.elektron2000.com/article/2206.html
6. L. Amusin. Dissolution of Gases in Liquids and the Formation of Dispersion Systems in the Mode of Torsion-Oriented Turbulization. iUniverse, 2022
7. L. Amusin. Title: Process of Prevention of Hazardous and Toxic Gases Emission. Provisional Patent Application. US 63/372,992. Dated April 19, 2022. US 2022.
8. I.S. Pearsall. Cavitation. Mills and Boon Limited. London. 1972.

9. А.Е. Акимов. Феноменологическое введение торсионных полей и их проявления в фундаментальных экспериментах. / В кн. "Горизонты науки и технологий XXI века", с.139-167.
10. Г.И. Шипов. Теория физического вакуума. М.: Наука,1997.
11. Е. С. Фрадкин. Избранные труды по теоретической физике. — М.: Наука, 2007
12. Д. М. Гитман, Е. С. Фрадкин, Ш. М. Шварцман. Квантовая электродинамика с нестабильным вакуумом. — М.: Наука, 1991
13. V. G. Bagrov, D. M. Gitman, A. S. Pereira, "Coherent and semiclassical states of a free particle", Phys. Usp., 57:9 (2014), 891–896
14. V. G. Bagrov, B. F. Samsonov, "Darboux transformation, factorization, supersymmetry in one-dimensional quantum mechanics", Theoret. and Math. Phys., 104:2 (1995), 1051–1060
15. V. G. Bagrov, V. V. Belov, M. F. Kondrat'eva, "The semiclassical approximation in quantum mechanics. A new approach", Theoret. and Math. Phys., 98:1 (1994), 34–38
16. D. Ivanenko, G. Sardanashvily The gauge treatment of gravity, Physics Reports 94 (1983) 1-45.
17. I. L. Buchbinder, S. D. Odintsov, I. L. Shapiro Effective_Action_in_Quant um_Gravity. CRC Press, 1992.
18. I. L. Buchbinder, S. M. Kuzenko Ideas_and_Methods_of_Supersymmetr y_and_Supergravity. — Bristol and Philadelphia: Institute of Physics Publishing, 1995.
19. I. L. Buchbinder, S. M. Kuzenko Ideas_and_Methods_of_Supersymmetr y_and_Supergravity. — второе издание, исправленное и дополнен ное. CRC Press, 1998.
20. D.I. Radin, R.D. Nelson. Evidence for conscious-related anomalies in random physical systems. Found. Phys., V.19, N12, 1989, p.1499-1514.
21. A.H. Jafary-AsL, S.N. Solanky, E. Aarcholt, C.W. Smith. Dielectric measurements on live biological material under magnetic resonance condition. J.Biol.Phys., 1983, v.11, p.15-22
22. H. Hayasaka, S. Takeuchi. Phys.Rev.Lett., 1989, v.63, N25, p.2701.
23. S. Imoushi, et all. J.Phys.Soc.Jap., 1991, v.60, N4, p.1150-1152.
24. V. de Sabbata, C. Sivaram. Fifth force as a manifestation of torsion. Int. J.Theor. Phys., 1990, v.29, N1, p.1-6.
25. V. de Sabbata, C. Sivaram. Strong spin-torsion interaction between spinning protons. Nuovo Cimento, 1989, V.101A, N2, p.273-283.
26. Физический Энциклопедический Словарь. Том 1. ГНИ «Советская Энциклопедия». Москва. 1960

27. Ю.Б. Румер, М.Ш.Рывкин. Термодинамика, Статистическая Физика и Кинетика. Издание 2, Москва. 1977.
28. В.А. Эткин. Об ориентационном взаимодействии. (http://zhurnal.lib.ru), 05-22-2005.
29. В.А. Эткин. К термодинамике ориентируемых систем. (http://zhurnal.lib.ru),
07-10-2005.
30. C. De Groom. П. Мазур. Неравновесная термодинамика. Москва. Мир. 1958.
31. Физический Энциклопедический Словарь. Том 3. ГНИ «Советская Энциклопедия». Москва. 1960
32. В. А. Эткин. Торсионно-ориентационные процессы. Материалы международной научной конференции. Хоста. Сочи. Август 25-29, 2009.
33. В. А. Эткин. Термокинетика. ТПИ. Тольятти. 1999.
34. В. А. Эткин. Энергодинамика. С-Пб. Наука. 2008.
35. G. Korn, T. Korn. Mathematical Handbook for Scientists and Engineers. Dover Publications, Inc. Mineola. New York. 2016.
36. В. А. Эткин. К математическому моделированию торсионных и ориентационных взаимодействий. (http.://sciteclibrary.ru/rus/catalog/pages/4956.html) 4-08-2003.
37. В.А. Эткин. О термодинамической направленности процессов самоорганизации. (http://zhurnal.lib.ru) 10-13-2007
38. В. А. Членов и Н. В. Михайлов. Явление возникновения статического перепада давления газа в виброкипящем слое. Государственный реестр открытий СССР. № 138. 4 июня 1963 г.
39. Р.А. Татевосян и Н.В. Михайлов. Способ получения дисперсных систем. Авторское свидетельство № 428768. Москва.
40. Р.А. Татевосян и Н.В. Михайлов. Способ получения дисперсных систем. Авторское свидетельство № 573177. Москва.
41. Р.А. Татевосян. Исследование закономерностей вибротурбулизации системы вода-воздух. Теоретические основы химической технологии. Том 11, № 4, 1977. Москва.
42. А.Н. Твердохлебов. Исследование и изменение плавучести упругих тел. Труды НИЛФХММ и ТП. «Наука» 1975

43. А.Н. Твердохлебов. Математическое описание процесса вибротурбулизации. Труды НИЛФХММ и ТП. «Наука» 1975
44. Л. Г. Андреева, М.А. Романчук и др. Способ выделения 1-окиси – 2-метобензола из водных растворов. Авторское свидетельство № 419504. Москва.
45. А.Н. Лаврова, Е.Н. Кузнецова и др. Способ обеззараживания осадков сточных вод. Авторское свидетельство № 439138. Москва.
46. В.И. Буканова, Н.М. Семихатова и А.Д. Поделько. Способ получения биомассы. Авторское свидетельство № 442204. Москва.
47. Л. Г. Андреева, М.А. Романчук и др. Способ выделения 1-окиси – 2-метобензола из водных растворов. Авторское свидетельство № 419504. Москва.
48. Л. Г. Андреева, Р.А. Татевосян и Н.В. Михайлов. Способ выделения органических соединений. Авторское свидетельство № 443020. Москва.
49. Н.В. Михайлов, А.Д. Поделько и Р.А. Татевосян. Аппарат для выращивания микроорганизмов. Авторское свидетельство № 449935. Москва.
50. Л. Г. Андреева, Р.А. Татевосян и Н.В. Михайлов. Способ выделения ванилина из реакционной массы. Авторское свидетельство № 497281. Москва.
51. Л. Г. Андреева, Р.А. Татевосян и Н.В. Михайлов. Способ получения соласодина. Авторское свидетельство № 547689. Москва.
52. Р.А. Татевосян и Н.В. Михайлов. О вибрационном способе аэрации для флотации сточных жидкостей. Труды НИЛФХММ и ТП. «Наука» 1972.
53. Р.А. Татевосян, Л.Г. Амусин, А.Д. Поделько и др. Исследование практического использования вибротурбулизации для пищевой промышленности. Промежуточный Отчет Всесоюзного Научно-исследовательского института продуктов брожения (ВНИИПрб). Межотраслевая лаборатория физико-химической механики. Москва. 1976.
54. Л.Г. Амусин, и др. Прибор для колориметрического анализа химических реакций в жидкостях и газах с фотодиодным преобразователем. Отчет Всесоюзного Научно-

исследовательского института продуктов брожения (ВНИИПрб). Межотраслевая лаборатория физико-химической механики. Москва. 1977.

55. Р.А. Татевосян, Л.Г. Амусин, А.Д. Поделько и др. Разработка реактора для исследования вибротурбулизации. Отчет Всесоюзного Научно-исследовательского института продуктов брожения (ВНИИПрб). Межотраслевая лаборатория физико-химической механики. Москва. 1977.
56. Р.А. Татевосян, Л.Г. Амусин, А.Д. Поделько и др. Исследование практического использования вибротурбулизации для парфюмерной промышленности. Промежуточный Отчет Всесоюзного Научно-исследовательского института продуктов брожения (ВНИИПрб). Межотраслевая лаборатория физико-химической механики. Москва. 1977.
57. Р.А. Татевосян, Л.Г. Амусин, А.Д. Поделько и др. Исследование практического использования вибротурбулизации для фармацевтической промышленности. Промежуточный Отчет Всесоюзного Научно-исследовательского института продуктов брожения (ВНИИПрб). Межотраслевая лаборатория физико-химической механики. Москва. 1977.
58. Л.Г. Амусин, А.Д. Поделько и др. Исследование практического использования вибротурбулизации для производства лаков и красок. Промежуточный Отчет Всесоюзного Научно-исследовательского института продуктов брожения (ВНИИПрб). Межотраслевая лаборатория физико-химической механики. Москва. 1977.
59. Л.Г. Амусин, А.Д.Поделько и др. Исследование практического использования вибротурбулизации для химической промышленности. Промежуточный Отчет Всесоюзного Научно-исследовательского института продуктов брожения (ВНИИПрб). Межотраслевая лаборатория физико-химической механики. Москва. 1977.
60. П.А. Ребиндер. Избранные труды. Издательство «Наука». Москва. 1979;
61. Е.Д. Щукин, А.В. Перцов, Е.А. Амелина, Коллоидная химия. Высшая школа. Москва. 1982;

62. Физико-химическая механика природных дисперсных систем. Под ред. Е.Д. Щукина, А.В. Перцов, и др. Изд-во МГУ. Москва. 1985.
63. Н.И. Гамаюнов, С.Н. Гамаюнов. Массоперенос в пористых и дисперсных материалах. УДК 536.2
64. Н.И. Гамаюнов, С.Н. Гамаюнов. Осмотические и электрокинетические явления в открытых системах. ТГТУ. Тверь. 2013.
65. Н.И. Гамаюнов. Процессы переноса энергии и вещества. ТГТУ. Тверь. 2004
66. Н.Б. Урьев. Физико-химические основы технологии дисперсных систем и материалов, М,, 1988.
67. Б.В. Дерягин, Н.В. Чураев, В.М. Муллер. Поверхностные силы. «Наука», Москва, 1985
68. Н.Б. Урьев. Физико-химическая динамика дисперсных систем. РАН. Успехи химии. 73 (1) Москва. 2004.
69. Н.Б. Урьев, И.В. Кучин. Моделирование динамического состояния дисперсных систем. Успехи Химии. РАН. Институт органической химии им. Зелинского. 75 (1) 2006.
70. Кавитационные явления при низко-частных колебаниях. Отчет Института Механики МГУ №198, Москва. 1962
71. Некоторые явления колеблющейся жидкости со свободной поверхностью. Отчет Института Механики МГУ №365, Москва. 1964
72. С.С. Григорян, Ю.Л. Акимов, Э.З. Апштейн. Поведение пузырьков воздуха в жидкости при вибрации. Сборник трудов симпозиума по механике в Юрате. Польша. 1965.
73. Э.З. Апштейн, С.С. Григорян, Ю.Л. Акимов. Об устойчивости роя пузырьков в колеблющейся жидкости. Известия АН СССР. Механика жидкости и газа. Том 3. Стр. 100-104. Москва. 1969.
74. Р.А. Восканян. Способ получения дисперсных систем. Авторское свидетельство № 1001988. Москва.
75. А.П. Бабичев. Технологическое применение колебаний или . . . вибрационные технологии. УДК 621.048.6
76. А.П. Бабичев. Технологическое применение колебаний или вибрационные технологии. Moksline Electronic Biblioteks. http://www.ebiblioteka.lt/...

77. М.А. Промтов. Перспективы применения кавитационных технологий для интенсификации химико-технологических процессов. Вестник Тамбовского ГТУ. Том 14, №4.
78. R. Krishna, J. Ellenberger and others. Utilisation of Bubble Resonance Phenomena to Improve Gas-Liquid Contact. Naturwissenschaften. (2000) 87:455-459.
79. R. Krishna, J. Ellenberger. Improving Gas-Liquid Contacting in Bubble Columns by Vibration Excitement. International Journal of Multiphase Flow. 28 (2002) 1233.
80. Е.А. Бобков. Явления вибротурбулизации и ее применение. УДК 664.021.040.
81. V.D. Lakiza. Study of Dynamic Processes in a Rigid Cylindrical Vessel with Elastic Bottom Partially Filled with a Liquid. International Applied Mechanics. Vol. 42. No 11, 2006.
82. R.Sh. Abner. Selection of the Rational Design of a Vibration Unit with Oscillation Vessels. Chemical and Petroleum Engireeng. Vol. 32, No 3, 1996.
83. И.И. Блехман и др. Вибрационные эффекты – эксперимент, теория, использование при обогащении руд и рецикленге. Институте проблем машиноведения РАН и НПК «Механоприбор». город Санкт-Петербург.
84. И.И. Блехман и др. Вибрационная механика. Москва. Физматлит. 1994
85. И.И. Блехман и др. Явление вибрационной инжекции газа в жидкость. Диплом № 187. Сборник «Научные открытия» Москва. РАЕН. 2002.
86. И.И. Блехман и др. О некоторых аномальных эффектов поведени сыпучей среды в сообщающихся вибрирующих сосудах. Ж. Обогащение руд. 2007 №5.
87. И.И. Блехман и др. Аномальные явления в жидкости при действии вибрации. Москва. ДАН 2008 Том 422. №4.
88. I. Blekhman, L. Blekhman, and others. Phenomenon of Inversion of the Stable States of "Gas-Fluid-Heavy Particles" System in the Vibrating Vessels. ENOC 2008, Saint Petersburg, Russia, June 30 – July, 4 2008.
89. Л.И. Блехман. Вибрационное взвешивание твердых тел в жидкости и сыпучей среде. Вестник ПНИПУ. Механика. 2013. № 2.

90. А.Ф. Кузаев. Экспериментальное исследование осредненного поведения твердых включений в полости с жидкостью при вибрациях. Автореферат диссертации на соискание ученой степени к.ф-м наук . Пермь. 2005
91. В.Б. Федосеев. О неэкстенсивном поведении термодинамической системы в условиях внешнего поля. Труды 9-ой Всероссийская научная конференция «Нелинейные колебания механических систем». Стр. 915 – 922.
92. В.Б. Федосеев. Термодинамическая интерпретация маятника Челомея и гипсометрические распределения для случая суперпозиции гравитационного, акустического и упругого полей. УДК 541.13; 539.1.075.
93. В.Б. Федосеев. Перераспределение вещества под действием внешних полей и стационарная модель маятника Челомея. Нелинейный мир. 2010. Том 2.
94. Г.А. Абакумов, В.Б. Федосеев. Ограниченно смешивающиеся жидкости в центробежном поле. ДАН. 2002 Том 383. № 5.
95. Г.А. Абакумов, В.Б. Федосеев. Фазовый переход в расслаивающихся жидких смесях под действием акустического поля. Сборник трудов 15 сессии Российского акустического общества. Москва. ГЕОС. 2004 Том 1.
96. Inventor(s): Stobbe Tech. Title: Biopharmaceutical Plant in a Column / Publishing date: Dec 5, 2012 / Publication No: EP 2379692 B1
97. Inventor(s): Meyer Behar, et al. Title: Device for Reaction between Liquid Phase and Gaseous Phase./Publishing date: May 16, 1972/Publication No: US 3662521 A
98. Inventor(s): Robert P Bannon. Title: Apparatus for Contacting a Gas and a Liquid. / Publishing date: Apr 7, 1992 / Publication No: US 5102583 A.
99. Inventor(s): Josefino Tunac. Title: Aeration/Publishing date: Dec 24, 1991/Publication No: US 5075234 A
100. Inventor(s): Gerhard Greller, et al. Title: Vibrational Mixer / Publishing date: Jan 1, 2013/Publication No: US 8342737 B2
101. Inventor(s): John W Schmidt, III. Title: Shaker for Paint Containers / Publishing date: Oct 28, 1986/ Publication No: US 4619532 A

102. Inventor(s): Ocamu Matsumato. Title: Gas and Liquid Mixture Generation Apparatus/ Publishing date: Oct 7, 2010/ Publication No: US 20090294996 A1
103. Inventor(s): Sang D Kim. Title: Bubble Column Reactor with Dispersing Devices/Publishing date: Sep 7, 1993/Publication No: US 5242643 A
104. Inventor(s): Eric Herbolzheimer, et al. Title: Slurry Bubble Column/Publishing date: Sep 20, 1994/Publication No: US 5348982 A
105. Inventor(s): Harless D Phillip. Title: Sealed-Bladdered Chemical Processing Method and Apparatus / Publishing date: Dec 14, 1999 /Publication No: US 6001327 A
106. Inventor(s): David C Pollock. Title: Apparatus for Biological Treatment of Wastewater / Publishing date: Mar 28, 2006 / Publication No: US 7018530 B2
107. Inventor(s): Alan G Wonders, et al. Title: Carried out in a bubble column reactor that provides for a highly efficient reaction at relatively low temperatures; oxidizing p-xylene to form terephthalic acid that can be purified more easily than if higher temperatures were required. / Publishing date: Mar 3, 2009/ Publication No: US 7498003 B2
108. Inventor(s): Arne Grislingas. Title: Slurry Bubble Column Reactor/ Publishing date: Mar 23, 2005/Publication No: WO 2005094979 A1
109. Title:Variable-Diameter Tower Reactor Capable of Carrying out Continuous Reaction/Publishing date: Nov 28, 2012/ Publication No: CN 202555255 U
110. Inventor(s): Bernd Best, et al. Title: Pulsation, Temporary Depressurization; Ozonolysis of Unsaturated Organic Acids./ Publishing date: Jan 28, 2003 /Publication No: US 6512131 B1
111. Inventor(s): Paolo Matteazzi. Title: Mechano-Chemical Reactors/ Publishing date: Oct 31, 2013/Publication No: US 20130284838 A1
112. Inventor(s): Andrew E Bloch. Title: Apparatus and Method for Providing Asymmetric Oscillations / Publishing date: Aug 14, 2014/ Publication No: WO 2014124440 A2
113. Inventor(s): Iginio Longo and Vittorio Ragaini. Title: Method for Activation of Chemical or Chemical-Physical Processes by a Simultaneous Use of Microwaves and Ultrasonic Pulses and Chemical

Reactor that Carries out this Method / Publishing date: Aug 23, 2007/Publication No: WO 2007093883 A2

114. Inventor(s): Jean-Pierre Nikolovski, Title: Cyril Delatter. Agitator of a Liquid Samples/ Publishing date: Jan 10, 2013/Publication No: US 20130010567
115. Inventor: Oleg V. Kozyuk. Title: Device for Creating Hydrodynamic Cavitation in Fluids/Publishing date: May 4. 2010/Publication No: US 7708453
116. Inventor: Oleg V. Kozyuk. Title: Fluid Impingement Mixing Device/ Publishing date: Sep 9, 2005/Publication No: US 7422360
117. Inventor: Oleg V. Kozyuk. Title: Device and Method for Creating Vortex Cavitation in Fluids/Publishing date: Apr 15, 2008/Publication No: US 7357566
118. Inventor: Oleg V. Kozyuk. Title: A Device and Method for Generating Bubbles in a Liquid Using Hydrodynamic Cavitation/Publishing date: Mar 4, 2005/Publication No: US 7338551
119. Inventor: Oleg V. Kozyuk. Title: Hydrodynamic Cavitation Crystallization Device and Process/Publishing date: Jan 1, 2004/Publication No: US 7314516
120. Inventor: Oleg V. Kozyuk. Title: A Homogenization Device and Method of Using the Same/Publishing date: Jan 1, 2008/Publication No: US 7314306
121. Inventor: Oleg V. Kozyuk. Title: Treatment Processes and Devices Utilizing Hydrodynamic Cavitation/Publishing date: Jul 24, 2007/Publication No: US 7247244
122. Inventor: Oleg V. Kozyuk. Title: Device and Method for Creating Hydrodynamic Cavitation in Fluids/Publishing date: Apr 24, 2007/Publication No: US 7207712
123. Inventor: Oleg V. Kozyuk. Title: Device and Method for Creating Vortex Cavitation in Fluids/Publishing date: Feb 20, 2007/Publication No: US 7178975
124. Inventor: Oleg V. Kozyuk. Title: Device and Method for Creating Vortex Cavitation in Fluids/Publishing date: Aug 8, 2006/Publication No: US 7086777

125. Inventor: Oleg V. Kozyuk. Title: Method of Preparing Metal Containing Components Using Hydrodynamic Cavitation/ Publishing date: Mar 22, 2005/ Publication No: US 6869586
126. Inventor: Oleg V. Kozyuk. Title: Device for Cavitation Mixing and Pumping and Method of Using the Same/ Publishing date: Feb 22, 2005/ Publication No: US 6857774
127. Inventor: Oleg V. Kozyuk. Title: Homogenization Device and Method of Using the Same/ Publishing date: Oct 12, 2004/ Publication No: US 6802639
128. Inventor: Oleg V. Kozyuk. Method of Preparing Metal Containing Components Using Hydrodynamic Cavitation/ Publishing date: Jul 8, 2003/ Publication No: US 6589501
129. Inventor: Oleg V. Kozyuk. Title: Device for Cavitation Mixing and Pumping and Method of Using the Same/ Publishing date: Feb 22, 2005 / Publication No: US 6857774
130. Inventor: Oleg V. Kozyuk. Title: Method and Apparatus for Conducting Sonochemical Reaction and Process Using Hydrodynamic Cavitation/ Publishing date: Jan 11, 2000/ Publication No: US 6012492
131. Inventor: Oleg V. Kozyuk. Title: Method for Changing the Qualitative and Quantitate Composition of a Mixture of Liquid Hydrocarbons Based on the Effect of Cavitation/ Publishing date: Oct 19, 1999/ Publication No: US 5969207
132. Inventor: Oleg V. Kozyuk. Title: Method and Apparatus for Conducting Sono-chemical Reaction and Process Using Hydrodynamic Cavitation/ Publishing date: Aug 17, 1999/ Publication No: US 5937906
133. Inventor: Oleg V. Kozyuk. Title: Method and Apparatus for Producing Ultra-Thin Emulsions and Dispersions/ Publishing date: Aug 3, 1999/ Publication No: US 5931771
134. Inventor(s): Edward W Smith. Title: Method of deaerating liquids/ Publishing date: Feb 21, 1939/ Publication No: US 2147677 A
135. Inventor(s): Harold W Howe, et al. Title: Method for Resonant-Vibratory Mixing/ Publishing date: Oct 7, 2010/ Publication No: US 20100254212 A1, also as: US7188993, US7866878
136. Title: Double-Vibration-Plate Ultrasonic Processing Unit/ Publishing date: Feb 12, 2014/ Publication No: CN 103566857 A

137. Inventor(s): Albert A Soldate. Title: Vibrating Chemical Reactor and Regenerator/ Publishing date: Oct 28, 1975/ Publication No: US3915890 A
138. Inventor(s): Lynn Faulkner, et al. Title: Resonance, Vibration/ Publishing date: Jul 13, 1982/ Publication No: US 4339247 A
139. Inventor(s): Francis G Firth. Title: Vibratory treatment apparatus and method/ Publishing date: Oct 5, 1982/ Publication No: US 4352570 A
140. .Inventor(s): Gregori Lishanski, Oleg Lishanski. Title: Vibratory Cavitation Pump Lishanski/ Publishing date: Oct 4, 2012/ Publication No: US 20120251338 A1
141. Yogesh G. Waghmare. Vibration For Improving Multiphase Contact. (A Dissertation. Louisiana State University. 2008);
142. Ashfag Shaikh. (A Dissertation. Washington University. Department of Energy, Environmental and Chemical Engineering. Saint Louis. Missouri. 2007);
143. Nasim Hooshyar. (A Dissertation. Hydrodynamics of Structured Slurry Bubble Column. Delft University of Technology. Delft. 2013).
144. Uzi Mann. Principles of Chemical Reactor Analysis and Design: New Tools for Industrial Chemical Reactor Operations by Uzi Mann (Texas Tech University. 2008).
145. K. Sival et al. Studies in Mass Transfer in Pulsed Bubble Column. Indian Institute of Science., 64 (A), July 1983, Pages 137–150.
146. B. Sohby et al. The Effect of Vibration on the Absorption of CO_2 with Chemical Reaction in Aqueous Solution of Calcium Hydroxide. World Academy of Science, Engineering and Technology. International Journal of Chemical, Nuclear, Metallurgical and Material Engineering.Vol:1 No: 5, 2007
147. В.Н. Челомей. Парадоксы в механике, вызываемые вибрациями. ДАН СССР, Том 270. Стр. 62. 1983
148. В. Карасев. http://fdisto.misis.ru/s/Hel/Laba/Matem/Ma_Pov2P/L_Ma_Pov2P.htm
149. Machinery's Handbook. 22nd Edition. P. 46. Industrial Press Inc. New York. 1984.
150. Физический Энциклопедический Словарь. Том 1. ГНИ «Советская Энциклопедия». Москва. 1960

151. Ю.Б. Румер, М.Ш.Рывкин. Термодинамика, Статистическая Физика и Кинетика. Издание 2, Москва. 1977.
152. R.L. Stallard. Lecture on Shock and Vibration. Boston 's Chapter of the Institute of Environmental Science and Center for Continuing Education Northeastern University. March, 1967.
153. Е.И. Бутиков, А.С. Кондратьев. Физика. Книга 1. Механика. Издательство «Наука». Москва. 1994.
154. М.Я. Выгодский. Справочник по высшей математики. Государственное Издательство физ-мат литературы. Москва. 1963
155. Р.И. Нигматулин. Динамика многофазных сред. Издательство «Наука». Москва. 1987.
156. В.Е. Накоряков, Б.Г. Покусаев, И.Р. Шрайбер. Распространение волн в газо- и парожидкостных средах. Издательство института теплофизики. Новосибирск. 1983.
157. В.К. Кедринский. Гидродинамика взрыва. Эксперимент и модели. Издательство СО РАН. Новосибирск. 2000.
158. Р.И. Нигматулин и др. Двумерные волны давления в жидкости, содержащей пузырьковые зоны. ДАН Том 378. Стр. 763-768. 2001
159. Р.Х. Болотнова, М.Н. Галимзянов, О.У. Агишова. Моделирование процессов взаимодействия сильных ударных волн в газожидкостных средах. Известия высших учебных заведений, Поволжский регион. Физико-математические науки. Выпуск 2-18. 2011.
160. Я.Б. Зельдович, Ю.П. Райзер. Физика ударных волн и высокотемпературных явлений. Издательство «Наука». Москва. 1966.
161. А.Н. Тихонов, А.А. Самарский. Уравнения математической физики. Издательство «Наука». Москва. 1977.
162. Д.А. Прокудин, Т.В. Глухарева, И.В. Казаченко. Уравнения математической физики. Кемеровский Гос. Университет. Кемерово. 2014
163. P. Jarman. Measurements Sonoluminescence from pure Liquids and some Aqueous Solutions. Proceedings of the Physical Society. Vol. 73, 628. 1959

164. Физический Энциклопедический Словарь. Том 2. ГНИ «Советская Энциклопедия». Москва. 1962
165. Яворский Е.М. Детлаф А.А., Справочник по физике. Москва, 1971
166. Краткий физико-технический справочник. Под Ред. К.П. Яковлева. Том 2. Государственное Издательство физ-мат. литературы. Москва. 1962
167. В.Н. Захарченко. Коллоидная химия. Издательство «Высшая школа». Москва. 1974.
168. Б.В. Бак. Современное состояние теории вязкости. Успехи Физических Наук. Том XV. Вып. 2, 1935
169. Болдырев В.В. Механохимия и механическая активация твердых веществ. Успехи Химии. 75. (3) 2006
170. В.А. Членов, Н.В. Михайлов. Виброкипящий слой. Издательство «Наука». Москва. 1972
171. А.С. Гинзбург. Тепло – и массообмен при разделении фаз в условиях воздействия внешних и внутренних полей. Материалы 5-й Всес. Конференции по тепло- и массообмену 1976. Издательство «Наукова думка». Минск. 1976
172. Н.К. Адам. Физика и химия поверхностей. ГИТТЛ. Москва-Ленинград. 1947
173. В.Б. Ратинов, Ф.М. Иванов. Химия в строительстве. Издательство литературы по строительству. Москва. 1969
174. И.Ф. Ефимов. Периодические коллоидные структуры. Издательство «Химия». Ленинград. 1971
175. Л.М. Щербаков. Об одной традиционной ошибке в теории капиллярности. Коллоидный журнал. Том 20. № 4, стр. 502.
176. H. Sonntag, K. Strenge. Koagulation und Stability Disperser System. VEB Deutscher Verlag der Wissenschaften. Berlin. 1970
177. G. Gouy. Journal Physics Radium. Vol. 9, 457. 1910
178. G. Gouy. Annual Physics. Vol 7, 129. 1917
179. D.L. Chapman. Philosophical Magazine. Vol. 25, 457. 1913
180. B.V. Deriagin. Ibid. Vol. 10, 333 (139)
181. Б.В. Дерягин. Коллоидный журнал. Том 6, 291. 1940
182. Б.В. Дерягин. Коллоидный журнал. Том 7, 285. 1941
183. Б.В. Дерягин. Известия АН СССР. Серия Химия № 5, стр. 1153, 1937
184. Б.В. Дерягин, Л.Д. Ландау. ЖЭТФ, Том 11, стр. 802, 1941

185. Б.В. Дерягин, Л.Д. Ландау. ЖЭТФ, Том 15. Стр. 662, 1945
186. Б.В. Дерягин. Труды 3-й Всес. Конференции по коллоидной химии. Издательство АН СССР, стр. 225, 1956
187. E.J. Verwey, J.Th. G. Overbeek. Theory of the Stability of Lyophobic Colloids. Amsterdam. 1948
188. В.М. Муллер. Сб. «Исследования в области поверхностных сил». Издательство «Наука». Стр. 270. Москва. 1967
189. H.C. Hamaker, Physika. Vol. 4, page 1058, 1937
190. А.В. Лыков. Теория сушки. Издательство «Энергия». Москва. 1968
191. Н.В. Чураев. Изучения механизма переноса влаги при сушке коллоидных капиллярно-пористых тел. Коллоидный журнал. Том 6. № 2, 1963
192. Б.В. Дерягин, С.В. Нерпин, Н.В. Чураев. Теория испарения жидкости из капилляра с учетом пленочного движения влаги. Сб. Трудов Агрофизического НИИ ВАСХНИЛ. Вып.11, Гидрофизика и структура почвы. Гидрометеоиздат, стр 5. Москва. 1965
193. С.В. Нерпин, Н.В. Чураев. Кинетика испарения влаги из капиллярно-пористых тел. Инженерно-физический журнал. Том 8, № 1, стр. 20. Москва. 1965
194. Б.В. Дерягин, С.В. Нерпин, Н.В. Чураев. К теории испарения жидкостей из капилляров. Коллоидный журнал. Том 26. № 3, стр. 301, Москва. 1964
195. Н.В. Чураев. Влияние пленочного движения на испарение влаги из пористых тел. Коллоидный журнал. Том 27. № 6, стр. 908, Москва. 1965.
196. Н.В. Чураев. Механизм переноса влаги в капиллярно-пористых телах. ДАН СССР. Том 148. Стр. 1361. Москва. 1963.
197. С.В. Нерпин, Б.В. Дерягин. Кинетика течения и устойчивости тонких слоев жидкости на твердой подкладке с учетом сольватной оболочки, как особой фазы. ДАН СССР, Том 100. Вып. 1, тр. 17. Москва. 1955
198. С.В. Нерпин, А.Ф. Чудновский. Физика почвы. Издательство «Наука». Москва. 1967.
199. П.А. Ребиндер. Исследования в области поверхностных явлений. ОНТИ. Москва-Ленинград. 1936
200. А.Ю. Давидов. Теория капиллярных явлений. Москва. 1951

201. Курс физики. Под редакцией Н.Д. Папалекси. Часть 1. Гостехиздат. Москва-Ленинград. 1948
202. Н.И. Гамаюнов, Л.Г. Амусин. Прибор для исследования капиллярных явлений. Информационный Бюллетень № 342/75. Калинин. 1975.
203. Н.И. Гамаюнов, Л.Г. Амусин. Разработка методики исследование и разработка прибора для измерений внутренних напряжений при формировании гидрофильных дисперсных систем. Отчет Калининского Политехнического института. Калинин. 1975.
204. Н.И. Гамаюнов, Л.Г. Амусин. Исследование тепло- и массопереноса при структурообразовании коллоидных капиллярно-пористых тел. Материалы 5-й Всесоюзной конференции по тепломассообмену. Высшая Школа. Т. 5. Стр. 88. Минск. 1976.
205. Н.И. Гамаюнов, Л.Г. Амусин. Исследование капиллярных явлений в клиновой щели. Инженерно-Физический журнал. Изд. АН СССР. Том 31. № 6. Стр. 1033. Минск. 1976.
206. Н.И. Гамаюнов, Л.Г. Амусин. Изучение механизма испарения влаги из капиллярной щели. Коллоидный Журнал. Т. 38. Выпуск 6. Стр. 1076. Академия Наук СССР. Москва. 1976.
207. Н.И. Гамаюнов, Л.Г. Амусин. Исследование явлений в процессе развития внутреннего напряженного состояния при сушке капиллярно-пористых структур. Тезисы Всесоюзной конференции по физической химии торфа. Академия Наук Белорусской ССР. Стр. 37. Минск. 1976.
208. N.I. Gamayunov and L.G. Amusin. Study of the Internal Pressure upon Structure Formation of Colloidal and Microheterogeneous Systems. Translated from Kolloidnyi Zhurnal, Vol. 38, No. 3, pp. 551-533, May-June, 1976.
209. N.I. Gamayunov and L.G. Amusin. Mechanism of Evaporation of Moisture from a Capillary Slit. Translated from Kolloidnyi Zhurnal, Vol. 38, No. 6, pp. 1076-1081, November-December, 1976.
210. N.I. Gamayunov, L.G. Amusin. Research of Capillary Phenomena on the Slot Model. Translated from Physical-Engineering Zhurnal. Vol. XXXI, No 6. December, 1976.

211. С.А. Гершгорин. Об изгибе пластинок нагрузками, распределенных по площади круга. Ж. Прикладная математика и механика. Том 1, № 2, стр. 159. 1933
212. А.М. Гуткин, И.П. Федоров. Погрешности при физических измерениях. Учебное пособие МЭИ. Москва. 1964
213. А.Н. Зайдель. Ошибки измерения физических величин. Издательство «Наука». Москва. 1966
214. И.М. Беленький. Введение в аналитическую механику. Издательство «Высшая школа» Москва. 1964
215. А.А. Померанцев. Курс лекций по теории тепломассообмена. Издательство «Высшая школа» Москва. 1965
216. А.Г. Касаткин. Основные процессы и аппараты химической технологии. ГНТ Издательство химической литературы. Москва. 1961
217. М.Д. Кузнецов. Определение коэффициентов скорости абсорбции по методу подобия. Журнал Прикладной Химии № 1, Москва. 1948
218. Д.С. Баранов. Выбор основных параметров грунтовых методов из условий наименьшего искажения измеряемых давлений. Развитие метода проволочной тензометрии для исследования строительных конструкций. Госстройиздат. Москва. 1962
219. Д.С. Баранов. О погрешностях при измерении давлений в грунтах. Ж. Основания, фундаменты и механика грунтов. № 2, 1962
220. Руководство по применению прямого метода измерения давления в сыпучих средах и грунтах. ЦНИИСК. Им. Кучеренко. Москва. 1965
221. Н.И. Гамаюнов, Л.Г. Амусин, А.Е. Афанасьев. Влияние поверхностных сил на структурообразование в торфяных системах. Сб. Структурные, реологические и физико-механические свойства торфа. Труды КПИ. Калинин. 1976
222. Н.И. Гамаюнов, Л.Г. Амусин. Прибор с тензометрическим преобразователем для измерения внутренних напряжений в дисперсных материалах. Информационный Бюллетень № 385/74. Калинин. 1974.
223. Н.И. Гамаюнов, Г.С. Берлин, Л.Г. Амусин. Прибор с механотронным преобразователем для измерения внутренних напряжений в

дисперсных материалах. Информационный Бюллетень № 6/75. Калинин. 1975.

224. Н.И. Гамаюнов, Г.С. Берлин, Л.Г. Амусин. Прибор с манотронным преобразователем для измерения внутренних давлений. Информационный Бюллетень № 6/75. Калинин. 1975.
225. Н.И. Гамаюнов, Л.Г. Амусин. Исследование внутреннего давления при структурообразовании коллоидных и микрогетерогенных систем. Коллоидный Журнал. Т. 38. Выпуск 3. Стр. 551. Академия Наук СССР. Москва. 1976.
226. Прочность, Устойчивость, колебания. Справочник под редакцией И.А. Биргера и Я.Г. Пановко. Том 1. Издательство «Машиностроение». Москва. 1968
227. Инженерные сооружения. Справочник. Том 1. Издательство «Машиностроение». Москва. 1950
228. Н.И. Гамаюнов, Л.Г. Амусин, Я.М. Юфик. Прибор для измерения внутренних напряжений в дисперсных материалах. Информационный Бюллетень № 121/74. Калинин. 1974.
229. Г.С. Берлин. Электронные приборы с механическими управляемыми электродами. Издательство «Энергия». Москва. 1971
230. Г.И. Зетгенидзе, Р.Ш. Гогсадзе. Математические методы в измерительной технике. Издательство Госкомстандартов. Москва. 1970
231. Приборостроение и средства автоматики. Справочник под редакцией А.М. Гаврилова. Издательство «Машиностроение». Том 2, Книга 1. Москва. 1962
232. Л.Е. Андреева. Упругие элементы приборов. Издательство «Машиностроение». Москва. 1962
233. А.С. Акопдженян. Гидравлические системы измерения усилий. Издательство «Машиностроение». Москва. 1972
234. И.П.Клоков и др. Тензодатчики для экспериментальных исследований. Издательство «Машиностроение». Москва. 1972
235. В.А. Глаговский, И.Д. Пивен. Электротензометры сопротивлений. Издательство «Энергия». Москва. 1964.

LIST OF AUTHOR'S PUBLICATIONS RELATED TO THIS SUBJECT

1. Л.Г. Амусин. Исследование механизма развития полей капиллярных давлений при высушивании коллоидных капиллярно-пористых тел с целью управления их структурно-механическими свойствами. Диссертация на соискание ученой степени к.т.н. Калининский Политехнический институт. Калинин. 1976.
   (Dissertation: ***Research of the Mechanism of the Development of Capillary Pressure Fields during Sorption of Colloidal Capillary-Porous Substances in order to control their structural and mechanical properties***. The Dissertation for the Ph.D. Doctorate. Kalinin Polytechnic University. City of Kalinin. Russia. 1976)
2. L. G. Amusin. Title: System and Method for Processing Dispersed Systems. United States Patent Application Publication. US 2015/0217244 A1. August 6, 2015.
3. L. G. Amusin. Title: System and Method for Processing Dispersed Systems. International Application Published Under The Patent Cooperation Treaty (PCT). International Publication Number WO 2015/119652 A1. August 13, 2015.
4. L. G. Amusin. Title: Method of Processing Molten Metals and Alloys. United States Patent Application Publication. US 2016/0040936 A1. February 11, 2016.
5. Л.Г. Амусин. Теоретические основы физико-химической динамики процесса формирования дисперсных систем в режимах вибрационной кавитации и резонансной турбулентности. Израиль. Июнь, 27 2019. http://www.elektron2000.com/article/2206.html
6. L. Amusin. Dissolution of Gases in Liquids and the Formation of Dispersion Systems in the Mode of Torsion-Oriented Turbulization. iUniverse, 2022
7. L. Amusin. Title: Process of Prevention of Hazardous and Toxic Gases Emission. Provisional Patent Application. US 63/372,992. Dated April 19, 2022. US 2022.
8. Р.А. Татевосян, Л.Г. Амусин, А.Д. Поделько и др. Исследование практического использования вибротурбулизации для пищевой

промышленности. Промежуточный Отчет Всесоюзного Научно-исследовательского института продуктов брожения (ВНИИПрб). Межотраслевая лаборатория физико-химической механики. Москва. 1976.

9. Л.Г. Амусин, и др. Прибор для колориметрического анализа химических реакций в жидкостях и газах с фотодиодным преобразователем. Отчет Всесоюзного Научно-исследовательского института продуктов брожения (ВНИИПрб). Межотраслевая лаборатория физико-химической механики. Москва. 1977.
10. Р.А. Татевосян, Л.Г. Амусин, А.Д. Поделько и др. Разработка реактора для исследования вибротурбулизации. Отчет Всесоюзного Научно-исследовательского института продуктов брожения (ВНИИПрб). Межотраслевая лаборатория физико-химической механики. Москва. 1977.
11. Р.А. Татевосян, Л.Г. Амусин, А.Д. Поделько и др. Исследование практического использования вибротурбулизации для парфюмерной промышленности. Промежуточный Отчет Всесоюзного Научно-исследовательского института продуктов брожения (ВНИИПрб). Межотраслевая лаборатория физико-химической механики. Москва. 1977.
12. Р.А. Татевосян, Л.Г. Амусин, А.Д. Поделько и др. Исследование практического использования вибротурбулизации для фармацевтической промышленности. Промежуточный Отчет Всесоюзного Научно-исследовательского института продуктов брожения (ВНИИПрб). Межотраслевая лаборатория физико-химической механики. Москва. 1977.
13. Л.Г. Амусин, А.Д. Поделько и др. Исследование практического использования вибротурбулизации для производства лаков и красок. Промежуточный Отчет Всесоюзного Научно-исследовательского института продуктов брожения (ВНИИПрб). Межотраслевая лаборатория физико-химической механики. Москва. 1977.
14. Л.Г. Амусин, А.Д.Поделько и др. Исследование практического использования вибротурбулизации для химической промышленности. Промежуточный Отчет Всесоюзного Научно-исследовательского института продуктов брожения (ВНИИПрб). Межотраслевая лаборатория физико-химической механики. Москва. 1977.

15. Р.А. Татевосян, Л.Г. Амусин, А.Д. Поделько и др. Исследование практического использования вибротурбулизации для пищевой промышленности. Промежуточный Отчет Всесоюзного Научно-исследовательского института продуктов брожения (ВНИИПрб). Межотраслевая лаборатория физико-химической механики. Москва. 1976.
16. Л.Г. Амусин, и др. Прибор для колориметрического анализа химических реакций в жидкостях и газах с фотодиодным преобразователем. Отчет Всесоюзного Научно-исследовательского института продуктов брожения (ВНИИПрб). Межотраслевая лаборатория физико-химической механики. Москва. 1977.
17. Р.А. Татевосян, Л.Г. Амусин, А.Д. Поделько и др. Разработка реактора для исследования вибротурбулизации. Отчет Всесоюзного Научно-исследовательского института продуктов брожения (ВНИИПрб). Межотраслевая лаборатория физико-химической механики. Москва. 1977.
18. Р.А. Татевосян, Л.Г. Амусин, А.Д. Поделько и др. Исследование практического использования вибротурбулизации для парфюмерной промышленности. Промежуточный Отчет Всесоюзного Научно-исследовательского института продуктов брожения (ВНИИПрб). Межотраслевая лаборатория физико-химической механики. Москва. 1977.
19. Р.А. Татевосян, Л.Г. Амусин, А.Д. Поделько и др. Исследование практического использования вибротурбулизации для фармацевтической промышленности. Промежуточный Отчет Всесоюзного Научно-исследовательского института продуктов брожения (ВНИИПрб). Межотраслевая лаборатория физико-химической механики. Москва. 1977.
20. Л.Г. Амусин, А.Д. Поделько и др. Исследование практического использования вибротурбулизации для производства лаков и красок. Промежуточный Отчет Всесоюзного Научно-исследовательского института продуктов брожения (ВНИИПрб). Межотраслевая лаборатория физико-химической механики. Москва. 1977.
21. Л.Г. Амусин, А.Д.Поделько и др. Исследование практического использования вибротурбулизации для химической промышленности. Промежуточный Отчет Всесоюзного Научно-исследовательского

института продуктов брожения (ВНИИПрб). Межотраслевая лаборатория физико-химической механики. Москва. 1977.

22. Н.И. Гамаюнов, Л.Г. Амусин. Прибор для исследования капиллярных явлений. Информационный Бюллетень № 342/75. Калинин. 1975.
23. Н.И. Гамаюнов, Л.Г. Амусин. Разработка методики исследование и разработка прибора для измерений внутренних напряжений при формировании гидрофильных дисперсных систем. Отчет Калининского Политехнического института. Калинин. 1975.
24. Н.И. Гамаюнов, Л.Г. Амусин. Исследование тепло- и массопереноса при структурообразовании коллоидных капиллярно-пористых тел. Материалы 5-й Всесоюзной конференции по тепломассообмену. Высшая Школа. Т. 5. Стр. 88. Минск. 1976.
25. Н.И. Гамаюнов, Л.Г. Амусин. Исследование капиллярных явлений в клиновой щели. Инженерно-Физический журнал. Изд. АН СССР. Том 31. № 6. Стр. 1033. Минск. 1976.
26. Н.И. Гамаюнов, Л.Г. Амусин. Изучение механизма испарения влаги из капиллярной щели. Коллоидный Журнал. Т. 38. Выпуск 6. Стр. 1076. Академия Наук СССР. Москва. 1976.
27. Н.И. Гамаюнов, Л.Г. Амусин. Исследование явлений в процессе развития внутреннего напряженного состояния при сушке капиллярно-пористых структур. Тезисы Всесоюзной конференции по физической химии торфа. Академия Наук Белорусской ССР. Стр. 37. Минск. 1976.
28. N.I. Gamayunov and L.G. Amusin. Study of the Internal Pressure upon Structure Formation of Colloidal and Microheterogeneous Systems. Translated from Kolloidnyi Zhurnal, Vol. 38, No. 3, pp. 551-533, May-June, 1976.
29. N.I. Gamayunov and L.G. Amusin. Mechanism of Evaporation of Moisture from a Capillary Slit. Translated from Kolloidnyi Zhurnal, Vol. 38, No. 6, pp. 1076-1081, November-December, 1976.
30. N.I. Gamayunov, L.G. Amusin. Research of Capillary Phenomena on the Slot Model. Translated from Physical-Engineering Zhurnal. Vol. XXXI, No 6. December, 1976.
31. Н.И. Гамаюнов, Л.Г. Амусин, А.Е. Афанасьев. Влияние поверхностных сил на структурообразование в торфяных системах. Сб. Структурные, реологические и физико-механические свойства торфа. Труды КПИ. Калинин. 1976

32. Н.И. Гамаюнов, Л.Г. Амусин. Прибор с тензометрическим преобразователем для измерения внутренних напряжений в дисперсных материалах. Информационный Бюллетень № 385/74. Калинин. 1974.
33. Н.И. Гамаюнов, Г.С. Берлин, Л.Г. Амусин. Прибор с механотронным преобразователем для измерения внутренних напряжений в дисперсных материалах. Информационный Бюллетень № 6/75. Калинин. 1975.
34. Н.И. Гамаюнов, Г.С. Берлин, Л.Г. Амусин. Прибор с манотронным преобразователем для измерения внутренних давлений. Информационный Бюллетень № 6/75. Калинин. 1975.
35. Н.И. Гамаюнов, Л.Г. Амусин. Исследование внутреннего давления при структурообразовании коллоидных и микрогетерогенных систем. Коллоидный Журнал. Т. 38. Выпуск 3. Стр. 551. Академия Наук СССР. Москва. 1976.
36. Н.И. Гамаюнов, Л.Г. Амусин, Я.М. Юфик. Прибор для измерения внутренних напряжений в дисперсных материалах. Информационный Бюллетень № 121/74. Калинин. 1974.

Printed in the United States
by Baker & Taylor Publisher Services